The Political Economy of Regio   ......ng

In this volume, scholars examine the efficacy of trade agreements, economic sanctions, and other strategies of economic statecraft for the promotion of peace both between rival states and across conflict-ridden regions more generally. In the introduction, Steven E. Lobell and Norrin M. Ripsman pose five central questions: (1) What types of economic statecraft, including incentives and sanctions, can interested parties employ? (2) Who are the appropriate targets in the rival states—state leaders, economic and social elites, or society as a whole? (3) When should specific economic instruments be used to promote peace—prior to negotiations, during negotiations, after signature of the treaty, or during implementation of the treaty? (4) What are the limits and risks of economic statecraft and economic interdependence? (5) How can economic statecraft be used to move from a bilateral peace agreement to regional peace?

The chapters that follow are grouped into three sections, corresponding to the three stages of peacemaking: reduction or management of regional conflict, peacemaking or progress toward a peace treaty, and maintenance of bilateral peace and the regionalization of the peace settlement. In each chapter, the contributors consider the five key questions from a variety of methodological, historical, cultural, and empirical perspectives, drawing data from the Pacific, the Middle East, Europe, Asia, and Latin America. The conclusion expands on several themes found in the chapters and proposes an agenda for future research.

Steven E. Lobell is Professor of Political Science at the University of Utah.

Norrin M. Ripsman is Professor of Political Science at Concordia University in Montréal.

Michigan Studies in International Political Economy

SERIES EDITORS: Edward Mansfield, Lisa Martin, and William Clark

Michael J. Gilligan
Empowering Exporters: Reciprocity, Delegation, and Collective Action in American Trade Policy

Barry Eichengreen and Jeffry Frieden, Editors
Forging an Integrated Europe

Thomas H. Oatley
Monetary Politics: Exchange Rate Cooperation in the European Union

Robert Pahre
Leading Questions: How Hegemony Affects the International Political Economy

Andrew C. Sobel
State Institutions, Private Incentives, Global Capital

Roland Stephen
Vehicle of Influence: Building a European Car Market

William Bernhard
Banking on Reform: Political Parties and Central Bank Independence in the Industrial Democracies

William Roberts Clark
Capitalism, Not Globalism: Capital Mobility, Central Bank Independence, and the Political Control of the Economy

Edward D. Mansfield and Brian M. Pollins, Editors
Economic Interdependence and International Conflict: New Perspectives on an Enduring Debate

Kerry A. Chase
Trading Blocs: States, Firms, and Regions in the World Economy

David H. Bearce
Monetary Divergence: Domestic Policy Autonomy in the Post–Bretton Woods Era

Ka Zeng and Joshua Eastin
Greening China: The Benefits of Trade and Foreign Direct Investment

Yoram Z. Haftel
Regional Economic Institutions and Conflict Mitigation: Design, Implementation, and the Promise of Peace

Nathan M. Jensen, Glen Biglaiser, Quan Li, Edmund Malesky, Pablo M. Pinto, Santiago M. Pinto, and Joseph L. Staats
Politics and Foreign Direct Investment

Yu Zheng
Governance and Foreign Investment in China, India, and Taiwan: Credibility, Flexibility, and International Business

Leslie Johns
Strengthening International Courts: The Hidden Costs of Legalization

Steven E. Lobell and Norrin M. Ripsman, Editors
The Political Economy of Regional Peacemaking

The Political Economy of
Regional Peacemaking

Edited by Steven E. Lobell
and Norrin M. Ripsman

UNIVERSITY OF MICHIGAN PRESS

ANN ARBOR

Published in the United States of America by the
University of Michigan Press
Manufactured in the United States of America
♾ Printed on acid-free paper

2019   2018   2017   2016   4   3   2   1

A CIP catalog record for this book is available from the British Library.

Library of Congress Cataloging-in-Publication Data

Names: Lobell, Steven E., 1964– editor. | Ripsman, Norrin M., editor.
Title: The political economy of regional peacemaking / edited by Steven E. Lobell and
    Norrin M. Ripsman.
Description: Ann Arbor : University of Michigan Press, 2016. | Series: Michigan studies in
    international political economy | Includes bibliographical references and index.
Identifiers: LCCN 2015037515| ISBN 9780472073078 (hardback : acid-free paper) | ISBN
    9780472053070 (paperback : acid-free paper) | ISBN 9780472121762 (ebook)
Subjects: LCSH: Peace-building—Economic aspects. | International economic
    relations. | Regional economics—Political aspects. | Commercial treaties—Political
    aspects. | Economic sanctions—Political aspects. | BISAC: POLITICAL SCIENCE /
    International Relations / Treaties. | POLITICAL SCIENCE / Peace.
Classification: LCC JZ5538 .P758 2016 | DDC 327.1/72—dc23
LC record available at http://lccn.loc.gov/2015037515

Acknowledgments

This book grew out of a long-standing conversation about the political economy of peacemaking and when or whether to target state leaders or economic elites in other states in the peace process. In May 2012, we hosted a workshop on this topic at Concordia University in Montreal, Canada. We would like to acknowledge gratefully the workshop support we received from the Social Science and Humanities Research Council of Canada, Concordia University's Aid to Research Related Events, the Fonds Québecois de la réserche sur la societé et la culture, the Research Group on Globalization and National Security (T. V. Paul, Principal Investigator), the Christopher H. Browne Center for International Politics at the University of Pennsylvania, and the Department of Political Science at Concordia University. We thank Shoghig Mikaelian, Brent Gerchicoff, and Jeannie Krumel for helping us organize this conference.

We are also grateful for the helpful comments we received on different drafts of this manuscript from Elizabeth Bloodgood, Mark Brawley, Michael Doyle, Yakub Halabi, Axel Huelsemeyer, Michael Lipson, Patrick Morgan, T. V. Paul, Krystof Pelcz, and Julian Schofield, as well as the participants in our May 2012 workshop. Several of the chapters were presented at the 2012 Annual Meeting of the American Political Science Association. A special thank-you goes to Paul Bernstein. We also thank Brittany Griffin for helping us prepare the manuscript for publication. We are especially grateful to Lisa Martin and William Clark, two of the series editors, for their support, and to Melody Herr for her expert guidance of this project through the publication process.

Finally, as always, we could not have completed this book without the loving support of our wives (Gwen and Nathalie) and our wonderful children (Hannah, Noah, and Eliana & Shira and Dafna).

Contents

Foreword

Yair Hirschfeld

This volume investigates an important subject that, though practiced by diplomats and track-two participants, has received scant attention by scholars: the political economy of peacemaking. The editors and contributors seek to understand what theoretical findings might help in the pursuit of economic statecraft to stabilize conflicts or promote peace. In order to create a systematic approach, the editors ask five guiding questions.

1. How should states and international institutions employ incentives and sanctions to encourage regional peacemaking?
2. Who should be targeted as the benefactors of incentives, and who should bear the consequences of sanctions?
3. When should economic instruments be used to promote peace?
4. What limits and risks do economic policy instruments carry with them?
5. How can economic statecraft be used to move from a bilateral peace agreement to regional peace?

As I have been involved in Israeli-Palestinian peace negotiations as a researcher, a track-two participant in the original Oslo back channel, and a behind-the-scenes actor for more than 30 years, I discuss these questions from my point of view as a practitioner.[1]

I begin with a short historical review of the failures and successes of economic statecraft in promoting an Israeli-Palestinian and a wider Israeli-Arab peace, which suggests some answers to these important questions.

In the period between 1968 and 1987, gross national product (GNP) in the

West Bank and Gaza rose from US$131 million to $1,783.5 million.[2] This was the result of a well-designed and politically motivated economic policy on the part of the Israeli government that aimed to stabilize the status quo of occupation. The policy had the effect of a tranquilizer, helping to avoid dealing with the conflict issues at stake. Although stability was temporarily achieved, it was not sustainable.

Between 1982 and 1987, Austrian chancellor Bruno Kreisky, following my suggestion, engaged in an exercise aimed at the economic empowerment of the Palestinian elite of the West Bank and Gaza. Then Shimon Peres and finally US secretary of state George Shultz engaged in a similar policy as a way to create supportive conditions for a bottom-up approach to Palestinian self-government. These attempts at economic statecraft failed. The main political stakeholders involved, the Palestine Liberation Organization (PLO), the Jordanian government, and Israeli military authorities, feared that they would lose control. The failing strategy was a contributing factor to the outbreak of the Palestinian intifada in December 1987.

The Palestinian intifada, from 1987 to 1991, caused a 27.7 percent decrease in the Palestinian GNP.[3] While on November 3, 1991, direct Israeli-Palestinian negotiations started, it would be difficult to argue that economic hardship got the Palestinians to the negotiating table.

The Madrid process provided for multilateral negotiations and, in this context, a regional economic development group. In business terms, it served to build bridges between Israel and many Arab states. The regional framework offered a convenient setting for Israeli-Palestinian meetings, which helped to set the Oslo negotiations in motion.

With the signing of the Israeli-PLO Declaration of Principles on the White House lawn on September 13, 1993, a new chapter in the peace process had begun. The aim was not simply to use economic statecraft to promote or sustain stability or to create incentives for peace building. Now the challenge was to employ economic policies as the essential device for Palestinian state building. Alas, it became obvious that economic statecraft cannot stand alone. The donor community, led by the United States, the European Union, and Norway, mobilized most substantial funds in support of the Palestinian Authority (PA). However, no effective measures were taken to prevent the use of funds to finance the purchase of arms. Perhaps worse, income resources were not used to create a monopoly on the use of force by the PA. On the contrary, competing Palestinian warlords were permitted to establish their own fiefdoms, which maintained the revolutionary setup of the PLO but prevented state building. Change was only achieved when, in 2007, Prime Minister Salam Fayyad successfully centralized the payment of salaries to each and every PA security employee by the Ministry of Finance. He thus put an end to the earlier system, which had permitted the various Palestinian warlords to pay salaries to their subordinates.

Only central control of the Palestinian security forces laid the basic foundation for Palestinian state building. This successful Palestinian security reform established a clear chain of command and initiated a chain reaction leading toward Israeli-Palestinian security coordination in the West Bank. This improved access and movement by diminishing roadblocks, creating the necessary minimal preconditions for trade and economic development, and permitting the PA to engage in institution building.

However, Salam Fayyad's state-building effort of 2007–11 documented a simple truth: economic state building cannot be based solely on the control of security forces and a joint effort to create the necessary stability for investment and economic growth; political headway toward an agreed peace and an end to occupation are also essential. The Palestinian security forces would only achieve sufficient public legitimacy to permit security cooperation with Israel if economic development did not simply contribute to the status quo but helped prepare the way for Palestinian sovereignty and independence.

By the time an end to the occupation of the Gaza Strip and the northern West Bank was being contemplated under Prime Minister Sharon's disengagement plan of 2004–5, the political conditions for economic statecraft had been created. At the time the government of Israel proposed to hand over the assets of the settlers in an orderly manner to the Palestinian government—assets valued at $4 billion. Fearing that those assets would be looted, as the Palestinians had not created the necessary security capacity to prevent looting, the PA, led on this issue by Mr. Muhammad Dahlan (one of the Gaza warlords), rejected these assets and demanded their destruction. In a failed attempt at economic state building, the donor community had already invested great amounts of taxpayer monies in the Palestinian economy. Instead of taking control of the settler assets and developing them with the aim of handing them over to the PA after the necessary Palestinian security capacity had been created, the donor community asked the government of Israel to destroy them. Whatever the motives of Sharon's disengagement plan might have been, it did offer an opportunity for Palestinian state building. The international community, however, failed to facilitate this real opportunity.

The evident conclusion is that economic statecraft has to be combined with the creation of an effective security capacity, as well as with a political process of conflict resolution. Thus, the political, security, and economic "baskets" of conflict resolution policies have to be combined to promote effective state building.

In 2007 Hamas took control of the Gaza Strip. Israel, the PA, Egypt, and the international community at large decided to impose a policy of economic sanctions with very little success: mortar, rocket, and missile attacks from Gaza against Israel not only undermined Israel's security, but they provoked two wars and had a major spoiler effect on the wider Israeli-Palestinian peace process. Whether the reverse policy of providing economic incentives to Hamas in Gaza would have been more effective, and could be today, remains unclear. The Israeli-Gaza war of November 2012 ended with a cease-fire (rather than an agreement) based on the premise quiet for quiet and stability for stability's sake. The emerging policy thus became to see how support for economic development in the Gaza Strip could contribute to stability. This policy will force the Hamas leadership in Gaza and elsewhere to face the dilemma of either maintaining effective governance by means of self-restraint and preventing competing radical Islamic groups from launching attacks against Israel, caring thereby for the good of the population, or pursuing ideological warfare against Israel by renewing mortar and rocket attacks in the name of "the right of resistance."

The presently unfolding peace initiative of US secretary of state John Kerry is drawing on lessons learned that may be summed up, as follows.

Lesson 1. The three baskets, political, security, and economic, must be pursued simultaneously. With the full backing of President Barack Obama, Kerry will personally pursue the political channel of negotiations while General John R. Allen has been put in charge of pursuing the security channel, leaving the economic channel to Quartet representative Tony Blair and his team.

Lesson 2. Economic statecraft cannot be reduced to incentives and sanctions but must have the wider political resolution concept in mind. If the international community, Israel, and the PLO/PA envisage a two-state solution, economic statecraft has to address the entire spectrum of what is needed for state building and the creation of good neighborly relations between Israel and Palestine. This must include planning for Palestinian physical infrastructure such as road and railway networks and sea- and airports, arrangements for border crossings and so on, the control of natural resources such as water and energy, and negotiations on a state-to-state economic agreement to replace the Paris Protocol of May 1994.

Lesson 3. The economic viability of the state of Palestine depends largely on maintaining peaceful relations with all its neighbors: Israel, the neighboring Arab states, and the Arab world at large. This necessitates a regional component with the ability to create a win-win-win situation for the entire Middle East.

Lesson 4. In the specific circumstances of Israeli, Palestinian, regional, and international politics, no political initiative and no policy of comprehensive economic statecraft can succeed without a strategy to deal with spoilers. Dealing with Hamas in Gaza has provided all sides with important insights showing that a policy of stability for stability's sake can work with control mechanisms to prevent incidents of violence from escalating. Since the military actions of November 2012, effective Israeli-Egyptian coordination has become a technique to control spoiler activity.

This short historical review has aimed to provide some insights necessary to answer the theoretical questions posed by the authors of this volume. In order to do so, it should be stated that the Israeli-Palestinian peacemaking effort represents a special (although not unique) case for economic statecraft. The aim is not simply to influence government or nongovernment actors to pursue a peace-building policy or refrain from conflict-provoking actions. The aim is far wider: to enable state building and the emergence of good neighborly relations between former enemies. Thus the instruments of economic statecraft have to be far more comprehensive than in the case of a more traditional state-to-state or government-to-government relationship. Our experience indicates that it is essential to develop four clusters of instruments: (1) a toolbox for investment promotion from within the Palestinian territories, from the Palestinian diaspora (which is economically and financially very strong), from the Arab world at large, and beyond; (2) a toolbox for donor support to minimize the political risks of investment and assist in creating the institutional structure necessary for state building; (3) political agreements with Israel to decrease Israeli control measures and permit the Palestinian government to develop its own administrative, monetary, and fiscal policies, as well as the necessary law enforcement capacity; and (4) an international community willing to assist the Palestinian government in its tasks and obligations to create the institutional structure, physical infrastructure, legal provisions, law enforcement, and anticorruption measures necessary to provide for economic growth and development.

Based on the strategic aim of creating a peaceful Israeli-Palestinian two-state solution and the comprehensive tasks of economic statecraft, the theoretical questions posed by the editors of this volume can be answered as follows.

1. **When should the economic instruments be used?** During the pre-negotiation period, the only effective means is to create personal relationships and supportive networks that can be put into action during and after negotiations. Any use of economic instruments to maintain the status quo will cause delays in the peacemaking effort. During the period of negotiations before a first agreement, the prevention of economic hardships for the population is essential to create the legitimacy needed for the negotiators to move forward. Economic statecraft with all its elements has to be put in place immediately after the agreement is concluded, as well as during the implementation period, in order to create sustainable conditions for economic growth and peace.

2. **Who are the targeted beneficiaries of incentives: state leaders, economic and social elites, or society as a whole?** Experience gained during the 1967–87 period shows that while permitting society as a whole to benefit does create a stabilizing effect, it has a negative impact on conflict resolution. Economic empowerment of elites without an agreed-upon governmental structure to guide them is doomed to fail. What happened in our experience is that different political stakeholders, the PLO, and the Jordanian and Israeli governments supported different groups of the social and economic elites; the PLO threatened some of them, and the entire effort resulted in greater internal friction and tension among the Palestinian elites of the West Bank and Gaza. After the signing of the Oslo Accords, economic statecraft was designed to benefit the state leaders, enabling them to build an effective self-government. In essence this policy made sense. However, two major mistakes were made. Chairman Yasser Arafat was permitted to retain the personal control structures he had developed in the "revolutionary" period of the PLO, which were counterproductive to the tasks of institution and state building, and no sufficient effort was made to achieve concomitant progress on the political, security, and economic fronts. When Salam Fayyad became prime minister in 2007, the necessary institution- and state-building measures were enforced. At that time, it became essential to benefit society as a whole in order to create the necessary legitimacy for the renewal or continuation of the negotiating process.

3. **How can incentives and sanctions best be employed in regional peacemaking?** Our experience shows that economic incentives as a stand-alone device are not effective, nor are sanctions. Both incentives and sanctions have to be embedded in a wider and more comprehen-

sive policy approach. In the Israeli-Palestinian context, instead of incentives, a comprehensive institution- and state-building policy is needed. In the case of sanctions, a five-component, coercive diplomacy strategy is called for: defining a specific policy aim, building a strong supportive coalition, creating painful sanctions, offering a quid pro quo in return for acceptance of the specified policy demand, and creating a modus operandi permitting the coerced side to maintain its prestige while giving in.

4. **What limits and risks do economic policy instruments carry with them?** Regarding limits, it is important to understand that the Weberian pattern of the impact of Protestant ethics on policy and economics relevant in most parts of the western world is not applicable to Islamic countries. Whereas in the United States the achievement of economic power has often been translated into political influence, the opposite pattern characterizes Islamic countries. There, as a rule, political power permits the creation of economic power and not vice versa. This state of affairs has two major repercussions: (1) it makes it necessary to promote the political process, as well as security arrangements, parallel to the use of economic instruments; and (2) it makes it politically awkward for Palestinian political leaders to ask for economic incentives, as they tend to be accused of promoting their own or specific group interests rather than the national good. The risks are many: as a stand-alone device, economic incentives may tend to favor one elite group over another and cause internal rifts; on the political front, economic policies may create the illusion of sustainable stability and prevent the concerned parties from engaging in a genuine conflict-resolution process; on the economic front, incentives may create a certain level of prosperity without economic growth and thus prevent necessary economic reforms; and on the social front, economic incentives may widen social gaps and thus create a destabilizing effect.

5. **How can economic policies be used to move from a bilateral to a regional peace?** In the case of the Israeli-Palestinian conflict, the Palestinian question is central to the wider Israeli-Arab relationship. Thus the approach pursued by the Madrid process of relating to the region, although useful, turned out to be unsustainable. When Israeli-Palestinian negotiations moved toward deadlock and crisis, the regional dialogue came to an end. Since then, the Arab states have adopted the opposite approach. In many circumstances, they have refused to support

Palestinian economic state building, as that might necessitate normalization of relations with Israel in some spheres. For instance, connecting the Jordanian and Egyptian electricity net to Palestine would automatically create a connection with the Israeli electricity net.

Under the emerging Kerry peace initiative, a more constructive approach is being planned: the support of the Arab states and Arab League for peace negotiations shall be political, diplomatic, and economic, as well as in the security sphere. On the economic front, this entails the participation of Arab states such as Jordan, Saudi Arabia, other Arab Gulf states, and Egypt in the Palestinian economic state-building effort. Undoubtedly, this can be a win-win-win recipe, permitting Israel, Palestine, and the Arab states to gain. This seems to be the best way to move from bilateral economic statecraft toward the creation of supportive regional economic coordination and cooperation structures.

Hopefully, this short essay from the perspective of a "reflective practitioner," together with the theoretical and empirical analyses in this book, will help promote a wider theoretical, policy-oriented discussion and provide decision makers and experts with useful insights for the promotion of peace.

Yair Hirschfeld

Senior Lecturer, Department of Middle East Studies

University of Haifa

Founder and Director General

Economic Cooperation Foundation, Tel Aviv

July 24, 2013

NOTES

1. For a detailed analysis of my involvement in the Israeli-Palestinian peace process from the beginning of the Oslo process, see Yair Hirschfeld, *Track-Two Diplomacy toward an Israeli-Palestinian Solution, 1978–2014* (Baltimore: Johns Hopkins University Press, 2014).

2. United Nations Conference on Trade and Development, *Palestinian External Trade under Israeli Occupation* (New York: United Nations, 1989), 19.

3. Ibid.

Introduction

Conceptualizing the Political Economy of Regional Peacemaking

Norrin M. Ripsman and Steven E. Lobell

Within the international relations literature, the political economy of national and international security has received comparatively little attention. In the late 1990s, surveying 50 years of research on international security, for example, Michael Mastanduno noted that "the study of economic statecraft, and economic issues more generally, tended to be conducted separately from the study of military statecraft, and national security issues more generally."[1] Jonathan Kirshner similarly lamented that, due to the Cold War, "In contemporary International Relations theory, there exists a sharp distinction between international political economy and security studies."[2] Since that time, to be sure, more scholarship has been conducted that recognizes the important nexus between economics and security, focusing on, among other topics, the application of political economy and domestic distributional models to security studies, liberal economic peace arguments about the inverse relationship between trade and conflict, the security externalities of trade, the link between domestic economics and foreign military policy (or the guns and butter debate), and the use of economic statecraft to discourage nuclear proliferation or humanitarian violations.[3] Nonetheless, the intersection of economics and security remains an understudied subject.[4] The political economy of peacemaking, at the dyadic and especially the regional/subsystemic levels, has received little attention in the field and has not been explored in a systematic manner.[5] The goal of *The Political Economy of Regional Peacemaking* is to address this gap.

Of course scholars have observed that adversaries do occasionally engage in commercial concessions, the provision of incentives, and trade with their rivals.[6] For example, during the 1930s, Britain extended credits, loans, trade concessions, market guarantees, and export earnings in sterling to Germany and Japan. Beginning in 1972, the United States proposed or extended capital and technology, Export-Import Bank financing, most favored nation (MFN) tariff treatment, and long-term credit to the Soviet Union. In the early 1970s, West Germany extended trade credits to East Germany.[7] More recently South Korea has established economic zones in North Korea, including the Kaesong Industrial Complex and Haeju, a port town. In each instance, American, British, West German, and Korean leaders identified the recipient state as a rival or threat, yet they carried through with the economic exchange.

Our interest, however, extends beyond occasional economic interactions between rivals and "trading with the enemy," focusing instead on the economic strategies leading to dyadic and ultimately regional peacemaking. The purpose of this introduction, therefore, is to map out the different ways in which belligerent states and interested third parties—states and international institutions—may be able to utilize economic statecraft to stabilize conflict between regional rivals and then to promote peace between them with the ultimate goal of achieving a regional peace. Similar to some of the questions raised by Etel Solingen in her study on the political economy of preventing nuclear proliferation, the contributors to this volume address five central questions: (1) What types of economic statecraft, including incentives and sanctions, can interested parties employ to advance regional peacemaking? (2) Who are the appropriate targets in the rival states—state leaders, economic and social elites, or society as whole? (3) When should specific economic instruments be used to promote peace—prior to negotiations, during the negotiations, or during the implementation phase after the treaty is signed? (4) What are the limits of and risks associated with economic statecraft? and (5) How can economic statecraft be used to move from a bilateral peace agreement to regional peace? The chapters in this volume address these questions and their interactions from a variety of methodological and empirical perspectives. In the balance of this introduction, we define the scope of our study by briefly explaining what we mean by the concept of "regional peacemaking," unpack the five questions that animate the book, explore possible relationships between them, and discuss how the contributors address the questions in their chapters.

One important clarification is in order. Typically when scholars refer to economic statecraft, they are referring to the deliberate and active manipulation of economic incentives and disincentives in order to achieve a desired policy payoff from a target state.[8] In this volume we broaden this definition to include the generation of economic interdependence between states to create more passive effects over time.[9] Interdependence and trade can have unintended and spillover effects on peacemaking, which allow it to take on a life of its own, apart from the initial economic statecraft effect. Some of our chapters, therefore, focus on the more direct effects of economic statecraft; others focus on the longer-term effects of economic interdependence on peacemaking.

I. Regions and Peacemaking

Before we discuss the questions that animate our study, a few words on the object of our inquiry are in order. Specifically, we need to explain what we mean by our use of the terms *region* and *peacemaking*. A *region* refers to a group of states within a geographically defined space that share both proximity and regularized patterns of interaction between them. Furthermore, a region requires natural and clearly demarcated boundaries—such as mountain ranges, oceans, or rivers—dividing it from neighboring regions.[10] Typically regions are characterized by regular patterns of interaction between regional participants and a high level of intensity of interactions due to strategic interdependence among them because of their geographic proximity.[11] States in these regions typically focus their security policies on other regional participants, trade disproportionately within their region, and have most of their disputes with regional rivals. For this reason, we understand a region as being characterized by a unique and common set of concerns or issues that constitute what Barry Buzan and Ole Waever refer to as a "regional security complex."[12] These regional dynamics, though informed by domestic political and systemic pressures, are also distinct from them.[13]

Although external great powers may play an important role in regional security dynamics, we view them as extraregional actors and not part of the region, since they are geographically remote. These extraregional actors are not compelled by geography to engage in regional power dynamics. They may simply withdraw from involvement in the area if more pressing concerns present themselves; regional participants do not have that luxury.

By "peacemaking" we mean the termination of a state of war or enduring rivalry between rivals with a public declaration of peace, preferably a formal treaty. Although there is a range of outcomes that can all be considered "peace"—from a cold peace, in which the former rivals agree to terminate their security competition but engage in little economic or cultural interaction, to a warm peace, characterized by a high degree of bilateral contact and cooperation, we consider any agreement of this type to be a kind of peace.[14] When peace is achieved, both sides have an expectation that the treaty will be respected, and they no longer invest as much time, energy, or resources in defending the border against the former enemy. Typically, states achieve peace by initiating bilateral negotiations leading to a peace treaty, which is then implemented. While cease-fires, disengagement agreements, and unilateral firing breaks can often be part of the steps states may go through in order to reach peace, these are not in and of themselves evidence of peacemaking or peace agreements. Similarly, while peace talks are necessary components of a peace process, we do not judge peacemaking as complete until a public and final agreement is reached by both parties.

In this volume some of the chapters examine how to promote peacemaking while others discuss the prior and necessary condition of regional conflict management. These important tasks are related and reflect different stages in the overall peacemaking process. We break regional peacemaking into a three-stage process: (1) a reduction or management of bilateral conflict in which outside actors use incentives and disincentives to dissuade the states from using force, as well as to limit the level of violence and create space for peacemaking; (2) peacemaking, or the negotiation and conclusion of a peace treaty or agreement to resolve the conflict rather than just deescalating it; and (3) the maintenance and deepening of bilateral peace after a treaty is signed, as well as the regionalization of the peace settlement.[15]

In addition, we need to discuss the scope of this book by considering what we are addressing and what is outside our purview. To begin with, we are investigating how economic statecraft can be used to encourage or deepen peacemaking between regional rivals, as broadly defined in the previous paragraph. By focusing on economic rather than military statecraft, we exclude attempts by great powers to impose an agreement on reluctant powers by means of military force or military coercion, such as the United States imposed on Japan after World War II.

Our object of study is peace agreements between states that are regional rivals. This excludes agreements between states and nonstate actors (such as the

Oslo Accords between Israel and the Palestine Liberation Organization [PLO] or the Good Friday Agreement between the United Kingdom and parties in Northern Ireland), as well as peace treaties between states not properly understood as belonging to the same region (such as the 1973 treaty between the United States and North Vietnam). We concentrate on public agreements rather than secret pacts, the details of which the rival societies might be unaware.

Finally, we are examining the impact of economic statecraft employed by states and international institutions comprised of state members (intergovernmental organizations or IGOs) in the service of peacemaking. This means that we are not focusing on attempts by nonstate actors (such as multinational corporations, diaspora groups, transnational societal actors or nongovernmental organizations [NGOs], and private investors) to influence regional peacemaking, even if they use economic strategies. Our assumption is that only states or groupings of states are likely to have an interest in mobilizing significant resources for the purpose of peacemaking, as well as the economic capacity to do so. As a result, we do not consider the effect of remittances, stock market fluctuations and private investors, relief and charitable organizations, and terrorist financial transactions on the politics of peacemaking.[16]

II. Unpacking the Five Questions

Question 1: The Types of Economic Statecraft

There are numerous types of economic instruments, involving both rewards and punishment, that actors might attempt to utilize in the service of building regional peace and stability.[17] On the rewards side, states and institutions can offer a variety of sweeteners, or what is sometimes termed "constructive engagement," to encourage belligerents to bury the hatchet, including foreign aid (loans, grants/credits, loan guarantees, subsidies, infrastructure, or technology), debt forgiveness, market access, loan or investment guarantees, and trade concessions (tariff reduction and preferential/MFN access).[18] Beyond ad hoc or episodic incentives, actors can also use a variety of institutionalized forms of incentives, such as bilateral and multilateral free trade agreements (FTAs), which eliminate tariff and nontariff barriers; qualified industrial zones (QIZs), which promote economic cooperation between states; trade and investment framework agreements (TIFAs), which establish legal protections for investors and are precursors to FTAs; bilateral investment treaties (BITs), which establish the terms and conditions for private investment; and general systems of preference (GSPs), which provide preferential duty-free entry for specific products.

On the punishment side, as an alternative to economic engagement or in concert with it, states and institutions can attempt to coerce recalcitrant belligerents with a range of economic sanctions. Trade sanctions may include embargoes, boycotts, tariffs and nontariff barriers, import duties, import or export quotas, or the withdrawal of MFN status. Other economic strategies used to penalize another state include financial or monetary sanctions such as freezing assets, import or export controls, aid suspension, restrictions on currency conversion, dumping goods or currency, preemptive buying, and divestment.[19] More extreme forms of economic punishment include economic blockades (both naval and air).[20] More recently there has been work on what is termed "smart" or targeted economic sanctions.[21]

In this volume, our contributors explore the utility of these economic tools as levers to encourage peacemaking between regional rivals. To this end, they address a range of related questions. For example, how are these tools used either separately or in combination? Do these strategies enhance or undermine each other? Are some of these tools better suited to the task of peacemaking than others?

Question 2: The Targets of Economic Incentives

In general, states and international institutions can target three distinct groups with economic statecraft: state leaders and the leadership; societal and economic elites; or society and the public as a whole. These targets are what we term the three "faces of security," in contrast to the frequent depiction of the state as Janus-faced.[22] Instead of the state consisting solely of decision makers that are oriented both inwardly and outwardly, the state is actually comprised of three distinct forces, each with its own unique mind-set, assets, and cluster of interests.[23] Each of these faces of security offers different prospects and possibilities for promoting and maintaining a peace settlement. We consider the implications of targeting each of these groups, particularly the types of economic incentives each would require, the timing of those incentives, and the risks of engaging each face of security. Of course each of these three faces exists in the sender state as well, although we do not focus on that side of the interaction in this book.[24]

The First Face

The first face of security refers to the state itself and its leadership. Essentially, this refers to the foreign policy executive (FPE) of the target state, including the head of state—such as the king, czar, dictator, or president—the head of government (i.e., the prime minister) and the officials and ministers tasked with making foreign policy, including the negotiation and signing of peace agreements.

There is compelling logic to engaging the leadership of belligerent states with economic incentives or sanctions. After all, statesmen are tasked with the responsibility and have the power to enact policy, whereas the public and economic elites cannot directly do so. Therefore, to foster the deescalation of a conflict, to inspire the negotiation and signature of a peace treaty, and to ensure its implementation, it makes sense to engage the foreign policy executives of the regional rivals.[25] Moreover, state leaders are few in number, are on balance more rational and better informed than the public, and are more attuned to a *raison d'état* rationale than the general public.[26] One might expect, therefore, that economic engagement could influence the state in shorter order than attempts to influence society and thus strengthen societal support for negotiations. In this respect, Norrin M. Ripsman argues that most successful peacemaking endeavors start as "top-down" settlements reached by states, often over initial societal objection. Only afterward, he argues, can the state use its power and resources to bring society onboard, once the settlement is a done deal.[27]

Based on the first face of security, could targeting rival states and their leadership with quid pro quo incentives be useful in an attempt to encourage flexibility in negotiations and reward concessions made?[28] Furthermore, do such incentives encourage leaders to adhere to any agreements they reach? Are particular types of incentives more likely to resonate with target state leaders? Are the foreign policy executives in target states likely to be compelled to embark on peacemaking by means of a strategy of economic sanctions and the costs it threatens or imposes? Or are state actors unlikely to be motivated to change their policies unless there is significant societal pressure from key interest groups or society as a whole? These are key questions that affect the utility of the first face of security.

The Second Face

The second face of security refers to key societal coalitions and power brokers in the target state. These include economic leaders, labor leaders, tribal authorities, financial interests, the clergy, and other key societal actors that can act either as drivers of a peace process by pressing the government to negotiate and make concessions or as veto players by preventing policies from being enacted and obstructing implementation.[29] Targeting these groups entails indirect attempts to engage a belligerent state by facilitating the formation of a foreign policy coalition that favors peacemaking and compromise. Some, such as Etel Solingen, argue that the purpose of economic statecraft is to strengthen the political and economic power of the internationalist-oriented elites in the rival states, who should be more receptive to peacemaking as a means of promoting their own economic interests, and/or to weaken the nationalist or inward-oriented elites, who actually stand to gain more economically through continuation of the conflict.[30] In principle, however, economic tools could be used to woo other groups that are ordinarily not part of the internationalist coalition to support peacemaking.[31] The assumption of second-face approaches is that, through concessions and inducements, the initiating state can concentrate benefits and thereby alter the domestic balance of political power in the target state. The beneficiaries or winners will subsequently pressure state leaders and the leadership to improve relations with the initiating state or the regional rival in order to maintain the economic benefit.[32] If so, second-face strategies could also enlarge the leadership's domestic base of support or win-set, which is necessary if leaders are to take the risky step of improving relations with a rival state.

Does altering the costs and incentives that key societal actors face present a reasonable strategy for driving and sustaining a peace process? If so, under what conditions? Which societal groups are most reasonable to target? Are societal groups more responsive to sanctions or incentives? Does the form of economic statecraft needed differ when it is directed at nationalist groups, as opposed to internationalists or those already leaning toward support for peacemaking? Is economic statecraft more effective at strengthening supporters of a peace process by giving them more economic and, consequently, political resources with which to build a peace coalition? Is it more effective in compensating opponents of a treaty with side payments in order to mute their opposition or woo them to support the peace process? Is it possible to sway economic nationalists and rejectionist elites by threatening or imposing economic sanctions? Or is targeting societal groups likely to be ineffective or even counterproductive?

The Third Face

The third face of security refers to targeting the population of a rival state as a whole, or at least large segments of it. The logic of third-face economic strategies is either to impose such extreme hardship on a population that it embraces peacemaking with the enemy as a means of alleviating its suffering or to provide tangible rewards for peacemaking that lead the population to embrace an agreement and implement it.

Could the provision of broad-based economic incentives that target rival populations as a whole, rather than the narrowly targeted strategies discussed above, help mobilize grassroots support for a peace agreement in rival states? If so, under what conditions? Are societies susceptible to economic punishment as well? Are societies likely, as economic sanctions theorists assume, to pressure their governments (or even societal elites) to change policies and make peace in order to escape debilitating costs?[33] Or are sanctions likely to backfire and create a rally-round-the-flag effect that opposes peacemaking?[34]

These three faces of security present a range of choices and challenges to sender states and institutions. Whom should states and institutions target with economic statecraft to promote peacemaking? Are different types of statecraft and tools more conducive to influencing different domestic targets? In other words, do state actors respond to different types of incentives and sanctions than the ones that societal elites or the public as a whole respond to? Does it pay to target all three faces simultaneously or is that unnecessary, counterproductive, or offsetting?

Question 3: The Timing of Economic Statecraft

When should economic instruments be utilized to facilitate peacemaking? Three distinct time periods emerge as possibilities: (1) the prenegotiation phase, before the rivals embrace the goal of peacemaking and initiate peace negotiations; (2) the negotiation phase, in which both parties engage in discussions aimed at resolving the conflict prior to signing a peace treaty; and (3) the postagreement phase, after the agreement is signed and is being implemented. In a successful peacemaking process, the parties move through these stages sequentially. Nonetheless, it is possible for backsliding to occur, such that states that were in the negotiation phase could return to the prenegotiation phase.[35] As we indicate below, each phase presents distinct opportunities and challenges that senders have to navigate.

In the *prenegotiation* phase, the sender's goals concern preparing the groundwork for peace negotiations. This involves finding a way to persuade the rival governments to engage each other in peace talks aimed at resolving the conflict. To some extent, this requires conflict management since leaders will be less willing to negotiate during periods of intense conflict and active hostilities.[36] How can economic statecraft be utilized at this early stage in the process? What economic instruments are most likely to gain sufficient traction to stabilize the conflict and jump-start talks? Are economic inducements or sanctions likely to be more productive? Which actors should senders target, those of the first, second, or third face? Should senders use different tools of economic statecraft to target different actors in the target state? Should economic incentives be conditional on progress, in the hope that linkage will compel actors to make concessions, or should they be open-ended, in the hope of building and enriching a vested interest in peacemaking?

In the *negotiation* phase, once the rivals are talking, the senders' goals revolve around getting the target to be flexible and make the concessions necessary to expand the peace camp's win-set and enable the parties to create an agreement that all can sign. How can economic statecraft be used at this stage? Can states and institutions use economic incentives to reward leaders who negotiate in good faith and make concessions? Could they include economic payoffs as part of the agreement both to reward the parties for reaching a settlement and to provide leaders with a tangible benefit they can present to their supporters and societies to justify the compromises made? Are economic sanctions appropriate at this stage to signal the costs of failing to reach an agreement? Which actors in the target state should senders engage at this stage: the leaders who are negotiating, key societal allies, potential veto players, or society as a whole? Should incentives be used freely throughout the process or held in reserve for a last-minute push to reach a final agreement?

Finally, in the *postagreement* phase the senders' goals are to ensure that all parties implement the agreement and increase the likelihood that it will endure. Once the former rivals have made their concessions and signed on the dotted line, do economic incentives and sanctions have any further role in maintaining peace? Can economic incentives be utilized as a means of cementing the agreement and socializing the rival populations to buy into an agreement that brings both peace and prosperity?[37] Can the rival states or third parties ensure that the treaty holds by threatening economic sanctions in cases of nonimplementation or lapses and setbacks in one party's implementation of the accord? Do the appropriate targets of economic statecraft differ at this stage? Should senders target rival states in order to offer them continued payoffs for cooperation? Or should they target societal actors and the general public to enhance the coalition in support of the agreement?

Of course, since slippage and backsliding can occur, this raises another set of questions about sequencing. For example, if senders use a set of economic instruments in the prenegotiation phase to jump-start peace talks, if those talks fail can the same senders employ the same set of tools or target the same groups to reignite the process? Does a relapsed process affect the appropriateness of economic sanctions as opposed to incentives?

Question 4: The Limits and Risks of Economic Statecraft

Assuming that economic statecraft has a role to play in regional peacemaking—something with which not all our contributors would agree—what are the limits of using such an approach? In other words, what can these policy instruments not accomplish? In the prenegotiation phase, can economic incentives credibly be used to encourage flexibility by actors that fear existential security threats or societal groups deeply committed to ideological or nationalist visions and claims? If the regional combatants have considerably divergent goals, can economic tools truly help bridge such wide gaps? Although the frequently cited distinction between security and sovereignty as high politics and economics as low politics may be overdrawn, when these fundamental priorities conflict can the lure of economic gains lead states to compromise over sovereignty and security?[38] In other words, can economic incentives do more than sweeten the pot for leaders already interested in peacemaking? Can they really drive states and societies concerned with security and contested territory to make peace? Can economic statecraft succeed when noneconomic interests dominate calculations in the rival states? Realists would surely doubt that economics can trump security concerns, especially in the prenegotiation phase, when the relative gains and cheating problems are most salient.[39] Are they correct or is it possible to overcome zero-sum thinking and fear of the sucker's payoff using economic statecraft under certain circumstances?

Once an agreement is reached, does economic statecraft lose its utility? In other words, are there reasonable prospects of using economic tools to sell the agreement to the rival societies and deepen it or is it merely useful as a means of pushing rival state leaders to make concessions and reach an agreement? Can economic interdependence be utilized in the postagreement stage to solidify the gains of peace, as commercial liberals believe?[40] Or are realists correct in believing that, since economic interdependence implies vulnerability due to the specialization and rationalization that are consequences of trade and comparative advantage, states will prefer to pursue relative autarky, at least in the security sphere, and resist attempts to enmesh them in networks of economic interdependence.[41]

Beyond mere limits, are there any risks involved in using economic statecraft as a means of fostering regional peace? Specifically, can the use of economic sanctions or incentives or the generation of economic interdependence paradoxically interfere with the task of peacemaking and have the unintended effect of making an agreement less likely? Can economic sanctions generate opposition to the sender and, consequently, a backlash against peacemaking? Are economic incentives likely to enrich and empower the opponents of a peace agreement? Are rewards likely to stigmatize pro-peace factions as tools of foreign powers and therefore traitors, thus limiting their ability to make concessions? In this regard, are public or private economic linkage strategies more likely to be effective? On one hand, public linkage may signal the importance of meeting expectations more effectively but be more likely to inspire a backlash. On the other hand, private linkage may be less likely to meet with resistance, although key societal actors might be unclear about what specifically is required of them and what the consequences of noncompliance will be. How do senders navigate these issues?

Finally, because of the security externalities of economics that realists identify, economic incentives might actually affect the regional military balance by enriching some states over others, thereby making conflict more likely between rivals.[42] Could this adversely affect the relationship between the target states and other regional participants, thereby undermining regional stability? What other unintended consequences might economic statecraft engender?

Question 5: Moving from Dyadic Peace to Regional Peace

Is reaching a bilateral peace agreement sufficient to stabilize a region and promote regional peace or are regions more than the sum of their parts? The literature on regional subsystems discusses regions as having their own dynamics, which are separate from domestic politics and systemic pressures.[43] If that is the case, resolving dyadic conflicts should be insufficient as a means of resolving enduring regional conflicts without addressing the major regional disputes among the regional participants. It follows, then, that once a dyadic peace agreement is achieved it will be important to move beyond the dyad to build a comprehensive regional peace.[44] Does this require more of the same economic statecraft and strategies from third parties and regional participants to move from a dyadic peace to a regional arrangement? Can economic statecraft shape regional dynamics in order to make it more likely that bilateral agreements will succeed? Can bilateral peace agreements become entrenched without resolving larger regional problems?

Alternatively, does it require distinctly regional economic strategies that institutionalize economic sanctions and incentives such as free trade regimes, preferential trade agreements (PTAs), currency unions, and regional economic integration to present regional states and societies with permanent incentives for cooperation and disincentives to defect?[45] Do regional solutions require multilateral and institutionalized regional cooperation or are regional economic institutions merely a by-product of stabilized regional dynamics? Which tools are most appropriate and which actors should be targeted to move from dyadic to regional peacemaking?[46]

Perhaps, however, the causal arrow should be reversed. Does regional economic cooperation precede and contribute to bilateral peacemaking between regional rivals? Can free trade zones, customs unions, or PTAs shape the calculations of conflict-ridden states and their societies so as to push them along the path to peacemaking? In which case, regional arrangements would be the starting point of rivalry termination rather than its endpoint.

III. Plan of the Book and Conclusion

The chapters in this volume reflect: a wide mix of qualitative and quantitative methodological approaches; a broad range of regions, encompassing diverse cultures, histories, and economies, including the Pacific, the Middle East, Europe, Asia, and Latin America; and dyads/regions in different stages of the peacemaking process. Besides the Ripsman, Lobell, and Press-Barnathan chapters, which address all five core questions raised in the introduction, the remaining chapters address different combinations of the questions. A number of factors restrict the range of possible cases in the volume. First, the scope of cases is limited by the selection of conflicts involving states with working and centralized government apparatuses. This state characteristic is essential for this project since both the top-down and bottom-up models recognize that statesmen are responsible for negotiating peace agreements. Weak, failing, and failed states lack a coherent central government, and thus there are no state leaders with whom to negotiate or to talk.

Second, given the small universe of cases of dyadic peacemaking, and especially regional peacemaking, there is overlap across the chapters, as many of our contributors weigh in on some of the crucial cases with different theoretical and empirical lenses. For instance, both Ripsman and Lobell examine peacemaking in and between Israel and Jordan; Ripsman, Press-Barnathan, and Thompson examine Franco-German peacemaking; Ripsman and Thompson investigate the Egyptian-Israeli peace treaty; and Blanchard, Kastner and Pearson, and Norris examine China's attempts at peacemaking with its neighbors. Consequently, as the authors draw very different conclusions from these key cases, the volume generates a series of lively debates that are engaged in both the individual chapters and the volume's conclusion.

The chapters in the volume, each of which addresses core questions raised in this introduction, are organized based on the stages of peacemaking. The initial chapters by Ripsman, Lobell, and Press-Barnathan address the influence of economic statecraft and economic interdependence during all three stages of peacemaking. These are followed by the Zahar chapter, which explores the prenegotiation/conflict management stage. The Thompson, Blanchard, Kastner and Pearson, and Norris chapters concentrate on the first two preagreement stages, considering the utility of economic statecraft and economic interdependence in the transition to peace during the prenegotiation and/or negotiation/agreement stages. The chapter by Mansfield and Pevehouse concentrates primarily on employing economic instruments in the service of peace maintenance and embedding bilateral peace agreements in regional arrangements in the postagreement stage. Finally, Peter Dombrowski's conclusion ties together these findings.

The book begins with paired minichapters in which we, the editors, present our own differing answers to our five questions. Norrin Ripsman's chapter 1 presents a first face of security set of answers, or a top-down approach, based on his research on peacemaking between France and Germany following World War II and the peace settlements between Egypt and Israel and Israel and Jordan. He argues that they key to economic peacemaking is engaging the target states with economic and other incentives to bring them to the bargaining table and encourage them to compromise. Engaging societal actors prior to the treaty is unlikely to be successful and may even be counterproductive.

Once a treaty is reached, however, the target of economic statecraft should change to encompass key societal actors and the public at large to build support for the settlement. In contrast, based on his research on Israeli-Palestinian and Israeli-Jordanian peace negotiations, Steven E. Lobell in chapter 2 presents a second-face argument or a bottom-up approach. He maintains that peacemaking requires third parties to boost the power and position of key societal actors to create the underlying constituency for peacemaking in the rival states. For Washington, the ultimate goal was to use economic statecraft to create a large constituency so that state leaders in Jerusalem and Amman could take the political risk of engaging in the peacemaking process. Absent such a coalition, the target states are unlikely to take risks for peace.

In addressing the five questions, Galia Press-Barnathan's chapter 3 examines the use of economic statecraft in the transitions to peace between France and Germany and Germany and Poland after World War II. Like Ripsman, she finds that in the initial stages of the peace process the targets are the leaders and economic elites, and only later in the process is the broader society brought in to normalize the peace agreement. She also notes a number of limitations of economic statecraft. One is the ability of the sender state to rally its business community to support economic statecraft. A second limitation is that economic statecraft can create hostility when there is economic disparity between the sender and receiver states, and especially if there is the perception of coercion and exploitation. Press-Barnathan's Franco-German case demonstrates that, under the right circumstances, bilateral peace can lead to regional peacemaking. Important facilitating factors include embedding economic statecraft within a regional institutional context and the active use of economic statecraft by third parties to advance regional arrangements.

The rest of the chapters focus on specific stages of the peace process. In chapter 4, Marie-Joëlle Zahar examines a critical aspect of the political economy of peacemaking that has received even less scholarly attention than the understudied topic as a whole: economic statecraft directed toward nonstate and armed actors in order to bring them into a peace process meant to end a regional conflict. She addresses three questions: which nonstate actors are the most appropriate targets, what types of economic statecraft are most likely to succeed, and what is the appropriate timing of economic statecraft? Zahar's findings are varied and often idiosyncratic, although she does find that economic statecraft alone might be insufficient to edge these groups toward the negotiation table absent concomitant military and political pressures for peacemaking. In terms of targets, one must consider the complexity of the organization and, consequently, its degree of dependence on outside resources for survival. Finally, using economic statecraft too early in the peace process can be problematic because it might divert actors' interest away from signing the treaty, although it can also create a ripe moment, especially if nonstate armed actors have suffered defeats.

In chapter 5, William R. Thompson assesses the role of economic incentives in rivalry termination in three cases spanning different regions: France and Germany, Egypt and Israel, and Argentina and Brazil. In assessing these cases, he finds that economic inducements matter most in reinforcing a process of deescalation that is already under way, although they do not drive regional peacemaking. According to Thompson's findings, although economic incentives can be important to a peace process, far more important factors include some combination of shocks such as military defeat, expectational revision, policy entrepreneurs, third and extraregional actors, and reciprocity between the rivals.

In chapter 6, Jean-Marc F. Blanchard assesses the different types of economic statecraft between China and Japan, including trade, foreign aid, low-interest loans, and foreign direct investment (FDI). He addresses the limits and risks of economic statecraft and especially why, despite massive Sino-Japanese trade ties and multiple realms of economic cooperation, these two states cannot surmount their frictions. He concludes that the central problem is that economic interactions occur within the context of power relations and the security dilemma. Consequently, economic incentives cannot generate sufficient traction and trust to overcome bilateral tensions.

In chapter 7, Scott L. Kastner and Margaret Pearson examine US-China and China-Taiwan relations. They assess why states use economic engagement strategies, whom they target, and the risks and limitations of these strategies. While they find that leaders have embraced engagement strategies, the policies themselves have enjoyed only limited success. One explanation, which is consistent with Press-Barnathan's conclusion, is that engagement strategies that target societal groups might backfire and, rather than the "winning hearts and minds," such policies can increase suspicions and decrease trust.

In chapter 8, William Norris examines the use of economic statecraft as a tool of peacemaking in China's relations with Russia and India. He assesses the targets, timing, and effectiveness of economic statecraft. Like Ripsman and Press-Barnathan, Norris finds that economic statecraft tends to solidify and reinforce regional peacemaking rather than initiate it. Like Blanchard, Norris concludes that economic statecraft can also feed regional suspicions and insecurities, especially if the gains are seen as uneven and therefore favoring one partner.

In chapter 9, Edward D. Mansfield and Jon C. Pevehouse examine the fifth question, regarding whether economic statecraft can be used to promote peacemaking in a geographic region. They are particularly interested in whether multilateral PTAs can reduce conflict. They conclude that multilateral PTAs characterized by a high level of trade among regional members can significantly reduce regional conflict, regardless of institutional design, and thereby are useful tools for reinforcing bilateral peace treaties between regional rivals.

In the conclusion, Peter Dombrowski acknowledges the novelty and importance of this volume in examining the valuable question of the political economy of peacemaking across warring states. He compares how the contributors address some or all of the five core questions raised by Ripsman and Lobell in the introduction. He finds that there is cautious support for the importance of economic statecraft, although, like the editors, the contributors identify some of its difficulties and limitations. Dombrowski also raises a number of important questions for future work on the political economy of peacemaking, including further theorizing on the role of economic statecraft, more discussion on the role of third parties, and expanding on how to move from dyadic peace to regional peacemaking.

The overall picture in this volume, therefore, is that using economic statecraft to promote peacemaking between regional rivals is complex and not a panacea. The contributors find that economic incentives and sanctions are but one factor among many in peacemaking, and some find that it is not the most important one. In addition, many of the authors find that there are serious limitations to using these economic tools, which can often be counterproductive and self-defeating. Thus, while most contributors find that economic statecraft can be useful at times as a means of promoting and especially cementing peace agreements, it is essential to employ it wisely toward the right targets, only under the right circumstances, and with an effort to control unintended consequences.

NOTES

1. Michael Mastanduno, "Economics and Security in Statecraft and Scholarship," *International Organization* 52, no. 4 (Autumn 1998): 825–54, at 826.

2. Jonathan Kirshner, "Political Economy in Security Studies after the Cold War," *Review of International Political Economy* 5, no. 1 (Spring 1998): 64–91, at 64.

3. See, for example, Jean-Marc F. Blanchard, Edward D. Mansfield, and Norrin M. Ripsman, eds., *Power and the Purse: Economic Statecraft, Interdependence, and International Conflict* (London: Frank Cass, 2000); Steven E. Lobell, *The Challenge of Hegemony: Grand Strategy, Trade, and Domestic Politics* (Ann Arbor: University of Michigan Press, 2003); Peter Dombrowski, ed., *Guns and Butter: The Political Economy of International Security* (Boulder: Lynne Rienner, 2005); Jonathan Kirshner, *Appeasing Bankers: Financial Caution on the Road to War* (Princeton: Princeton University Press, 2007); Patrick J. McDonald, *The Invisible Hand of Peace: Capitalism, the War Machine, and International Relations Theory* (Cambridge: Cambridge University Press, 2009); and Etel Solingen, ed., *Sanctions, Statecraft, and Nuclear Proliferation* (Cambridge: Cambridge University Press, 2012).

4. Michael Mastanduno, "The Strategy of Economic Engagement: Theory and Practice," in Edward D. Mansfield and Brian M. Pollins, eds., *Economic Interdependence and International Conflict: New Perspectives on an Enduring Debate*, 175–86 (Ann Arbor: University of Michigan Press, 2003).

5. For exceptions, see Ruth Arad, Seez Hirsch, and Alfred Tovias, *The Economics of Peacemaking: Focus on the Egyptian-Israeli Situation* (New York: St. Martin's, 1983); Galia Press-Barnathan, "The Neglected Dimension of Commercial Liberalism: Economic Cooperation and Transition to Peace," *Journal of Peace Research* 43, no. 3 (May 2006): 261–78; Galia Press-Barnathan, *The Political Economy of Transitions to Peace* (Pittsburgh: University of Pittsburgh Press, 2009); and David Cortright, *The Price of Peace: Incentives and International Conflict Prevention* (New York: Carnegie Commission on Preventing Deadly Conflict, 1997).

6. Raymond L. Garthoff, *Détente and Confrontation: American-Soviet Relations from Nixon to Reagan* (Washington, DC: Brookings Institution, 1985); Peter Liberman, "Trading with the Enemy: Security and Relative Economic Gains," *International Security* 21, no. 1 (Summer 1996): 147–75; Katherine Barbieri and Jack S. Levy, "Sleeping with the Enemy: The Impact of War on Trade," *Journal of Peace Research* 36, no. 4 (July 1999): 463–79; Steven E. Lobell, "Second Face of Security Strategies: Anglo-German and Anglo-Japanese Trade Concessions during the 1930s," *Security Studies* 17, no. 3 (2008): 438–67.

7. Patricia Davis, *The Art of Economic Persuasion: Positive Incentives and German Economic Diplomacy* (Ann Arbor: University of Michigan Press, 1999).

8. David A. Baldwin, *Economic Statecraft* (Princeton: Princeton University Press, 1985); Jean-Marc F. Blanchard and Norrin M. Ripsman, *Economic Statecraft and Foreign Policy: Sanctions and Incentives and Target State Calculations* (London: Routledge, 2013).

9. See, for example, Robert O. Keohane and Joseph S. Nye Jr., *Power and Interdependence* (New York: Addison Wesley Longman, 2001).

10. David A. Lake and Patrick M. Morgan, "The New Regionalism in Security Affairs," in David A. Lake and Patrick M. Morgan, eds., *Regional Orders: Building Security in a New World,* 3–19 (University Park: Pennsylvania State University Press, 1997), 11.

11. William R. Thompson, "Regional Subsystem: A Conceptual Explication and a Propositional Inventory," *International Studies Quarterly* 17, no. 1 (March 1973): 89–117.

12. Barry Buzan and Ole Waever, *Regions and Powers: The Structure of International Security* (Cambridge: Cambridge University Press, 2003).

13. Leonard Binder, "The Middle East as a Subordinate International System," *World Politics* 10, no. 3 (April 1958): 408–29; Malcolm Kerr, *The Arab Cold War: Gamal 'Abd al-Nasir and His Rivals, 1958–1970* (New York: Oxford University Press, 1971); Paul C. Noble, "The Arab System: Pressures, Constraints, and Opportunities," in Bahgat Korany and Ali E. Hillal Dessouki, eds., *The Foreign Policies of Arab States,* 2nd ed., 50–60 (Boulder: Westview Press, 1991).

14. On variations from cold to warm peace, see Benjamin Miller, "Explaining Variations in Regional Peace: Three Strategies for Peacemaking," *Cooperation and Conflict* 35, no. 2 (June 2000): 155–92. See also Kenneth Boulding, *Stable Peace* (Austin: University of Texas Press, 1978); Benjamin Miller, *States, Nations, and the Great Powers* (Cambridge: Cambridge University Press, 2007); and Arie M. Kacowicz, "Introduction," in A. Kacowicz, Y. Bar-Siman-Tov, O. Elgstrom, and M. Jerneck, eds., *Stable Peace among Nations,* 1–8 (Boulder: Rowman and Littlefield, 2001).

15. On conflict management versus peacemaking, see Yaacov Bar-Siman-Tov, "The Arab-Israeli Conflict: Learning Conflict Resolution," *Journal of Peace Research* 31, no. 1 (February 1994): 75–92.

16. Brian M. Pollins, "Conflict, Cooperation, and Commerce: The Effect of International Political Interactions on Bilateral Trade Flows," *American Journal of Political Science* 33, no. 3 (August 1989): 737–61; Gerald Schneider and Vera E. Troeger, "War and the World Economy," *Journal of Conflict Resolution* 50, no. 5 (October 2006): 623–45. On charitable organizations, see Dean Dilley and Elizabeth Ryan, "Developing New Mechanisms to Promote the Muslim Charitable Sector," in *U.S.-Islamic World Forum Papers* (Washington, DC: Brookings Institution, 2012), 1–17.

17. Baldwin, *Economic Statecraft,* 29–50.

18. On constructive engagement, see David Shambaugh, "Containment or Engagement of China? Calculating Beijing's Responses," *International Security* 21, no. 2 (Autumn 1996): 180–209.

19. Baldwin, *Economic Statecraft*, 41–42; Daniel Byman and Matthew Waxman, *The Dynamics of Coercion: American Foreign Policy and the Limits of Military Might* (Cambridge: Cambridge University Press, 2002), 9–10; Yuan-li Wu, *Economic Warfare* (New York: Prentice Hall, 1952); Jean-Marc F. Blanchard and Norrin M. Ripsman, "Measuring Vulnerability Interdependence: A Geopolitical Approach," *Geopolitics* 1, no. 3 (Winter 1996): 225–46.

20. Byman and Waxman, *Dynamics of Coercion*.

21. See David Cortright and George A. Lopez, eds., *Smart Sanctions: Targeting Economic Sanctions* (Lanham, MD: Rowman and Littlefield, 2002).

22. Michael Mastanduno, David A. Lake, and G. John Ikenberry, "Toward a Realist Theory of State Action," *International Studies Quarterly* 33, no. 4 (1989): 457–74.

23. This term draws on Scott C. James and David A. Lake's three faces of hegemony, which emphasize different instruments and targets of hegemonic influence: positive and negative sanctions directed at a foreign government (first face), societal actors (second face), and public opinion (third face). Scott C. James and David A. Lake, "The Second Face of Hegemony: Britain's Repeal of the Corn Laws and the American Walker Tariff of 1846," *International Organization* 43, no. 1 (Winter 1989): 1–30; Lobell, "Second Face of Security Strategies."

24. Etel Solingen, *Regional Orders at Century's Dawn: Global and Domestic Influences on Grand Strategy* (Princeton: Princeton University Press, 1998).

25. On the foreign policy executive, see David A. Lake, *Power, Protection, and Free Trade: International Sources of U.S. Commercial Strategy* (Ithaca: Cornell University Press, 1988); Norrin M. Ripsman, *Peacemaking by Democracies: The Effect of State Autonomy on the Post–World War Settlements* (University Park: Pennsylvania State University Press, 2004); Steven E. Lobell, Norrin M. Ripsman, and Jeffrey W. Taliaferro, *Neoclassical Realism, the State, and Foreign Policy* (Cambridge: Cambridge University Press, 2009); and Norrin M. Ripsman, Jeffrey W. Taliaferro, and Steven E. Lobell, *Neoclassical Realist Theory of International Politics* (New York: Oxford University Press, 2016).

26. Stephen Krasner, *Defending the National Interest* (Princeton: Princeton University Press, 1978); Jeffrey W. Taliaferro, Steven E. Lobell, and Norrin M. Ripsman, "Introduction: Neoclassical Realism, the State, and Foreign Policy," in Steven E. Lobell, Norrin M. Ripsman, and Jeffrey W. Taliaferro, *Neoclassical Realism, the State, and Foreign Policy,* 1–41 (Cambridge: Cambridge University Press, 2009).

27. In this regard, see Norrin M. Ripsman, *Peacemaking from Above, Peace from Below: Ending Conflict between Regional Rivals* (Ithaca: Cornell University Press, 2016); "Top-Down Peacemaking: Why Peacemaking Begins with States and Not Societies," in T. V. Paul, ed., *International Relations Theory and Regional Transfor-*

mation (Cambridge: Cambridge University Press, 2012); "Two Stages of Transition from a Region of War to a Region of Peace: Realist Transition and Liberal Endurance," *International Studies Quarterly* 49, no. 4 (December 2005): 669–93; and "The Politics of Deception: Forging Peace Treaties in the Face of Domestic Opposition," *International Journal* 60, no. 1 (Winter 2004–5): 169–96.

28. See, for example, the contributions in Cortright, *Price of Peace*.

29. George Tsebelis, *Veto Players: How Political Institutions Work* (Princeton: Princeton University Press, 2002).

30. Etel Solingen, *Regional Orders at Century's Dawn: Global and Domestic Influences on Grand Strategy* (Princeton: Princeton University Press, 1998). Others that use this nationalist versus internationalist model include Peter Gourevitch, *Politics in Hard Times: Comparative Responses to International Economic Crises* (Ithaca: Cornell University Press, 1986); Jeffrey A. Frieden, *Debt, Development, and Democracy: Modern Political Economy and Latin America, 1865–1985* (Princeton: Princeton University Press, 1991); Benjamin O. Fordham, *Building the Cold War Consensus: The Political Economy of U.S. National Security Policy, 1949–51* (Ann Arbor: University of Michigan Press, 1998); Peter Trubowitz, *Defining the National Interest: Conflict and Change in American Foreign Policy* (Chicago: University of Chicago Press, 1998); Lobell, *Challenge of Hegemony*; Scott L. Kastner, "When Do Conflicting Political Relations Affect International Trade?," *Journal of Conflict Resolution* 51, no. 4 (August 2007): 664–88; and Kevin Narizny, *The Political Economy of Grand Strategy* (Ithaca: Cornell University Press, 2007).

31. Guy Ben-Porat, "Between Power and Hegemony: Business Communities in Peace Processes," *Review of International Studies* 31, no. 2 (April 2005): 325–48; *Global Liberalism, Peace, and Conflict in Israel/Palestine and Northern Ireland* (Syracuse, NY: Syracuse University Press, 2006).

32. Harald Müller and Thomas Risse-Kappen, "From the Outside In and from the Inside Out," in David Skidmore and Valerie Hudson, eds., *Limits of State Autonomy: Societal Gaps and Foreign Policy Formulation*, 25–48 (Boulder: Westview Press, 1993); Thomas Risse-Kappen, *Bringing Transnational Relations Back In: Non-state Actors, Domestic Structures, and International Institutions* (Cambridge: Cambridge University Press, 1995).

33. For an optimistic view of the ability of economic sanctions to persuade a target society to compel policy changes, see Gary C. Hufbauer, Jeffrey J. Schott, and Kimberley Ann Elliott, *Economic Sanctions Reconsidered: History and Current Policy*, 2nd ed., vol. 1 (Washington, DC: Institute for International Economics, 2008). Robert Pape offers a more skeptical view in "Why Economic Sanctions Do Not Work," *International Security* 22, no. 2 (1997): 90–136.

34. See, for example, Johan Galtung, "On the Effects of International Economic

Sanctions with Examples from the Case of Rhodesia," *World Politics* 19, no. 3 (April 1967): 378–416.

35. For example, while Israel and Syria were negotiating a peace agreement in the early to mid-1990s, those talks broke down. The parties are now back in a pre-negotiation phase.

36. See, for example, Paul Wehr, *Conflict Regulation* (Boulder: Westview Press, 1979); and Richard L. Kuenne, "Conflict Management in a Mature Rivalry," *Journal of Conflict Resolution* 33, no. 3 (September 1989): 554–66.

37. See, for example, Ripsman, *Peacemaking from Above, Peace from Below.*

38. Norrin M. Ripsman, "False Dichotomy: Why Economics Has Always Been High Politics," in Peter Dombrowski, ed., *Guns and Butter: The Political Economy of International Security,* 15–31 (Boulder: Lynne Rienner, 2005).

39. Joseph M. Grieco, "Anarchy and the Limits of Cooperation: A Realist Critique of the Newest Liberal Institutionalism," *International Organization* 42, no. 3 (Summer 1988): 485–507; *Cooperation among Nations: Europe, America, and Non-tariff Barriers to Trade* (Ithaca: Cornell University Press, 1990).

40. Richard Rosecrance, *The Rise of the Trading State: Commerce and Conquest in the Modern World* (New York: Basic Books, 1986); Michael W. Doyle, *Ways of War and Peace* (New York: W. W. Norton, 1997), 230–50; Bruce Russett and John R. Oneal, *Triangulating Peace: Democracy, Interdependence, and International Organizations* (New York: W. W. Norton, 2001).

41. Kenneth N. Waltz, *Theory of International Politics* (New York: Random House, 1979), 139–46. For a more nuanced realist perspective, see Dale Copeland, "Economic Interdependence and War: A Theory of Trade Expectations," *International Security* 20, no. 3 (Spring 1996): 5–41.

42. Joanne Gowa, *Allies, Adversaries, and International Trade* (Princeton: Princeton University Press, 1994); Edward D. Mansfield, *Power, Trade, and War* (Princeton: Princeton University Press, 1994).

43. Binder, "Middle East as a Subordinate International System."

44. Emanuel Adler and Michael Barnett, "A Framework for the Study of Security Communities," in Emanuel Adler and Michael Barnett, eds., *Security Communities,* 29–66 (Cambridge: Cambridge University Press, 1998).

45. See, for example, Yoram Haftel, *Regional Economic Institutions and Conflict Mitigation: Design, Implementation, and the Promise of Peace* (Ann Arbor: University of Michigan Press, 2012), which argues that under the right circumstances regional economic organizations can foster peace within a region.

46. This is the approach taken in Ripsman, *Peacemaking from Above, Peace from Below.*

CHAPTER 1

The Economics of Peacemaking

Lessons from Western Europe and the Middle East

Norrin M. Ripsman

The introduction to this volume posed five questions regarding the prospects for and limitations of using economic statecraft to promote regional peacemaking. In this chapter, I will briefly provide a set of answers to these questions based on my research on the peacemaking processes between France and Germany after World War II, between Egypt and Israel in the late 1970s, and between Israel and Jordan in 1993–94. In contrast to the paired essay by Steven Lobell that follows, my conclusion here is that peacemaking is a top-down, statist endeavor, with attempts to bring societies onboard after the fact.[1] Thus, economic statecraft, to the extent that it can contribute to peacemaking, must in the first instance target state leaders. Only after a state-to-state agreement is reached are the second and third faces of security strategies useful to help sell an agreement to the rival societies.

Before I begin my overview of the use of economic tools in fostering peace between these states, a word about the importance of these cases is in order. As I indicate elsewhere, very few peace treaties (only about a dozen) were reached between regional rivals of roughly equal power during the twentieth century.[2] Of these, only four rivalries—the three I analyze here and the Sino-Japanese rivalry—can be considered the most intense, featuring three or more wars between the rival states. The strategies that were able to terminate these most intense rivalries should be useful in resolving not only other intense conflicts but also less intense ones.

Question 1: Which Instruments of Economic Statecraft Are Most Effective in the Service of Peacemaking?

The Franco-German, Egyptian-Israeli, and Israeli-Jordanian peace settlements were all facilitated with the promise of large economic assistance programs or grants. Reconciliation between France and Germany was jump-started with a massive American-led aid program known as the Marshall Plan. Prior to the extension of Marshall Plan aid, the French government was reluctant to rebuild the West German economy and was even conducting wholesale plunder of the French occupation zone in Germany, moving coal, timber, industrial equipment, and other tractable goods to France.[3] The French also resisted American attempts to soften the implementation of the Permitted and Limited Industries Agreement, which restricted German production of defense-related goods and dismantled excess German production capacity beyond allowed limits.[4] A primary purpose of Marshall Plan aid, therefore, was to link French economic recovery to German and European recovery as a means of overcoming French economic punishment of Germany.[5]

The Egyptian-Israeli peace treaty was encouraged by the promise of direct American aid to Egypt in the form of PL-480 food aid, project-related economic development assistance, and military sales credits.[6] In total, as soon as the treaty was signed and ratified, the United States augmented existing aid to Egypt by $1.8 billion in 1979.[7] On the Israeli side, $3 billion in American aid was required to defray the costs of dismantling the two Israel air bases in the Sinai and reconstructing them on the Israeli side of the agreed-upon border.[8] Furthermore, the United States agreed to provide oil to Israel at market prices if Egypt were to renege on its commitment to sell Israel oil from its Sinai wells.[9]

Once again, the Israeli-Jordanian peace treaty was encouraged by a large aid package for Jordan, including American promises to forgive about $1 billion of Jordanian debt, a US appeal to the London and Paris clubs for additional debt forgiveness of Jordanian debts totaling over $4 billion, and additional incentives such as the termination of US maritime inspections on shipping in the Gulf of Aqaba and US support for Israeli-Jordanian joint development projects.[10] After the treaty was signed, the United States explored other means of cementing peace, such as qualified industrial zones (QIZs) in Jordan (1998), which gave preferential access to the US market to goods produced in these zones with joint Israeli-Jordanian input.[11]

Overall, then, to stimulate these successful peacemaking enterprises, the

United States relied on a relatively narrow range of economic tools of statecraft. It did not employ economic sanctions in the service of peacemaking, nor did it use instruments such as reduced tariffs, free trade agreements, quota reductions, or individual- or business-specific incentives in the presignature period.

Questions 2 and 3: Which Actors Should Be Targeted at Which Stages of Peacemaking?

The three settlements I examined suggest that, at least in an effort to jump-start a peace process and facilitate an agreement, first-face of security approaches targeting the leadership of the belligerent states, rather than their societies, are most effective. Galia Press-Barnathan, in chapter 3, reaches a similar conclusion. In the European settlement, the United States overcame French reluctance to rehabilitate Germany with the massive Marshall Plan aid program. Most of this money was spent on the importation of American goods, reconstruction and infrastructure projects, and, after the outbreak of the Korean War, military upgrades for the recipient countries. Thus, although some of the money went to help rebuild firms and industrial sectors in war-ravaged European countries, the bulk of American aid served governmental purposes of promoting economic recovery and rearmament.[12] This aid was clearly tied to peacemaking, as the French, in particular, were told that American support for French reconstruction under the plan would be dependent on French support for German economic recovery and a viable postwar political statute for western Germany.[13] Consequently, the French government was compelled to allow German economic reconstruction where it had previously imposed punitive economic policies in the French occupation zone, to administer the French zone collaboratively with the British and American bizone for the purposes of jump-starting the German economy, and to allow the establishment of the Federal Republic of Germany (FRG).[14] Economic incentives were thus state to state and did not seek to persuade states to make peace by mobilizing economic interest groups or society as a whole in support of peacemaking.

In the Middle Eastern cases, economic statecraft also targeted the leadership of the belligerent states, rather than societal elites or the public, in the first instance. Instead of seeking to engage business elites in Egypt with promises of tariff reduction, free trade agreements, or firm- or sector-level incentives, American aid to Egypt consisted of items that Anwar Sadat desired as a means of overcoming the challenges his regime faced: food aid; development assistance; and, most of all, military assistance. Similarly, American assistance to Israel consisted of practical assistance to the state to defray the costs of its redeployment from the Sinai and to ensure its access to oil. To facilitate the Israeli-Jordanian settlement, the United States granted Jordan what King Hussein requested: debt forgiveness and military assistance.[15] Thus, the initial stage of economic statecraft aimed to satisfy the leaders of belligerent states rather than their societies.

Needless to say, all these state-to-state grants entailed spinoffs that would affect business interests in the target country. Nonetheless, the primary effect of this aid was to advance the target government's economic and political goals as opposed to those of the business elites or the general public. Moreover, its principal purpose was to tempt the state itself into rivalry termination rather than to generate economic pressure on the state.

Only after the belligerent governments signed peace treaties were efforts made to engage society. Thus, in Europe the 1954 London Accord and Paris Agreement preceded the negotiation and signature of the Treaty of Rome among France, Germany, and other regional participants, establishing the European Economic Community (EEC), which by 1968 had eliminated most tariffs between member states and established common pricing for agricultural goods. Similarly, only four years after the Israeli-Jordanian peace treaty did the United States introduce a QIZ program that allowed duty-free imports into the United States of goods made in specially designated zones in Jordan if they contained a minimum of 8 percent Israeli inputs as a percentage of their total cost (or only 7 percent for high-tech goods).[16] These measures engaging economic interests in the former rivals were thus intended to bring societal groups onboard the settlement after its conclusion by providing tangible benefits of peace rather than to motivate peacemaking.[17]

Question 4: What Are the Limits of Economic Statecraft?

Although economic statecraft played a role in the Western European and Middle Eastern settlements, they also suggest that we should temper our expectations regarding the importance of economic considerations in peacemaking. Indeed, in none of the three episodes did economic statecraft drive the peacemaking process. The political settlement reintegrating the FRG into the West and ending Franco-German antagonism was principally motivated by a need for regional players to unite in the face of a far greater Soviet threat than any of the weakened Western European states posed. A peace treaty was further made possible by American hegemonic pressure and security guarantees to ensure the French that they would not stand alone again against a remilitarized Germany.[18] While economic incentives were useful as a means of prodding the French to bury the hatchet and stabilizing regional relations after a peace agreement, they were certainly insufficient to produce peace on their own and may even have been unnecessary.

In the Egyptian-Israeli settlement, Sadat was clearly concerned about the domestic political implications of the economic crisis Egypt faced, as the bread riots in Egypt in 1977 could potentially threaten his hold on power. For this reason, he wanted food aid and other economic assistance from the United States to help stabilize his regime.[19] Had Sadat been motivated primarily by a desire to seek economic aid, however, he could have maintained Egypt's relationship with the Soviet Union, which he terminated in 1972, or sought more aid from the oil-rich Arab states without making peace with Israel.[20] Instead, Sadat's economic goals paled in comparison with his overriding goal of recovering the Sinai, core Egyptian territory, which Israel had captured in 1967. Since he had concluded that he was unable to recapture the Sinai by force with Soviet arms, realignment with the United States and a peace treaty with Israel presented themselves as the only logical way to attain his objective.[21] From the Israeli perspective, while US economic assistance was useful as a means of defraying the costs of the agreement, particularly the relocation of Israeli air bases from the Sinai and its military reorganization, Israel was motivated to make peace by the far more important goal of taking the most powerful Arab state out of the Arab-Israeli conflict and thereby bolstering its fragile security.[22] Thus, once again, while economic statecraft may have been necessary as a means of greasing the skids, it was by no means sufficient, or even the key ingredient, for peacemaking.

Similarly, in 1993 King Hussein was motivated in part by an economic crisis in Jordan, which was exacerbated by the effects of international economic sanctions against Iraq, Jordan's principal trading partner. In this vein, he presented a list of economic needs that he wanted the United States to fill as part of a peace deal, including debt forgiveness and military aid. Peacemaking for the king, however, was designed to achieve more fundamental strategic objectives, such as repairing Amman's relationship with the United States, which had soured because of the king's decision not to side with the United States during the 1991 Gulf War, and, after the 1993 Oslo Accords, preventing Israel and the Palestine Liberation Organization (PLO) from reaching decisions on security in the West Bank without Jordanian participation, as that could harm Jordanian strategic interests.[23] Consequently, economic statecraft was important to Jordanian calculations but was insufficient to bring about peacemaking and may not have been a necessary condition for peace.

Based on these three important cases, therefore, it would appear that economic statecraft may play a supporting role in peacemaking, but we cannot expect that regional rivals that have few strategic or political incentives to make peace would be motivated to conclude a treaty on the basis of economic incentives and sanctions alone. This point is reinforced by the similar findings in chapter 6, Jean-Marc F. Blanchard's essay on Sino-Japanese economic relations. Therefore, policy makers should not treat economic incentives as a magic wand for the promotion of peacemaking but should keep them in their arsenal of policy tools to grease the skids of peacemaking between rivals that have other compelling reasons to negotiate peace.[24] Similarly, economic sanctions might also be used to signal the costs of a failure to make peace by leaders who have reasons to contemplate peacemaking in the first place. Furthermore, economic sweeteners can be used after an agreement is reached to help leaders sell an agreement to reluctant societal elements and to solidify the domestic coalition maintaining the peace.

Moreover, the evidence from these cases suggests that economic statecraft in the service of peacemaking can even be counterproductive at times. In the Jordanian case, although economic incentives were tendered to strengthen the peace coalition, it might paradoxically have undermined pro-peace elements, as opponents of the peace treaty were able to paint those who capitalized on economic gains from trade with Israel as traitors in the service of foreign governments. In this regard, during the 1990s, professional associations in Jordan (including those representing dentists, engineers, doctors, lawyers, journalists, and writers) opposed those who supported normalization of relations with Israel. Supporters have been blacklisted and expelled from the guilds, thereby denying them basic social benefits such as pensions and health care.[25] Moreover, a list of the names of companies and individual normalizers, called the "List of Shame," is available on the Internet, and boycotts are publicly urged against all those who work with Israel or Israelis in any context.[26] Consequently, rather than empowering moderates, economic statecraft might operate to isolate them. In this regard, Scott Kastner and Margaret Pearson's conclusion in chapter 7 that economic statecraft works best when its goals are not publicly stated may have some merit.

Furthermore, given the Egyptian experience, in which dire domestic economic performance led to pressure on the regime, which confirmed Sadat's strategic inclination to contemplate peacemaking, we can hypothesize another risk of economic incentives in the service of peace. To the extent that economic incentives tendered prior to a signed agreement improve economic conditions in the belligerent states, they may reduce economic and domestic political pressure on the leaders to make peace, thereby undermining the peace process rather than fueling it. Finally, although this did not occur significantly in the peace settlements I investigated, poorly targeted economic incentives might actually enrich opponents of peace and empower them to obstruct a settlement.[27]

In light of these limitations, policy makers should not expect too much from economic instruments in promoting peace and should target them carefully to avoid undermining progress toward peace.

Question 5: How Can Economic Tools Embed Bilateral Peacemaking in a Regional Context?

The European and Middle Eastern cases suggest two alternative endpoints for peace treaties between regional rivals. Peace between France and Germany occurred not at a bilateral but at a regional level, involving other regional and extraregional actors. The London Accord and Paris Agreement were negotiated and signed with Great Britain and the United States as cosignatories and equal partners. This ensured not only that the peace treaty was embedded in a broader regional settlement but that the former rivals had guarantees from other states to allow them a greater measure of security and trust in the settlement. Moreover, the economic dimension of the settlement was regionalized as well. Before the settlement, France, Germany, Italy, and the Benelux countries created a regional coal and steel industry in the European Coal and Steel Community (ECSC). After the 1954 agreements, this regional instrument was deepened with the 1957 Treaty of Rome, creating the EEC, and eventually expanded to include other regional participants. As a result of these broader regional frameworks, the bilateral peace treaty was embedded in a regional transformation and stabilized over time.

In contrast, the two Middle Eastern settlements were bilateral agreements that were never entrenched in broader regional arrangements. Following the Egyptian-Israeli peace treaty, the Arab boycott of Israel and companies doing business with Israel remained in force, making it impossible to envision a regional economic institution that could entrench the peace settlement as the EEC had done in Europe.[28] While many regional Arab states (including Egypt, Jordan, Morocco, and the Gulf states) suspended application of the boycott (though in some cases only the secondary and tertiary boycotts of companies doing business with Israel) after the Oslo Accords and the Israeli-Jordanian peace treaty, other, harder-line states did not, preventing the regionalization of economic arrangements.[29] In this context, aside from the rather ineffectual Union for the Mediterranean initiated in July 2008, no regional institutions of note have ever included both Arab states and Israel as members.[30] As a result, the treaties—if they endure in the wake of the "Arab Spring" that is transforming Arab governments in the region—are likely to remain bilateral.

In light of these contrasting experiences, it is tempting to suggest that the key to stabilizing peace agreements is to embed them in broader regional economic and political arrangements. After all, the Franco-German rapprochement was cemented within Western European political institutions and remains, in Benjamin Miller's terms, a "warm peace," while the two Arab-Israeli settlements failed to do and remain "cold peaces."[31] Nonetheless, it remains possible that the causal arrow points in the other direction, namely, that regional economic arrangements are only possible if the bilateral peace agreement resolves the core issues of the regional conflict. If possible, however, regionalizing economic arrangements after a bilateral peace treaty is achieved should help stabilize the peace settlement.

Conclusion: Top-Down Peacemaking

In contrast to chapter 2, by Steven E. Lobell, my conclusion drawn from my analysis of three successful and high-profile peace processes between regional rivals—successful in that they each culminated in peace treaties—is that peacemaking begins as a top-down endeavor driven by state interests. Some of these state interests, as I discuss elsewhere, had little to do with economics but instead centered on threats from other states, great power pressure (in these cases, especially from the United States), and regime survival interests.[32] To the extent that states or international institutions wish to promote regional peacemaking with economic instruments, however, first-face-of-security strategies targeting the belligerent states and their leadership are likely to be more effective than broad-based approaches engaging the second and third faces of security.

Moreover, as I observe elsewhere, second- and third-face approaches, which seek to promote peace by changing societal attitudes, necessarily postpone the project of peacemaking, often at great cost in blood and treasure. After all, societal attitudes change in glacial time, often over generations, whereas states are often more flexible and can change policy in the face of changing international conditions and incentives. Consequently, not only are top-down approaches likely to be more effective in promoting peacemaking than societal approaches, but when they work they are likely to show results sooner than second- and third-face approaches.[33]

This is not to downplay the importance of engaging societal elites and the general public with second- and third-face economic tools *after* a peace treaty is concluded as a means of bringing societal groups onboard and thereby entrenching the settlement. Societal engagement is critical to maintaining peace, and economic tools can help build and enlarge peace coalitions. The bottom line is that the type of economic engagement needed to foster peacemaking between regional rivals varies depending on the stage of negotiations.

NOTES

1. See Norrin M. Ripsman, "Top-Down Peacemaking: Why Peacemaking Begins with States and Not Societies," in T. V. Paul, ed., *International Relations Theory and Regional Transformation*, 255–82 (Cambridge: Cambridge University Press, 2012); "Two Stages of Transition from a Region of War to a Region of Peace: Realist Transition and Liberal Endurance," *International Studies Quarterly* 49, no. 4 (December 2005): 669–93; and "The Politics of Deception: Forging Peace Treaties in the Face of Domestic Opposition," *International Journal* 60, no. 1 (Winter 2004–5): 169–96.

2. See Norrin M. Ripsman, *Peacemaking from Above, Peace from Below: Ending Conflict between Regional Rivals* (Ithaca: Cornell University Press, 2016). For the list of twentieth-century rivalries used to compile this list, see Paul F. Diehl and Gary Goertz, *War and Peace in Enduring Rivalries* (Ann Arbor: University of Michigan Press, 2000), 145–46.

3. On French occupation policy, see Marc Hillel, *L'Occupation française en*

Allemagne (Paris: Balland, 1983); and Frank Roy Willis, *The French in Germany* (Stanford, CA: Stanford University Press, 1962).

4. Norrin M. Ripsman, *Peacemaking by Democracies: The Effect of State Autonomy on the Post–World War Settlements* (University Park: Pennsylvania State University Press, 2002), 164–87; Alec Cairncross, *The Price of War* (Oxford: Basil Blackwell, 1986).

5. John Gimbel, *The Origins of the Marshall Plan* (Stanford, CA: Stanford University Press, 1976).

6. Patrick Clawson and Zoe Danon Gedal, *Dollars and Diplomacy: The Impact of U.S. Economic Initiatives on Arab-Israeli Negotiations* (Washington, DC: Washington Institute for Near East Policy, 1999), 63–64.

7. Carter to Church, April 2, 1979, Jimmy Carter Presidential Library, WHCF, Subject File, Countries, Box CO-24, CO 45 1/1/79–6/30/79.

8. Ibid.

9. Moshe Dayan, *Breakthrough: A Personal Account of the Egypt-Israel Peace Negotiations* (New York: Knopf, 1981), 276–77.

10. Asher Susser, "Jordan: Al-Mamlaka al-Urdunniyya al-Hashimiyya," in Ami Ayalon, ed., *Middle East Contemporary Survey, 1993*, 449–89 (Boulder: Westview Press, 1995), 473; Martin Indyk, *Innocent Abroad: An Intimate Account of American Peace Diplomacy in the Middle East* (New York: Simon and Schuster, 2009), 127.

11. Howard Rosen, "Free Trade Agreements as Foreign Policy Tools: The US-Israel and US-Jordan FTAs," in Jeffrey J. Schott, ed., *Free Trade Agreements: US Strategies and Priorities*, 51–78 (Washington, DC: Institute for International Economics, 2004), 60; Steven E. Lobell, "The Second Face of American Security: The U.S.-Jordan Free Trade Agreement as Security Policy," *Comparative Strategy* 27, no. 1 (2008): 1–13.

12. Michael J. Hogan, *The Marshall Plan: America, Britain, and the Reconstruction of Western Europe, 1947–1952* (Cambridge: Cambridge University Press, 1987), 414–15.

13. Gimbel, *Origins of the Marshall Plan.*

14. Ripsman, *Peacemaking by Democracies*, 176–87.

15. Dennis Ross, *The Missing Peace: The Inside Story of the Fight for Middle East Peace* (New York: Farrar, Straus and Giroux, 2004), 171–75; Indyk, *Innocent Abroad*, 127–29.

16. Rosen, "Free Trade Agreements as Foreign Policy Tools," 60; Lobell, "Second Face of American Security," 1–13.

17. See, for example, Abdul Salam Majali, Jawad A. Anani, and Munther J. Haddadin, *Peacemaking: The Inside Story of the 1994 Jordanian-Israeli Treaty* (Norman: University of Oklahoma Press, 2006), 158–59.

18. Ripsman, "Two Stages of Transition from a Region of War to a Region of Peace."

19. Ibrahim A. Karawan, "Sadat and the Egyptian-Israeli Peace Revisited," *International Journal of Middle East Studies* 26, no. 2 (May 1994): 249–66, at 261; Mohamed Heikal, *Secret Channels: The Inside Story of Arab-Israeli Peace Negotiations* (London: Harper Collins, 1996), 248; Etel Solingen, *Regional Orders at Century's Dawn: Global and Domestic Influences on Grand Strategy* (Princeton: Princeton University Press, 1998), 177–78. Arad, Hirsch, and Tovias, therefore, note that Sadat's desire to make peace was at least partially motivated by economic concerns. Ruth Arad, Seez Hirsch, and Alfred Tovias, *The Economics of Peacemaking: Focus on the Egyptian-Israeli Situation* (New York: St. Martin's, 1983), 3.

20. On Sadat's break with Moscow, see Alvin Z. Rubinstein, *Red Star on the Nile: The Soviet-Egyptian Influence Relationship since the June War* (Princeton: Princeton University Press, 1977), chaps. 5–6.

21. Raphael Israeli, *Man of Defiance: A Political Biography of Anwar Sadat* (Totowa, NJ: Barnes and Noble, 1985), 216–20.

22. Israeli Foreign Minister Moshe Dayan, for example, noted, "[I]f you take one wheel off a car, it won't drive. If Egypt is out of the conflict, there will be no more war." William B. Quandt, *Peace Process: American Diplomacy and the Arab-Israeli Conflict since 1967* (Washington, DC: Brookings Institution, 2001), 190.

23. King Hussein of Jordan, "Remarks on the Peace Process, Amman, 9 July 1994," *Journal of Palestine Studies* 24, no. 1 (Autumn 1994): 134–36, at 135; Itamar Rabinovich, *Waging Peace: Israel and the Arabs, 1948–2003* (Princeton: Princeton University Press, 2004), 60.

24. As Patrick Clawson and Zoe Danon Gedal observe, "In the Middle East, politics does come before business, but business can help to reinforce politics. Although economic efforts will rarely be enough of a force to pave a path from hostility to peace, they can be useful in supporting and cementing progress along that path." Clawson and Gedal, *Dollars and Diplomacy*, 127.

25. Danishai Kornbluth, "Jordan and the Anti-Normalization Campaign, 1994–2001," *Terrorism and Political Violence* 14, no. 3 (Autumn 2002): 80–108, at 91.

26. "The Free Arab Voice," February 12, 2001, accessed March 11, 2013, http://www.freearabvoice.org/ArabZionstConflictInJordan.htm.

27. See Norrin M. Ripsman, "Promoting Regional Peacemaking," *International Journal* 67, no. 2 (Spring 2012): 434–36.

28. On the Arab boycott, see Dan Chill, *The Arab Boycott of Israel: Economic Aggression and World Reaction* (New York: Praeger, 1976); and Gil Feiler, *From Boycott to Economic Cooperation: The Arab Boycott of Israel* (London: Taylor and Francis, 1998).

29. David Makovsky, *Making Peace with the PLO* (Boulder: Westview Press, 1995), 121; Martin A. Weiss, "Arab League Boycott of Israel," CRS Report RS22424, April 19, 2006, Foreign Press Centers, accessed February 19, 2007, http://fpc.state.gov/documents/organization/65777.pdf.

30. On the limited political significance of the Union for the Mediterranean, which is like "a balloon that lost its air," see Rosa Balfour, "The Transformation of the Union for the Mediterranean," *Mediterranean Politics* 14, no. 1 (March 2009): 99–105, at 99.

31. Benjamin Miller, *States, Nations, and the Great Powers* (Cambridge: Cambridge University Press, 2007); "Explaining Variations in Regional Peace: Three Strategies for Peacemaking," *Cooperation and Conflict* 35, no. 2 (June 2000): 155–91.

32. Ripsman, *Peacemaking from Above, Peace from Below*.

33. Ripsman, "Promoting Regional Peacemaking," 435–36.

CHAPTER 2

The Second Face of Regional Peacemaking

Israel and Jordan, 1985–2001

Steven E. Lobell

This chapter addresses the five questions outlined in the introduction to this volume and discusses the role of the United States in the peace processes in Israel and Jordan between 1985 and 2001. In contrast to chapter 1 by Norrin Ripsman, which emphasizes top-down peacemaking, I present a bottom-up or second-face-of-security model of peacemaking.[1]

Peace treaties are negotiated by the foreign policy executive (FPE) or state leaders who are tasked with making foreign security and economic policy.[2] A second-face-of-security strategy entails including societal actors and interest groups in the peacemaking process rather than state leaders alone.[3] According to this deliberate strategy, a state (and often an extraregional great power) uses economic incentives, including different types of trade agreements, foreign aid, and loans, to enable or strengthen a pro-peace domestic interest bloc or win-set in the target state. Concomitantly, this strategy can weaken or disable an anti-peace coalition by driving a wedge between societal elites and state leaders. The ultimate goal is to create a large pro-peace win-set or constituency to allow the state leaders to take the political risks that are inherently involved in engaging a rival power in the peacemaking process.

Question 1: Which Instruments of Economic Statecraft are Most Effective in the Process of Peacemaking?

The United States has signed a number of trade arrangements with Middle Eastern states. These include bilateral free trade agreements (FTAs), which eliminate tariff and nontariff barriers to trade, with Israel, Jordan, and Morocco; qualified industrial zones (QIZs), which promote economic cooperation between states (i.e., duty-free export to the United States of certain Egyptian and Jordanian goods that contain Israeli inputs); trade and investment framework agreements (TIFAs), which establish legal protections for investors and were precursors for FTAs with Kuwait, Qatar, Egypt, and Tunisia; bilateral investment treaties (BITs), which establish the terms and conditions for private investment; and general systems of preference (GSPs), which provide preferential duty-free entry for specific products.[4]

In 1985 Washington and Jerusalem signed the US-Israel Free Trade Agreement.[5] The FTA reduced rates of duty and in some cases eliminated all duties on merchandise exported from Israel to the United States. The agreement covers merchandise exported from Israel, the Gaza Strip, and the West Bank. In 1995 all products produced in Israel that were eligible for reduced duties under the agreement became duty free.

In the aftermath of the 1994 Jordan-Israel peace treaty, the United States established several QIZs.[6] For Jordanian goods to enter the United States duty free (the relationship was nonreciprocal), two conditions had to be met: the product had to be produced in a QIZ, and at least 8 percent of the appraised value of any product had to come from Israeli sources.[7] With King Abdullah II's ascension to the throne, the United States and the king took additional steps to further link Jordan to the global economy. In 2001, superseding the QIZs, the US-Jordan Free Trade Agreement was signed into law.[8]

Questions 2 and 3: Which Actors Should Be Targeted and at Which Stages of Peacemaking?

In targeting economic and societal elites in another state rather than the leaders alone, the FPE's intention in using economic statecraft is threefold and reflects the different stages of the peace process. The first goal is to strengthen the power of societal actors and interest groups that have a vested economic, political, or social stake in deepening international ties (the internationalist bloc) and to weaken the opponents of such policies (the nationalist bloc) both politically and economically.[9] The second goal is to create a large domestic pro-peace win-set. Both goals will allow state leaders to undertake the politically risky steps that are necessary to engage a rival power's leaders in the prenegotiation stage of the peace process and to make difficult and unpopular compromises in the negotiation stage. The third goal is to promote the growth of domestic groups with a vested interest in the peace agreement. This goal is important in the implementation phase in order to make the agreement sticky and more difficult to reverse under successive leaders or if relations worsen.[10]

The United States used economic statecraft, and in particular preferential trade agreements and intergovernmental organization (IGOs), to strengthen and enlarge the membership of the pro-peace blocs in both Israel and Jordan. Specifically, Washington used the 1985 US-Israel Free Trade Agreement, the creation of QIZs in 1996, the 2001 US-Jordan Free Trade Agreement, and International Monetary Fund (IMF) and World Bank programs to boost the power and position of outward-oriented economic and societal elites. In the case of Israel, the target was to increase the size and power of the internationalists' win-set in order to assist the prime minister engage the Arabs and Palestinians. As one author summarizes it, "Israeli moderation toward the Palestinians, the recognition of the PLO [Palestine Liberation Organization] . . . under the Rabin-Peres governments, should be understood as part and parcel of a broader process of liberalization in Israeli society which continues to sustain peace making."[11] In the case of Jordan, the target was to increase the size of the internationalists' win-set in order to assist the palace in its risky domestic and international realignment toward commercial liberalization, political democratization (renewal of Parliament), and normalization of relations with Israel.

Israel: Targets of Economic Statecraft

From the creation of Israel in 1948 to the mid-1980s, the ruling Labor Party adopted a highly state-interventionist economic policy and a heavily subsidized economy. By the late 1970s, the Histadrut, the ruling trade union of workers, owned or controlled 25 percent of Israel's economy, its membership rolls accounted for one-third of Israel's population, and it included roughly 85 percent of all wage earners.[12] The decade after the 1973 Yom Kippur War is known as the "lost years" (1974–85) since Israel's economic growth slowed, inflation rose, and government expenditures and deficits increased. By 1984 inflation in Israel was close to 450 percent.

The American FPE, in combination with the IMF and the World Bank, pushed the ideas of the Washington Consensus on Israel. Washington prescribed that Israel adopt anti-inflationary policies, open its economy to both foreign trade and investment, expand market forces, and adopt macroeconomic stabilization (known as "Herb's ten points"). In return Washington promised a safety net of $1.5 billion, transformed its annual loans of $3 billion to a grant, and established the United States–Israel Free Trade Agreement.[13]

Jerusalem's response was the 1985 Emergency Stabilization Plan (ESP), undertaken by Shimon Peres's National Unity Government (1984–86). The plan called for significant cuts in government spending, devaluation of the Israeli shekel, tax cuts, temporary wage and price controls, and limiting the ability of the Bank of Israel to print money.[14] Market reforms contributed broadly to the privatization, liberalization, the reduction of monopolies, a decline in state intervention and government control, and deregulation of Israel's economy; the ESP replaced the heavily subsidized and state-owned economy with market-based economic incentives and liberalized capital markets.[15] Specifically, the ESP allowed private enterprises to raise capital by issuing securities through the stock exchange without government control and relaxed foreign capital borrowing.[16] Israeli companies were also listed on the New York Stock Exchange (as well as the Tel Aviv Stock Exchange) and offered securities.[17]

The ESP, the FTA, and the IMF and World Bank programs contributed to growth in the size, scope, and power of Israel's outward-oriented and internationalist bloc. Specific beneficiaries of America's targeted economic statecraft in Israel included export-oriented high-tech industries such as telecommunications, electronics, and agro-chemicals; the private sector; and a growing, autonomous, Israeli business community. Other Israeli winners included such representatives of the Israeli business community such as the Israeli Manufacturers' Association (Dov Lautman, president); the Israeli Chamber of Commerce (Danny Gillerman, chairman); the Federation of Chambers of Commerce; and large private corporations such as Koor, Delta Galil Industries, Osem, and Teva Pharmaceuticals.[18]

Empowered by the FTA and ESP, the outward-oriented and internationalist bloc campaigned and lobbied the Israeli FPE on several fronts. Members of this bloc argue that political instability and the Arab-Israeli-Palestinian conflict, the Arab boycott and secondary boycott of Israeli goods and services, and the lack of progress in the peace talks with the PLO are barriers to attracting foreign investment and capital and greater Israeli access to the global economy.[19] According to Etel Solingen, the internationalist bloc lobbied the Israeli FPE for (1) access to foreign capital, investments, and technology; (2) a stable regional environment, which would attract foreign investment and firms; and (3) a reduction in the size and cost of the military-industrial complex and domestic defense spending.[20] Similarly, according to Guy Ben-Porat, internationalists pushed for (1) economic and political liberalization, (2) termination of the conflict with the Palestinians, and (3) global integration.[21] Moreover, the internationalist bloc rejected Likud's platform of "Greater Israel," or retaining the territory of the West Bank and Gaza Strip, since it was incompatible with greater Israeli integration into the global community and terminating the primary and secondary boycotts. Instead, internationalists favored the Labor Party's "land for peace" platform, or Israeli withdrawal in exchange for peace. In 1989 John Rossant wrote in *Business Week,* "The pragmatic Israeli business community is putting behind-the-scene pressure on the Shamir government to negotiate with the Palestinians."[22]

The ESP, and more broadly the push for Israeli economic liberalization and greater global integration, was opposed by the inward-oriented and nationalist bloc, including labor-intensive sectors, farmers, labor unions, settlers, religious/confessionalist groups (Gush Emunim), and religious rightist parties.[23] While Likud, the more right-wing party, had a strong commitment to a market-based economy, in retaining the support of Greater Israel it lost the favor of the internationalist-oriented business community. Retrenchment of the welfare state further weakened the Histadrut and trade unions. Low-tech producers, such as food manufacturers, opposed the reduction of tariff barriers. According to Gershon Shafir and Yoav Peled, workers in labor-intensive industries (including farming and the textile, food, wood, leather, and plastics industries), whose views were more national and domestic than international and global, also resisted these moves as they were vulnerable to competition from Palestinian workers with their lower wages.[24] Other businesses that benefited from Israel's self-sufficiency doctrine, especially in the military sector, also benefited from protection of the domestic market.

In the 1992 Israeli national elections, as a clear alternative to the right-wing Likud government of Yitzhak Shamir, the Yitzhak Rabin-led Labor Party campaigned on the promise of reaching an agreement with the Palestinians within nine months. More broadly, the Labor Party identified itself as the territory-for-peace party in opposition to Likud's Greater Israel platform.[25] Public support for recognition of the PLO came from leaders of the Israeli business community. The export industry supported the subsequent 1993 Oslo Accords, or Declaration of Principles (DOP), and the postinterim agreements. As Ben-Porat notes, "In the months that followed the revelation of the Accords and the ceremonial signing of the agreement . . . statements made by the Israeli government were backed by businessmen's optimistic scenarios."[26]

Jordan: Targets of Economic Statecraft

Similar to the experience in Israel, in 1988 the Jordanian government entered into structural adjustment agreements with the IMF to restructure its debt payments and restore its economy.[27] In return for the IMF austerity program and World Bank loans, Jordan agreed to economic reforms, cuts in government spending and subsidies, reductions in tariffs and nontariff barriers (NTBs), and tax increases to boost government revenues. In the aftermath of the 1994 Jordan-Israel peace treaty, to help further lock in the agreement and pave the way for more progress in the normalization of relations, the United States established QIZs. In 2001, superseding the QIZs, the US-Jordan Free Trade Agreement was signed into law, granting Jordan unfettered access to the American economy.

The IMF and World Bank structural adjustment programs, the QIZs, and the FTA accelerated economic liberalization in Jordan. Furthermore, these liberalization measures enlarged the rolls and strengthened the political power of the "new actors" in Jordan.[28] The king's pro-western supporters include military personnel, top bureaucrats and cabinet appointees, private sector elites and Palestinian businessmen close to the palace, and a westernized Palace elite.[29] These supporters benefit as a result of their ties to companies in the United States and Europe, government spending on defense contracts, and capital intensive projects. The predominantly Transjordanian Army also shares the king's pro-western orientation. The leadership of the army receives its training in the West and in particular in the United States and Britain.

One tangible outcome of US, IMF, and World Bank economic statecraft has been the emergence of a Palestinian business elite. This elite is young and foreign educated and willing to engage in joint ventures with foreign partners, including Israeli companies.[30] While Transjordanians control the public sector, Palestinians (of East Jordanian background) and Palestinian-owned companies dominate the private sector, especially the key areas of banking and commerce.[31] Due to their close ties to the palace, they are able to defy opposition from inward-oriented professional associations and support the QIZs, normalization with Israel, and the FTA with the United States. While the king's support for the private sector will increase the Palestinians' political influence in Jordan, thus far Palestinians have been slow to convert their economic gains into political power.[32]

Southern and rural Transjordanians, the king's historical constituency, are the swing voting bloc in Jordan. Transjordanians are an overwhelming proportion of state employees, the bureaucracy is under their control, and they manage a majority of state-owned companies. There exists a revolving door between public companies and government officials. Transjordanians dominate public sector jobs, including those in education, agriculture, transportation, and public works. Finally, Transjordanians serve as the backbone of the armed forces, police, intelligence community, and security system.

As state and public sector employees, Transjordanians were harmed by the FTA and the IMF and World Bank structural adjustment programs. These programs translate into the elimination of subsidies, reductions in social services, and layoffs of public employees. The king has used "side-payments" to compensate his traditional supporters for their losses. For instance, following the signing of Jordan's peace treaty with Israel, salaries for schoolteachers (the largest group of state employees) were increased and the military and security services were modernized with American financial assistance.[33]

The inward-oriented economic nationalist bloc has suffered most under the QIZs, FTA, and structural adjustment programs. Nationalists call for the cancellation of government and IMF-mandated economic austerity packages, oppose further liberalization of Jordan's economy, and reject improved relations with the United States and normalization with Israel. Combating the normalization of relations with Israel is the lightning rod of opposition to broader integration into the global economy. For instance, in 1996 a broad and log-rolled coalition of anti-peace Islamists, centrists, and leftists united to oppose an Israeli trade and industrial fair to be hosted in Amman.[34] Unable to block the peace treaty, anti-normalizers campaigned against full relations with Israel and more broadly against the king and the internationalists' worldview and agenda. For anti-normalization members, QIZs and the FTA are external threats to their domestic power and positions.

Anti-normalization members represent groups that are harmed politically, economically, socially, or culturally by an outward-oriented and international-ist foreign policy. These include Islamists and especially the Muslim Brother-hood and its political party, the Islamic Action Front (IAF), ultranationalists, trade union syndicates, leftist parties and pan-Arabists (who fear being dis-tanced from the Arab world), and trade and professional associations.[35]

Question 4: What Are the Limits of Economic Statecraft?

There are several limits to the use of economic statecraft in the peace process. One is the creation of domestic losers who become spoilers.[36] Specifically, the risk is that economic statecraft can backfire and ignite a nationalist, anti-American, and extremist backlash. Moreover, in the case of Jordan, the FTA and QIZs heightened intercommunal tensions between the Transjordanian-dominated public sector and the Palestinian-dominated private sector—both constituencies of the crown. Finally, a gap often exits between the business community's support for the peace process, which can outpace the general public's support.

A second problem is the linking of negotiations and a settlement with promises of economic growth and prosperity. One common theme in both the Israeli and Jordanian internationalist blocs was the belief that peace would bring greater prosperity in the form of trade and investment. Moreover, both the Palestinians and the Jordanians believed their territory would serve as a "land bridge" between Israel and the Arab world for goods, services, and tour-ism. Israeli business interests believed that peace with Jordan and the Palestin-ians would roll back the secondary boycotts, which were blocking Israeli access to the global market.

The positive externalities resulting from US, IMF, and World Bank eco-nomic statecraft have been limited by the Arab states' fear of Israel's economic superiority and the perception that the peace dividends have been insufficient for both the Palestinians and the Israeli general public. Moreover, the expected economic peace dividends from creating a New Middle East Market have not materialized.[37] Unemployment remains high, population growth is rapid, and poverty and income disparities are growing.[38] Anticipated increases in tourism (a new source of foreign exchange), trade, foreign investment and international funding, and American (and British) debt relief and bilateral and multilateral aid on the scale of the 1978 Camp David Accords have failed to occur in significant amounts.[39] The 1993 Oslo Accords and the 1994 Israel-Jordan peace treaty even created some popular images of a Benelux-style economic entity consisting of Israel, Jordan, and the Palestinian Authority.[40] Finally, proponents suggested that Jordan would become the gateway among Israel, the Arab world, and Asia.[41] Many of those who expected the peace treaty with Israel to yield such a peace dividend have subsequently joined the ranks of the opposition.

Meanwhile, Israeli industry looked beyond trade with the Arab world. In addition to opening the Arab markets closed by primary boycotts, it was hoped the peace dividend would open other markets closed by secondary boycotts of Israeli goods and services.

Question 5: How Can Economic Tools Embed Bilateral Peacemaking in a Regional Context?

There have been several attempts to move beyond the dyadic peace among Israel, Egypt, and Jordan. These initiatives call for regional economic cooperation with the ultimate goal of regional peacemaking in the Middle East.[42] In his 1993 book *The New Middle East*, Shimon Peres outlined a plan that would increase regional cooperation based on a common market of Israeli, Palestinian, and Jordanian economies and contribute to the growth of region-based institutions.[43]

One attempt to move from a dyadic peace to a regional process was the Middle East and North Africa (MENA) economic summits. Beginning in 1994, multinational corporations, governments, and businesses from the MENA countries held a series of economic summits, which included Israel. The summits were held in Casablanca (1994), Amman (1995), Cairo (1996), and Doha (1997). In addition to other opportunities for multilateral economic coordination, the summits highlighted joint investment opportunities and regional infrastructure projects. According to Jonathan Paris, one goal of MENA was to "reinforce the peace process and Israel's normalization of relations with its Arab neighbors by building an economic scaffolding."[44] Paris contends that MENA was a reward for Israel's progress in the Oslo peace process. However, beginning in 1996, MENA was undermined by a perceived lack of progress in the peace process.

A second opportunity to move beyond a dyadic peace was the Regional Economic Development Working Group (REDWG), which emerged from the 1991 Madrid Conference.[45] REDWG sought to coordinate regional infrastructure projects on water conservation, power and electricity, pipelines, pollution control, and transportation among Egypt, Israel, the Palestine Authority, Jordan, and the United States. Coordination among the REDWG members declined after 1996, with only a few joint projects moving forward.

A third attempt to move beyond dyadic peace was President George W. Bush's proposed a Middle East Free Trade Area (MEFTA). The intent is to "increase trade and investment with the United States and the world economy, and to assist these countries in implementing domestic reforms, instituting the rule of law, protecting private property rights (including intellectual property), and creating a foundation for openness, economic growth, and prosperity."[46]

One major problem with MEFTA and the use of FTAs in the Middle East is that many of the states are poor candidates. The combination of freer trade, liberalization of market forces, and privatization would cause destabilizing sociopolitical and economic dislocations and thereby strengthen the power and position of the hard-liners who oppose the peace process. Broadly, FTAs can undermine preexisting social and political arrangements. For instance, privatization and deregulation of a local economy can affect a bloated public sector, contributing to a loss of jobs among state employees, which might result in grievances, strikes, and potential public unrest. Foreign competition could destroy inefficient and unprofitable state-owned public sector enterprises. Skilled labor would then abandon the public sector for private manufacturing, threatening those who favor preserving the role of government-run enterprises in the national economy. At odds with public sector managers and party-state officials, rising commercial interests would try to divert scarce resources from social welfare and the military services to domestic investment. In this instance, FTAs would greatly strengthen supporters of the economic nationalist bloc, who oppose increased integration.

In the short to medium term, the most constructive US trade policy might include opening its economy unilaterally or nonreciprocally to specific exports from the region while allowing the target country to maintain its trade barriers. Under the second face of security—as the target country's pro-peace bloc experiences the benefits of increased trade—empowered internationalists will pressure the government for further international engagement.

NOTES

1. Also see Jonathan Nitzan and Shmshon Bichler, "From War Profits to Peace Dividends: The New Political Economy of Israel," *Class & Capital* 17, no. 60 (September 1996): 61–94; Gershon Shafir and Yoav Peled, eds., *The New Israel: Peacemaking and Liberalization* (Boulder: Westview Press, 2000); Guy Ben-Porat, "Between Power and Hegemony: Business Communities in Peace Processes," *Review of International Studies* 31, no. 2 (April 2005): 325–48; and Guy Ben-Porat, *Global Liberalism, Local Populism: Peace, and Conflict in Israel/Palestine and Northern Ireland* (Syracuse: Syracuse University Press, 2006). For an extended discussion of the second-face-of-security strategies, see Steven E. Lobell, "Second Face of Security Strategies: Anglo-German and Anglo-Japanese Trade Concessions during the 1930s," *Security Studies* 17, no. 3 (2008): 438–67.

2. On the FPE, see Steven E. Lobell, Norrin M. Ripsman, and Jeffrey W. Taliaferro, eds., *Neoclassical Realism, the State, and Foreign Policy* (Cambridge: Cambridge University Press, 2009).

3. For my commentary on President Barack Obama's use of second-face-of-security strategies during his visit to Israel in 2013, see Steven E. Lobell, letter to the editor, *New York Times,* March 22, 2013, http://www.nytimes.com/2013/03/23/opinion/obama-in-the-mideast-sampling-the-reviews.html?_r=1&.

4. An FTA with Bahrain is awaiting congressional approval, and the US government has initiated negotiations with Oman and the United Arab Emirates. See http://www.ustr.gov/Trade_Agreements/Bilateral/Section_Index.html; http://www.ustr.gov/Trade_Agreements/TIFA/Section_Index.html; and http://www.ustr.gov/Trade_Agreements/BIT/Section_Index.html.

5. The European Economic Community (EEC) and Israel signed the Israel Free Trade Agreement in 1975. See http://tcc.export.gov/Trade_Agreements/All_Trade_Agreements/exp_005439.asp.

6. Congress authorized the QIZs in 1996, and the first QIZ was officially designated in 1998 in Irbid. The QIZs encouraged foreign investment in Jordan through "free currency transactions, full repatriation of profits and salaries, and the elimination of tariff restrictions on US goods." Robert J. Bookmiller, "Abdullah's Jordan: America's Anxious Ally," *Alternatives* 2 (Summer 2003): 177.

7. Mutual trade between Israel and Jordan rose from $13 million in 1996 to $130 million in 2003. Israel holds the sixth spot on Jordan's export list. Israeli exports to Jordan made an even greater leap, increasing in the same period by $78 million, a rise of 40 percent. See Marc Lynch, *State Interests and Public Spheres: The International Politics of Jordan's Identity* (New York: Columbia University Press, 1999).

8. Jordanian exports to the United States rose from around $16 million in 1998 to $670 million in 2003, with a total of around $3 billion in annual exports.

9. On the internationalist and the nationalist blocs, see Benjamin O. Fordham, *Building the Cold War Consensus: The Political Economy of U.S. National Security Policy, 1949–51* (Ann Arbor: University of Michigan Press, 1998); Etel Solingen, *Regional Orders at Century's Dawn: Global and Domestic Influences on Grand Strategy* (Princeton: Princeton University Press, 1998); and Steven E. Lobell, *The Challenge of Hegemony: Grand Strategy, Trade, and Domestic Politics* (Ann Arbor: University of Michigan Press, 2003).

10. Etel Solingen, "The Multilateral Arab-Israeli Negotiations: Genesis, Institutionalization, Pause, Future," *Journal of Peace Research* 37, no. 2 (March 2000): 171.

11. Gershon Shafir and Yoav Peled, "Peace and Profits: The Globalization of Israeli Business and the Peace Process," in Gershon Shafir and Yoav Peled, eds., *The New Israel: Peacemaking and Liberalization* (Boulder: Westview Press, 2000), 243.

12. Lev Luis Grinberg and Gershon Shafir, "Economic Liberalization and the Breakup of the Histadrut's Domain," in Gershon Shafir and Yoav Peled, eds., *The New Israel: Peacemaking and Liberalization* (Boulder: Westview Press, 2000), 103.

13. Emma Murphy, "Israel," in Tim Niblock and Emma Murphy, eds., *Economic and Political Liberalization in the Middle East* (New York: British Academic Press, 1993), 243–44.

14. Ibid.

15. Ben-Porat, *Global Liberalism*, 152–59.

16. Shafir and Peled, "Peace and Profits," 246.

17. Ibid.

18. Ben-Porat, *Global Liberalism*, 158–66.

19. Shafir and Peled, "Peace and Profits," 247, 252, 259, 260; Uri Ram, "The Promised Land of Business Opportunities: Liberal Post-Zionism in the Global Age," in Gershon Shafir and Yoav Peled, eds., *The New Israel: Peacemaking and Liberalization* (Boulder: Westview Press, 2000), 231.

20. Solingen, "Multilateral Arab-Israeli Negotiations," 171.

21. Ben-Porat, *Global Liberalism*.

22. John Rossant, quoted in Shafir and Peled, "Peace and Profits," 247.

23. Ibid., 181.

24. Ibid., 260–61.

25. Asher Arian and Michal Shamir, "Two Reversals: Why 1992 Was Not 1977," in Asher Arian and Michal Shamir, eds., *The Elections in Israel in 1992* (Albany: State University of New York Press, 1995), 17–54.

26. Guy Ben-Porat, "Markets and Fences: Illusions of Peace," *Middle East Journal* 66, no. 2 (Spring 2000): 316.

27. For an extended discussion of the second face of security in the case of

Jordan, see Steven E. Lobell, "The Second Face of American Security: The U.S.-Jordan Free Trade Agreement as Security Policy," *Comparative Strategy* 27, no. 1 (2008): 1–13; and "Power Disparities and Strategic Trade: Domestic Consequence of U.S.-Jordan Trade Concessions, in Kristen P. Williams, Steven E. Lobell, and Neal G. Jesse, eds., *Beyond Great Powers and Hegemons: Why Secondary States Support, Follow, or Challenge* (Stanford, CA: Stanford University Press, 2012), 81–96.

28. Oliver Wils, "Competition or Oligarchy? The Jordanian Business Elite in Historical Perspective," in Hamed El-Said and Kip Becker, eds., *Management and International Business Issues in Jordan* (New York: Haworth Press, 2001).

29. A small internationalist bloc exists in Syria. See Susan Sachs, "Syria Businessmen Yearn for Reforms," *New York Times,* January 27, 2000, http://www.nytimes.com/2000/01/27/world/syria-businessmen-yearn-for-reforms.html?pagewanted=all&src=pm. On US trade policy toward other Islamic states, see Joseph Kahn, "A Business Plan for Islam Inc.," *New York Times,* December 20, 2001, http://www.nytimes.com/2001/12/30/weekinreview/30KAHN.html.

30. Markus E. Bouillon, "The Failure of Big Business: On the Socio-economic Reality of the Middle East Peace Process," *Mediterranean Politics* 9, no. 1 (Spring 2004): 3, 9.

31. Yitzhak Reiter, "The Palestinian-Transjordanian Rift: Economic Might and Political Power in Jordan," *Middle East Journal* 58 (Winter 2004): 1–28.

32. Ibid.

33. Glenn E. Robinson, "Defensive Democratization in Jordan," *International Journal of Middle East Studies* 30, no. 3 (August 1998): 405.

34. Danishai Kornbluth, "Jordan and the Anti-normalization Campaign, 1994–2001," *Terrorism and Political Violence* 14, no. 3 (Autumn 2002): 80–108.

35. Robinson, "Defensive Democratization in Jordan." Prior to 1992, political parties were illegal. Only the Muslim Brotherhood was tolerated as a semilegal party since it was viewed as counter to leftist, pan-Arab, and Nasserist groups. The leadership also comes from well-established families that are unlikely to press for the overthrow of the regime.

36. Ben-Porat, *Global Liberalism*; Lobell, "Second Face of Security Strategies."

37. Lynch, *State Interests and Public Spheres*; Ben-Porat, "Markets and Fences."

38. Pete W. Moore, "The Newest Jordan: Free Trade, Peace, and an Ace in the Hole," *Middle East Report Online,* June 26, 2003, http://merip.org/mero/mero062603 (accessed Sept. 9, 2015).

39. For instance, from 1990 to 1997 Washington extended $1.65 billion in a combination of grants, loans, and loan guarantees. See Russell E. Lucas, "Jordan: The Death of Normalization with Israel," *Middle East Journal* 58, no. 1 (Winter 2004): 108.

40. Avraham Sela, "Politics, Identity, and Peacemaking: The Arab Discourse

on Peace with Israel in the 1990s," *Israel Studies* 10, no. 2 (Summer 2005): 15–71. It was also anticipated that joint Israeli-Jordanian-Palestinian ventures would create a vested interest in the continuation of the peace process.

41. Paul L. Scham and Russell E. Lucas, "'Normalization' and 'Anti-normalization' in Jordan: The Public Debate," *Middle East Review of International Affairs* 5, no. 3 (September 2001): 141–64.

42. For a good discussion of the multilateral Arab-Israeli peace process, see Solingen, "Multilateral Arab-Israeli Negotiations," 167–87.

43. Shimon Peres, *The New Middle East* (New York: Henry Holt, 1993).

44. Jonathan Paris, "Regional Cooperation and the MENA Economic Summits," in Gershon Shafir and Yoav Peled, eds., *The New Israel: Peacemaking and Liberalization* (Boulder: Westview Press, 2000), 267.

45. Ibid., 296–70.

46. Fact Sheet, Office of the Press Secretary, "US-Middle East Free Trade Area" (June 9, 2004), http://georgewbush-whitehouse.archives.gov/news/releases/2004/06/text/20040609-37.html (accessed on Sept. 9, 2015).

CHAPTER 3

Economic Statecraft and Transitions to Peace

France, Germany, and Poland

Galia Press-Barnathan

This chapter addresses the five questions raised by Norrin M. Ripsman and Steven E. Lobell in the introduction to this volume through an examination of two cases: the use of economic statecraft (ES) in the transition to peace between France and Germany after 1945 and its use in the transition to peace between Germany and Poland. These German experiences demonstrate several points. First, the use of economic rewards can be very effective when such rewards are high but even more so when the target faces or foresees very high costs if no cooperation ensues. Second, as Ripsman indicates in chapter 1, the targets of ES in the early stages of the transition have to be the leaders and economic elites—those who can actually make policy. In later stages, though, in order to further normalize the peace, the broader society needs to be targeted and must enjoy the peace dividends. Finally, while a state can target the society of its counterpart, the deepening of peaceful relations involves greater and more diverse economic interaction between the two societies. This implies that, in the long run, effective ES should create the conditions for nongovernmental economic cooperation. Consequently, as peace deepens, the actual role of ES (a statist strategy) is likely to diminish.

The German experience also raises several points with regard to the limits and risks associated with ES. First, at the international, geostrategic level, ES can work effectively in relatively benign international circumstances. The defeat of Germany, its disarmament, and the firm American security commitment to European security created special circumstances that made it easier for ES to work.[1] This being said, German-Polish relations demonstrate that even under challenging geopolitical circumstances ES can be used to sow the seeds of a future successful transition to peace when those circumstances change. The German case also points to the importance of looking at the capacity of the sender state to practice ES effectively. This, in part, is determined by the economic conditions on the ground, which determine what economic rewards (or costs) are at stake. It also depends, however, on the capacity of the sender government to use its economic resources effectively, and especially to enlist and maneuver the cooperation of its own key economic actors, whose cooperation and support greatly enhance the effectiveness of ES strategies. A strong state, with a well-organized big-business sector that works closely with it, stands the best chance of using ES effectively. In other words, practicing effective ES involves a two-level game that needs to be played well.

Another lesson is that the ability of ES to promote a transition to peace is complicated by broad economic power disparities between the states. This, on the one hand, can create strong leverage for the use of ES in the early transitional stage. On the other hand, it also creates several problems. It narrows the potential for expanding the actual base of economic cooperation in the longer run. And it also creates political problems because it may seem either coercive or exploitative—two perceptions that may limit the willingness of the weaker party to join—and, similar to Scott L. Kastner and Margaret Pearson's observation in chapter 7, it can generate a lot of ill will that is not conducive to long-term peace building.[2] These dilemmas are evident in German-Polish relations.

Finally, the two German cases illustrate three key points regarding the shift from bilateral to regional peace. First, a bilateral transition to peace between two states that form a regional strategic dyad (such as Germany and France) will have a spillover effect at the regional level as well, given the centrality of this bilateral cooperation in changing regional dynamics. This is exemplified in the central role of the Franco-German axis in the formation of the European Economic Community (EEC) in 1957. Second, embedding ES within a regional institutional context can play an important role in both expanding the peace and institutionalizing it within regional multilateral frameworks. This is reflected by the institutionalization of Franco-German relations within the European Community (EC) and in the institutionalization of German-Polish relations within the European Union (EU). Finally, the ability of third parties to use ES to advance regional peace is enhanced if it is used to promote such regional institution building. This point is well exemplified in the US role in promoting regional cooperation in Europe via the Marshall Plan.

The cases explored here, and especially the Franco-German case, suggest that looking at ES as a unidirectional process in which state A uses economic tools to change the preferences and policies of state B may be deceiving.[3] In the first case, the focus is on France as the initiator of ES and Germany as the target state, and in the second case Germany is the initiator of ES and Poland is the target state. However, ES can be used by both sides in the transition process. This is most likely in cases like the Franco-German transition, in which both sides were to receive significant economic gains from the transition to peace and therefore could, to some degree, use ES strategies vis-à-vis each other. Future research can explore the strategic interactions involved in ES, but that is beyond the scope of this chapter.

The Franco-German Transition to Peace

Type of Economic Statecraft

In the Franco-German case, the use of inducements or positive ES (reward granting) was central. The expected economic gains from a transition to peace did not have to be seriously manipulated by the two governments nor by the key external actor, the United States. This was due to the natural complementarities of the French and German economies.

The economic potential of a transition to peace was of major importance to both France and Germany. France found itself in poor economic shape after the war. French industry had languished for four years, the occupation had drained and disrupted the economy, and France had lost Britain as its main coal supplier. While the early postwar French vision of peace was based on keeping Germany weak and divided, this initial plan was not viable for economic reasons. The Monnet Plan (the French Modernization and Re-equipment Plan) strove to make the French economy more internationally competitive and turn France into Europe's largest steel producer. This could only be achieved by increasing inputs of German coal and coke into the French economy. Consequently, from the outset French reconstruction was tied to German economic reconstruction.[4]

Germany, for its part, stood to gain both economically and politically from a transition to peace with France. Beyond the vivid understanding at the time of the cost of military conflict, West Germany's postwar strategy was based on an export-led growth strategy and, as such, was highly dependent on the desire of the rest of Europe to trade with it.[5] Indeed, strong commercial interests on both sides wanted to move to peace so as to reap economic benefits. Andrew Moravcsik argues that it was those commercial interests, rather than any geostrategic considerations, that pushed France and Germany into each other's arms.[6] There was a basic complementarity in strategic and economic terms between France and Germany after the war, and the relations fulfilled specific functional needs. They served the French interest in securing access to German energy sources and in playing a preponderant political role within the European communities, and they served the German interests in regaining independence and market access.[7] This is exactly the type of natural interdependence that gave the transition process its underlying logic and driving power.

From initial French relations with occupied Germany to the 1954 Paris Agreements, which marked the achievement of an official peace (and creation of a new sovereign Federal Republic of Germany [FRG]), and the 1963 Elysée Treaty, several economic tools were used. One was the 1950 Franco-German tariff agreement, which allowed goods to pass freely from France to the French-controlled occupation zone in Germany and into German markets.[8] Another was the creation of the European Coal and Steel Community (ECSC) in 1952, and the third was the signing in 1955 of a commercial treaty between the two states, which turned them into each other's largest and second-largest trading partners.[9] I do not consider the signing of the Treaty of Rome in 1957 as a form of ES, as its main goals on both sides were economic and not the deepening of peace between the states.

Attempts to use ES to promote a transition to peace were made as early as the aftermath of World War I, when France initiated the 1920 Seydoux Plan, which was to create a revolving fund in order to commercialize the reparations debt and give German manufacturers an economic stake in French reconstruction. This was followed in 1926 by the creation of the International Steel Cartel (among France, Germany, Belgium, and Luxemburg), an agreement reflecting the belief that market-sharing agreements could be used for diplomatic purposes.[10] This did not prevent Nazi Germany from invading France, but it shows that in the aftermath of World War II a precedent for using ES to build cooperation existed.

The focus on the leverage generated by expected benefits from renewed trade and investments is amplified if the costs of ongoing conflict or lack of an agreement are perceived as high. In the Franco-German case, Germany clearly felt the costs associated with its defeat and conquest. More immediately, one negative ES tool used by the Allies created significant pressure on Germany to push for an agreement with France. This was the law adopted by the Allied High Commission in April 1950, which provided the juridical basis for the deconcentration of the larger German *Konzernes*. The law was followed by the liquidation of six large steel-producing firms and the deconcentration of the mining industry.[11] This leads to the central question of the targets of ES.

Who Were the Targets of ES?

A central question raised in this volume deals with the appropriate targets of ES: leaders, elites, or broader segments of society. This is directly linked to the previous discussion on economic gains. Those gains should be assessed at two levels: the level of the state and the level of society (i.e., which domestic actors stand to gain economically from the transition). This case demonstrates that the powerful domestic actors in the target state need to foresee significant gains from economic interaction, gains that will make it worthwhile to endure the potentially high political costs of ending conflictual relations. The key actors here are state leaders and big business. They represent what Lobell and Ripsman call the first and the second faces of security. Etel Solingen's internationalist liberalizing domestic coalitions are a key concept in this regard. If a domestic ruling coalition sees potential in opening up to the global economy, export-led growth, and foreign direct investment (FDI), it will also perceive that ending its conflictual relations with its neighbor(s) will be very beneficial in this regard.[12] However, state leaders do not necessarily need to adopt a liberal economic approach to perceive such expected gains if a transition to peace entails more immediate economic benefits such as debt relief or a major inflow of aid.[13] At the same time, in the transition to peace we also need to consider the domestic economic losers on both sides. The existence of major losers (spoilers) on either side is sufficient to undermine the effectiveness of an ES strategy. All in all, then, the domestic balance between winners and losers is crucial for predicting the effectiveness of an ES strategy in promoting peace. A central goal of an ES strategy is therefore also to downplay or mitigate the potential economic costs for various domestic actors on both sides.

The process of the transition to peace between France and Germany was guided from above, by state agents who perceived a clear link between building economic ties with the former enemy and establishing a more solid and reliable strategic partnership between the two states. The best example of ES is the Schuman Plan and the subsequent creation of the ECSC. The ECSC initiative was guided by French foreign minister Robert Schuman. Although Schuman promised that his plan would make war between France and Germany unthinkable and materially impossible, the plan's immediate appeal was still based on his claim that the establishment of common bases of economic development would bring major economic advantages to both countries.[14] As noted earlier, the French motivation was not only geopolitical but also economic, given that the Monnet Plan to boost French industry could not be realized without German coal and steel.

Schuman's targets were the new German state leaders and the big industrialists in Germany. On the German side, the transition was managed by a German government, led by Konrad Adenauer and his economics minister Ludwig Erhard, which adopted a growth strategy based on free market competition (with a social twist) and an emphasis on foreign trade. German reliance on external markets for its economic rehabilitation after the war gave the French significant leverage. Also it led to greater domestic political influence for the export sector within Germany over the formation of foreign economic policy. This influence was further enhanced by the close links between business interests and the ministries of finance and economics.[15] As noted earlier, German coal and steel producers had a vital interest in achieving an agreement that would both bring to a halt the dismantling of German factories and open to them foreign markets for exports.[16] In fact by mid-1948, even before the Schuman Plan was announced, major German and French industrialists began meeting and examining potential cooperative projects.[17] The nature of government-industry relations within Germany meant that the French were, in practice, targeting both. This is not necessarily the case elsewhere and depends on the domestic institutional setting.

Despite the expected economic benefits for France, Schuman still had to use political maneuvering and vision to push this plan forward in the face of a general domestic sentiment of hostility toward and distrust of Germany within France.[18] He advanced the plan in the face of domestic opposition from the French steel industry's trade association, as well as other industries, which felt threatened by the chance of further pooling of resources later on.[19] Ripsman argues that the Schuman Plan was meant to reconcile French public opinion with the eventuality of German economic resurgence.[20] This demonstrates again how ES can be seen as a two-level game. Given such domestic opposition, it was clearly a state-led strategy and not a strategy driven by domestic private interests.

The ECSC proved to be a dramatic success as an ES tool. The impressive gains in productivity and trade volume two years after its creation converted many of its critics into supporters. It had important implications also for the broader German society. One of the central challenges in the transition to peace and normalization of relations is the need over time to expand the peace dividends to broader segments of society. This can be achieved either by explicitly targeting society (the third face of security) in the use of ES or, in the easier case, through a positive spillover of the earlier ES strategies targeted at the state. Germany in the early postwar years was an easy case in this regard for two main reasons. First of all, the decade and a half since the beginning of rapprochement with France was a period of rapid economic growth and rehabilitation. To illustrate, GNP (in deutschmarks) rose from DM98 billion in 1950 to approximately DM303 billion in 1960, DM679 billion in 1970, and DM1.497 billion in 1980. This dramatic growth was based largely on the country's industry, and about a third of its industrial production was exported. This tremendous overall growth of the national economic pie was also translated into a dramatic rise in workers' salaries. The nominal average hourly gross earnings of a German industrial worker rose between 1950 and the early 1980s almost tenfold and by about 300 percent in real terms![21] The fact that the crucial decade of the transition to peace was accompanied by dramatic economic growth and an equally dramatic rise in citizens' standard of living clearly facilitated the process of upgrading the peace. It was easy to view German society as a whole as a winner. The idea of "peace dividends" was not an academic notion but a vivid description of reality for most Germans. Society, however, was not directly targeted by the French. Their peace dividends trickled down naturally and, also thanks to German domestic policies and the unique nature of industrial relations in West Germany, were characterized by collective bargaining and workers' participation in management. Such participation was prevalent in the coal, iron, and steel companies—three of the central players in the postwar economic game.[22] Such participation also created a greater sense of involvement in the policy process among German workers and ensured that they would share in the economic benefits of peace and integration.

The Timing of Specific Instruments

A transition to peace should be perceived as a long and dynamic process. Consequently, ES can play different roles at different stages of the transition. As noted in the introduction to this volume, many scholars have made a distinction between different stages in the transition to peace. Most would accept the basic distinction between the initial stages of the transition to a formal, cold peace and the long process of warming, normalizing, and stabilizing that peace. Normalization includes various steps that bring relations closer to a warm peace. The previous section demonstrated this process well. The success of the early initiatives stemmed from the successful targeting of the German government and German big business, which in turn worked closely with each other.

At the same time, in phase 3 (the postagreement phase), economic incentives helped stabilize and normalize relations by broadening its targets. In terms of the goals of ES, the target in this stage should be expanded to the third face of security, broader society. If the fruits of peace do not trickle down, peace will remain an elitist construct. Furthermore, the same economic incentives that played an important role in the early stages may in fact compromise the enhancement of cooperation, as the perception of a peace that only benefits elites might create further resentment and frustration. As was described in the previous section, this trickling down did occur in the Franco-German case. Throughout the decade of the 1950s various business organizations were promoting reconciliation and creating numerous economic agreements (examples include an agreement between Air France and Lufthansa, the creation of many chambers of commerce, and the formation of an agricultural committee to coordinate agricultural policies). More channels were created in the 1963 agreement.[23] The notion of a stable or warm peace is characterized by crosscutting and multiple links between societies. Economic engagement is obviously an excellent tool with which to achieve this, but only after it is broadened.[24] Once such crosscutting, multiple economic links emerge between societies, the role of ES is likely to become less central. Put differently, successful ES can make ES less relevant in the long run.

The second dramatic signpost in upgrading the peace between France and Germany, namely, their decision to create the EC and sign the Rome treaty, already reflects a different process. This was a joint venture of two states driven by clearly complementary economic interests. The basic bargain struck between France and Germany as they entered the new community was a trade-off between the French insistence on the Common Agricultural Policy (CAP) and the German insistence on opening up industrial markets.[25] It is telling that the debate within France surrounding the decision to enter the EC revolved around economic matters only and not geopolitical issues related to relations with Germany.[26] Consequently, while this was a significant step in deepening and stabilizing the Franco-German partnership, and while it was driven by economic considerations, it does not qualify as an example of using ES.

The Limits and Risks Associated with ES

A central problem with extrapolating from the Franco-German experience to other cases stems from the fact that while the two states did indeed overcome a horrible, bloody, conflictual past, the use of ES in the process was greatly facilitated by other, noneconomic circumstances. First, when the transition process began, Germany was divided and would remain so for the foreseeable future (as it seemed in the early 1950s). Second, under the Paris Agreements, which led to the creation of a sovereign FRG in 1954, Germany took on itself various safeguards to prevent a resurgence of militarism.[27] This commitment was enhanced by the American commitment to maintain ground forces in Germany. These geopolitical guarantees were obviously of crucial importance.[28] Still, such guarantees on their own would not have provided the necessary fuel for a full transition to peace. The fuel was the strong economic logic of cooperation and the clear mutual gains for both parties. The ES strategies used by the French, such as the ECSC, reflected bilateral interests and preferences, not those induced by the United States (which was actually concerned about the illiberal nature of the ECSC arrangement). Finally, with the onset of the Cold War, France and the FRG came to share a common threat perception vis-à-vis the Soviet Union.

All in all, given the unique geopolitical circumstances of this case, neither the French nor the Germans faced very high risks in following the logic of economic cooperation. One such risk was that the use of ES can strengthen the target state to the extent that it might threaten the initiating state. Conversely, if the target state is economically much weaker, then allowing it to go along with the ES strategy of its partner runs the risk of increasing its dependence on it, as Albert Hirschman warned. These concerns are likely to be higher among former enemies. Such concerns were also mitigated in this case. Due to Germany's unique political condition after regaining its sovereignty, what developed over the years between the two states was a special partnership in which German economic power was balanced by French political influence. While relations were asymmetric, they were clearly complementary.[29] The Germans did expect to become economically much stronger in the future and therefore were willing to acquiesce to the French in their efforts to realize the Monnet Plan. Adenauer believed time was on his side and that the real danger was that a stronger Germany moving too fast would rekindle old fears and suspicions and prolong the occupation.[30] However, this did not generate strong French fears because the transition began at a time when economic disparities were relatively small due to the occupation regime. Concerns regarding the risks of ES are more evident in the Polish-German case.

ES and the Shift from Bilateral to Regional Peace

One of the most interesting questions addressed in this volume is how ES can be used to bring about regional, rather than only dyadic, peace. The Franco-German transition to peace highlights several insights on this question. First, a dyadic transition to peace can play a crucial role in advancing regional peace when the dyad in question is a *strategic regional dyad*. By that I mean a dyadic relation that is central to the overall regional dynamics, negative and positive. The Franco-German dyad is a classic example. As noted earlier, the transition to peace between France and Germany was crucial in enabling the evolution of broader European integration. To begin with, the ECSC was not a bilateral framework. The creation of the EC further expanded and deepened European integration. This was driven by the Franco-German bargain, yet it further entrenched and stabilized those bilateral relations as well. Similarly, in the creation of the EU, France and Germany served as the linchpins of the arrangement, yet at the same time this wide regional institutional network further deepened and stabilized their relations, eliminating to a large extent the option of armed conflict between them. A large part of this regional institution-building project revolved around economic cooperation. Once created, this dense institutional environment could be used as the playing field for future use of ES between states.

The Franco-German transition also highlights a second important mechanism that links ES directly to broader regional peace. This mechanism was advanced in this case not by the parties themselves but by the most pertinent third party, the United States. Beyond the crucial American role as a security provider ameliorating a possible security dilemma between France and Germany, the United States explicitly used ES strategies to force the French into a more accommodating position vis-à-vis Germany, as well as to foster greater Western European cooperation in building a joint European economic framework into which a rehabilitated Germany could fit. The main tool used by the United States was the aid provided by the Marshall Plan. The Americans refused to offer aid to individual Western European states and insisted that they work together to devise a European recovery plan. This was a direct and blunt use of the promise of positive sanctions, accompanied by a clear emphasis on the threat of withholding aid should a joint regional effort fail. This led eventually to the creation of the Organization for European Economic Cooperation (OEEC) in April 1948. Beyond forcing initial inter-European cooperation, this effort was directly linked to the revival of Germany. The Americans concluded that the only way to revive Germany (as part of a common anti-Soviet front) without also reviving the threat of German militarism was by reintegrating it into a strong European framework. The Americans used additional ES tools to ensure the reintegration of Germany by inserting into their bilateral treaties with individual European states a clause demanding that they grant most favored nation (MFN) treatment to German trade for two years.[31] This American strategy ensured that the dyadic transition to peace between France and Germany would be intrinsically linked to the broader regional transition to peace in Western Europe.

The second part of this chapter examines a different dyadic transition to peace, one in which Germany was the initiator and the target state of ES was Poland. This case offers interesting variation compared to the first one and is explored along similar lines based on the questions set out in the introduction to this volume.

The Transition to Peace between Germany and Poland

German-Polish relations carry with them a very heavy historical load dating back to the late eighteenth century, when Germans ruled over Poles.[32] The period following the German occupation of Poland in 1939 was a brutal one. Mass expulsions of Poles from territories annexed to Germany were conducted, more than 6 million Poles perished during the war, and Polish culture was nearly destroyed.[33] To complicate things further, in the aftermath of the war and following Germany's defeat and the creation of the new border with Poland along the Oder-Neisse line, nearly a million Germans who lived in Poland were expelled. Many perished along the way, and others found themselves refugees in either the German Democratic Republic (GDR) or the FRG, dreaming of returning to their homes in what was now a sovereign Poland. Despite this historical burden, as most observers acknowledge, economic factors played a central role in this transition to peace, though somewhat differently for each side. For Poland, even under Communist rule and more clearly after the democratization process, there was a clear and strong economic incentive to develop peaceful relations with Germany. For Germany, while normalizing relations did hold economic benefits, the driving force in the relations was political, and economic tools were utilized to promote *Ostpolitik* in Eastern Europe in general and Poland in particular. This was a much more classic case of ES.

After World War II, the two states found themselves in two opposite ideological camps. Their relations were marred by a host of thorny problems (the central ones being the Oder-Neisse border, the "lost territories," the German minority in Poland, and Polish demands for compensation). The first major breakthrough in relations between the two states was the Warsaw Treaty, signed in 1970, which followed the German policy shift since the mid-1960s known as Willy Brandt's *Ostpolitik*. The treaty affirmed that the Oder-Neisse line forms the People's Republic of Poland's western frontier and that neither side has a territorial claim against the other. Official permanent recognition of the border was to wait for German unification 20 years later.[34] The treaty called for the economic and cultural normalization of mutual relations and indeed was followed by a mutual effort to facilitate and institutionalize wide cooperation. Polish imports from West Germany grew by over 80 percent by 1972, West German business subsidiaries were formed in Poland, and a permanent Polish business representative lived in the FRG. Official visits between government leaders grew significantly, and following the 1975 Helsinki Accords there was also an increase in contacts and formal meetings between labor groups, scientists, educators, and others, as well as an increase in the number of tourists.[35] Against the setting of the Helsinki Accords, one of the most explicit political-economic deals was made between the FRG and Poland when Chancellor Helmut Schmidt signed a package of agreements with Polish Edward Gierek, among them a German loan of DM1 billion at a low interest rate in exchange for Polish permission for 120,000 to 125,000 Germans to leave Poland over the following four years.[36] Throughout the 1980s, economic relations between the two states continued to develop, although further warming was difficult in the face of the political realities of the region.

The next dramatic milestone signifying the upgrading of relations between the two states came only after the historical events of 1989–90: the fall of the Berlin Wall and the beginning of talks on German unification, the fall of the Communist government in Poland, and the creation of the first democratically elected government in Poland. On November 14, 1990, Poland and Germany signed a treaty permanently fixing the mutual border along the Oder-Neisse line.[37] On June 17, 1991, Poland and Germany, after eight months of arduous negotiations, signed the Treaty of Good Neighborliness and Friendly Cooperation. Poland finally acknowledged the existence of a German minority and agreed to grant it rights, whereas Germany committed to help Poland enter the EC and other multilateral organizations, including the North American Treaty Organization (NATO), and deal with its foreign debt issues. Since the signing of the treaty, there has been an intensification of cooperation between the two states, including significant growth in bottom-up cooperation. There has been an explosion of trade and travel across the Oder-Neisse border, with more than 100 million people crossing in 1993.[38] A wide variety of institutions and bilateral consultation mechanisms were created to further institutionalize the relations, drawing on the Franco-German model. At the local level, cooperation developed especially along the border, the most prominent example being the developing Nysa Euroregion.[39] On December 20, 2007, a historic step was taken when Poland officially joined the Schengen Area, that is, the area within which EU citizens can move freely, without the need for a visa or border inspections. The once contentious Oder-Neisse border became an open border.

While an economic rationale for normalizing relations did exist, it was not the driving force for Germany. Germany was motivated to normalize its relations with Poland, as well as other states in Eastern Europe, first and foremost for political reasons: to demonstrate its benign intentions to the larger international community and to support reform in Eastern Europe. Economic cooperation was used to advance these political goals.[40] By contrast, Poland's interest in improving relations with the FRG was largely driven by economic factors. This gave German ES clear leverage. There was a basic economic complementarity between the FRG and its Eastern European neighbors, Poland being a central one of them. The FRG was able to supply manufactured goods and technology that Poland needed. At the same time, especially after its division and the loss of its raw material and energy supplies in the eastern territories (e.g., Silesian coal), the FRG needed to import them and other primary goods such as natural gas and basic chemicals.[41] For the Germans, this was an opportunity to enter a large consumer market with a relatively high demand for industrial and consumer goods. Furthermore, by 1962 there was growing competition among Western European states over Eastern European markets.[42] Finally, expansion of trade with Eastern Europe served another goal of both German business and the government: reducing German dependence on US imports and improving the FRG's dollar balance.[43] On the Polish side, the need for an outlet for its products and a dire need for technology created a strong incentive to trade with the FRG, even under Communist rule.

The Types of ES Used

Germany's extensive use of positive sanctions since the initiation of *Ostpolitik* was in part a result of the conclusion that the previous policy toward Eastern Europe—one of an official boycott (negative sanctions)—had simply failed.[44] German ES toward Poland, both in the 1970s and in the second round of the transition after 1989, was based on the promise and provision of low-interest loans, private credit, and state-led support for and facilitation of enhanced trade relations. By 1989 Germany was Poland's largest creditor and primary source of private credit. Germany clearly used economic sweeteners to promote its political goals vis-à-vis Poland. The Warsaw Treaty of December 1970, for example, was preceded by a Treaty on Trade and Economic Cooperation. Then, in 1989, as part of the negotiations toward a treaty with Poland, Germany agreed to unilaterally reschedule all the payments, which had been due from 1986 to 1988, on German government loans to Poland. The final Joint Declaration resulting from a historic summit meeting in 1989 between Chancellor Helmut Kohl and Prime Minister Tadeusz Mazowiecki included a clear economic component, for example, the provision of DM2.5 billion in Hermes credits over two years. Germany offered an additional economic carrot in the form of active advocacy in favor of Poland with major economic institutions, such as the International Monetary Fund (IMF) and World Bank, as well as vis-à-vis German corporations and other western states.[45]

The Targets of ES

Many authors note the elitist nature of this transition process, especially since on the German side political considerations played a significant role, whereas on the Polish side the prominent economic logic driving normalization was closely guided by the Communist state. This means that the transition in the 1970s–80s focused on the first face of security. In Poland a prolonged domestic economic crisis had created ongoing social restlessness, which threatened the regime's stability. Consequently, even the Communist rulers (in Warsaw and Moscow) encouraged some economic interaction with West Germany, despite the countries' clear ideological and political differences.[46] There was a basic understanding that in order to improve economic conditions (and ultimately save the regime as well), expansion of trade and especially importation of modern technology were inevitable and West Germany was the most logical partner.[47] The enduring economic crisis led eventually to the fall of Władysław Gomułka, who was replaced by Gierek. Gierek's economic blueprint for 1970–75 proposed a dramatic upgrading of commercial relations with the capitalist countries.[48] This fledgling liberalizing coalition turned into a real one after the fall of the Communist government, as the new Solidarity government embarked on a dual program of democratization and economic liberalization, two processes aimed at leading Poland "back to Europe" via West Germany.[49]

On the sender side, this case, even more than Germany's relations with France, demonstrates the importance of close cooperation between the government and private business. Specific branches of West German industry were quite dependent on eastern trade. Thus, for example, in the mid-1970s, as much as 20 percent of Germany's exports of iron and steel went to Eastern Europe. Leaders of the iron and steel industries, together with the banks that supported them, acted as an important lobby in Bonn. Thus, even if the original interest in developing eastern trade was mainly political, the effect of this politically driven expansion was an increase in economic interest as well.[50] West Germany's neocorporatist institutional structure enabled a smooth and efficient process of government-business cooperation to advance its economic diplomacy vis-à-vis Poland. The German commercial sector was able to exert significant influence over policy thanks to its efficient organization through peak associations and its developed and institutionalized links to bureaucratic ministries and the government.[51] At the same time, the top-down process is also exemplified by the important role the German government played in reassuring private businessmen and ensuring (e.g., via export credit guarantees) that they would reap major benefits despite the high risks involved in investing in Poland.

The two potential economic losers in West Germany—labor and agriculture—were protected. Clauses were inserted to protect against dumping by Polish firms.[52] And German agriculture was under little threat during Communist rule in Poland.[53] The German government, then, played an effective two-level ES game.

The use of an ES strategy vis-à-vis Poland was facilitated in the 1970s by the fact that Germany had to deal with a centralized regime in Poland. This of course was true only once the Communist regime became threatened by the terrible state of the Polish economy. Interacting with a democracy can be more complicated, as at some point ES will need to address the needs of various domestic groups that have political power. In the Polish case, as well, this dilemma became apparent and found its perhaps clearest expression in the German reaction to the attempted revolution by the Solidarity movement in 1980. While it was supportive of the attempt to advance democracy and human rights in Poland, the German government was also very concerned lest the Solidarity revolution create such havoc that it would sabotage Germany's carefully crafted *Ostpolitik* and have a detrimental effect also on its developing relations with East Germany and the Soviet Union. Consequently, in the end Germany chose to accept and endorse the declaration of martial law in Poland by General Wojciech Jaruzelski in December 1980 as a peaceful internal solution to a domestic Polish problem.[54] This German reaction demonstrates that it is easier to craft a cold peace, or even a normal one, at the state and elite level, whereas societal interaction is much harder to carefully manage from above.

Timing and Phases

For the FRG in the late 1960s and 1970s, "normalization of relations" with Poland meant the development of normal economic relations. Economic statecraft was used well before actual official relations existed with Poland, as Germany maintained a large trade mission in Warsaw, which sought to promote business contacts and served as a quasi embassy. This is a good example of the use of ES in a preagreement stage as an important tool in preparing the ground for an official political breakthrough.[55] The Germans wanted first to advance economic normalization and only then talk about formal ties. Conversely, the Poles wanted first to resolve all the basic problems and then move to normalization.[56] As described earlier, major economic promises of credits and debt relief were used as sweeteners just before official breakthroughs. However, the institutionalization of bilateral economic cooperation played a crucial role in the later stages of consolidating relations. This was apparent in active interministerial cooperation and ongoing government activity to facilitate and encourage German companies to trade with Poland. This was done via participation in trade fairs and by providing benefits to German companies (such as export credit guarantees) to reduce the potential risks of doing business in Poland.

In the second round of the transition, after 1989, German ES strategies gave greater weight to the promise of helping Poland enter the Common Market. This strategy was obviously irrelevant earlier, when Cold War realities made such an option impossible.

Risks and Limits of ES

A central challenge of the use of ES in promoting peace that is reflected in this case is the impact of great economic disparities between Germany and Poland. Despite having a population half as large as Germany's, Poland had an economy only about 10 percent as large. It exported low-value-added raw materials and semifinished products to Germany while importing machinery and other high-value-added products. Its trade with Germany has been at least 10 times more important for Poland than it has been for Germany.[57] This underlying asymmetry has not changed dramatically over the years, despite the significant changes that Poland has undergone. After the 1991 agreement, this asymmetry was only exacerbated, with Germany accounting for about half of Poland's trade with the EU (27 percent of its total trade in 1992), whereas Poland accounted for merely 1.1 percent of Germany's foreign trade in the same year. This wide disparity enabled Germany to successfully use ES in promoting a transition to peace. One could argue that due to these disparities Poland had little choice but to cooperate.

These economic disparities, despite their positive implications, also created serious limits to how much ES could be used to promote the transition to peace, especially in the long run, in the later phases. Despite the political motivation to cooperate, the development of more advanced forms of economic relations, especially in the fields of finance and investment, was disappointing. Germans perceived the risks of investing in such forms of cooperation to be relatively high and preferred to wait for the Poles to undertake reforms and improve their efficiency.[58] Wide disparities in levels of economic development can thus serve as a brake on unlimited expansion of economic cooperation and can limit the potential for bottom-up initiatives. The structural economic power disparities created a basic problem of German lack of interest on the one hand and Polish mistrust on the other, especially in the more advanced stages of the transition.[59] These concerns created problems for devising a means of practical cooperation. One example is the Stolpe Plan, a July 1991 proposal for regional cooperation, which was to create a cooperative zone along the entire German-Polish border, extending 100 kilometers into Poland and 50 into Germany. Development in that zone was to be promoted by a joint German-Polish development bank, with Germany providing 70 percent of the capital and holding a majority on the board of directors. The Germans were surprised at the outrage this proposal created in Poland. It was seen as unfair, disproportionately favorable to Germany, and a threat to Polish sovereignty in these regions. The specializations assigned to the German and Polish regions seemed to Poles unfair, as Germany could again specialize in modern manufacturing projects while Polish tasks would include simple processing of food and raw materials. It was seen as exploitation rather than cooperation.[60] Similar problems are abundant when one looks at German-Polish cooperation at local levels.[61]

Finally, the final negotiations on the Oder-Neisse border just before German reunification reveal the limits of using ES on issues of strategic importance. The various economic benefits that Germany could offer Poland could not influence the Polish position on the Oder-Neisse border. Economic aid or trade credits could not replace an official and explicit German commitment to the permanent nature of that border. Only after the Germans conceded on this point did the economic dimension kick in again. This is important since it shows that even very large economic incentives cannot overrun what are perceived to be existential political and security concerns. This should lead to a very cautionary conclusion concerning the power of ES to actually shift positions regarding the core of the conflict.

Moving from Dyadic to Regional Peace

Unlike the Franco-German dyad, a strategic regional dyad that generated on its own significant spillover effects at the regional level, the German-Polish dyadic relationship was advanced by its nesting within the broader regional framework of the EU. Initially, Germany was able to use the promise of helping Poland enter the EU as a source of significant political leverage. Membership in multilateral European institutions was seen by the Poles as a way to mitigate the asymmetry between Poland and Germany, but at the same time cooperation with Germany was seen as a crucial element in the strategy of rejoining Europe. A circular logic was created, using cooperation with Germany in order to join the EU and the belief that this would also reduce asymmetries with Germany. This Polish perspective, in turn, was compatible with Germany's own postwar strategy, which stressed the wielding of power only via multilateral institutions.

Germany adopted the European option in the 1950s initially for instrumental reasons, but over time its interests were fundamentally shaped by the institutional context of Europe and the Europeanization of the identity of the German state that took place in the following decades. It has become, as Peter Katzenstein describes it, a "tamed power."[62]

This German leverage disappeared once Poland entered the EU, but embedding the relations within this regional institution had two positive effects: it reduced concerns over Germany because German foreign policy was now constrained by the EU, and at the same time it provided Poland with new opportunities to actively reduce the power disparities and play a politically more significant role in shaping the future of Europe. The feeling in Poland was that Germany had become Europeanized and consequently there was no longer a need to fear German hegemony or political dependence on Germany.[63] The Polish ambassador to Germany explained that embedding its neighbor's policies in a wider European framework was the only way to ensure that Poland would not fall victim to great power politics in Europe as it had several times in the past. Poland, therefore, pursued a pro-European foreign policy.[64]

Embedding German-Polish relations within multilateral integration also facilitated the emergence of a stable peace by encouraging habits of mutually beneficial cooperation based on deepening trust and common interests.[65] Within EU institutions, Poland and Germany interact on a regular basis, and within those institutions the very asymmetric relations appear more balanced.[66] Joint activities of Poland and Germany within the EU have also enhanced cooperation levels,[67] while situations such as the June 2007 crisis surrounding Poland's refusal to accept the German reform plan for EU voting are more easily contained and diffused thanks to the embeddedness of their relations in the wider multilateral setting. The enduring nature of this peace found expression in the historic opening of the borders between the two states on December 20, 2007, only half a year after the June crisis.

Conclusion

To conclude, the German experience in Europe after World War II and in the post–Cold War transition period is often seen as the poster-child case of successful ES. This chapter suggests that this was indeed the case in Germany's relations with Poland. In its relations with France, Germany was more the target than the initiator of ES policies. Both cases demonstrate the power of significant inducements or positive sanctions as a means of stabilizing regional rivalries, especially when coupled with the specter of high costs for no cooperation. The effectiveness of these sanctions, however, hinges on three central factors: the potential economic benefits emerging from the underlying nature of the economies involved; the existence of favorable geostrategic circumstances; and the ability of the government to target both the first and second faces of security in the initial transition stages. Furthermore, ES is often a two-level game, and it requires a strong state that can play it well. Such a state can target its own economic players effectively to bring them into agreement with its external ES strategy. Wide economic power asymmetries generate greater leverage for the more powerful state, but they also create challenges for the effective use of ES for the purpose of promoting peace (rather than, e.g., for the purpose of creating greater dependence). Finally, to be successful ES must generate greater economic interaction in the long run, interaction that is not driven by the state and thus is no longer part of an ES strategy. Embedding the dyadic relations in broader multilateral institutions can help achieve this goal, as well as help to promote regional peace.

NOTES

1. See Galia Press-Barnathan, *The Political Economy of Transitions to Peace* (Pittsburgh: University of Pittsburgh Press, 2009).

2. On the strategic use of trade, illustrated in Germany in the 1930s, see Albert O. Hirschman, *National Power and the Structure of Foreign Trade,* 2nd ed. (Berkeley: University of California Press, 1969), chap. 2.

3. See Steven E. Lobell, "Winning Friends and Influencing Enemies among Great Power Rivals: The Case of Washington, Beijing, and Moscow, 1969–1979," *Chinese Journal of International Politics* 4, no. 2 (2011): 205–30.

4. Alan S. Milward, *The Reconstruction of Western Europe, 1941–51* (Berkeley: University of California Press, 1984), 127–29; John Gillingham, *Coal, Steel, and the Rebirth of Europe, 1945–1955: The Germans and French from Ruhr Conflict to Economic Community* (New York: Cambridge University Press, 1991), 95–96, 137–77.

5. On West Germany's export-led growth strategy, see Michael Kreile, "West Germany: The Dynamics of Expansion," in Peter J. Katzenstein, ed., *Between Power and Plenty: Foreign Economic Policies of Advanced Industrial States* (Madison: Uni-

versity of Wisconsin Press, 1978). On Germany's reliance on external markets, see Haig Simonian, *The Privileged Partnership: Franco-German Relations in the European Community, 1969–1984* (Oxford: Clarendon Press, 1985), 18–20.

6. Andrew Moravcsik, *The Choice for Europe: Social Purpose and State Power from Messina to Maastricht* (Ithaca: Cornell University Press, 1998).

7. Alistair Cole, *Franco-German Relations* (Harlow, UK: Pearson Education, 2001), 23.

8. Gillingham, *Coal, Steel, and the Rebirth of Europe*, 224–29.

9. Frank Roy Willis, *France, Germany, and the New Europe, 1945–1967* (Oxford: Oxford University Press, 1968), 235–36.

10. Gillingham, *Coal, Steel, and the Rebirth of Europe*, chap. 1.

11. Willis, *France, Germany, and the New Europe*, 120–22.

12. Etel Solingen, *Regional Orders at Century's Dawn: Global and Domestic Influences on Grand Strategy* (Princeton: Princeton University Press, 1998).

13. In her later work Solingen broadened her focus to include leaders' "survival strategies," a framework that better incorporates these types of considerations. See Etel Solingen, "Pax Asiatica versus Bella Levantina: The Foundations of War and Peace in East Asia and the Middle East," *American Political Science Review* 101, no. 4 (2007): 757–80.

14. Willis, *France, Germany, and the New Europe*, 88.

15. Simonian, *Privileged Partnership*, 20, 61–62.

16. Gillingham, *Coal, Steel, and the Rebirth of Europe*, 62–64.

17. Ibid., 189–204.

18. Craig Parsons, "Showing Ideas as Causes: The Origins of the European Union," *International Organization* 56, no. 1 (2002): 47–84.

19. Willis, *France, Germany, and the New Europe*, 94–98.

20. Norrin Ripsman, *Peacemaking by Democracies: The Effect of State Autonomy on the Post–World War Settlements* (University Park: Pennsylvania State University Press, 2002), 185–86.

21. Gunther Kloss, *West Germany: An Introduction* (Basingstoke: Macmillan Education, 1990), 121–23, 117–18.

22. Kloss, *West Germany*, 132–36. For more on industrial relations in Germany, see Peter J. Katzenstein, *Policy and Politics in West Germany: The Growth of a Semisovereign State* (Philadelphia: Temple University Press, 1987), chap. 3.

23. Cole, *Franco-German Relations*, 49–51.

24. I should note, though, that the clear distinction between formal peace and normalization is rarely as clear-cut in real life. The distinction between state- and society-centered economic initiatives is not straightforward either.

25. Cole, *Franco-German Relations*, 69–71.

26. Moravscik, *Choice for Europe*, 116–18.

27. For a thorough analysis of the debate over German rearmament and the Paris Agreements, see Ripsman, *Peacemaking by Democracies*, 190–212.

28. See Norrin Ripsman, "Two Stages of Transition from a Region of War to a Region of Peace: Realist Transition and Liberal Endurance," *International Studies Quarterly* 49, no. 4 (2005): 669–94.

29. For a concise description of the changing power disparities with the growth of German economic power during the 1970s and 1980s and their impact on political relations with France, see Cole, *Franco-German Relations*, 13–17.

30. Gillingham, *Coal, Steel, and the Rebirth of Europe*, 233.

31. See Michael Hogan, *Marshall Plan: America, Britain, and the Reconstruction of Western Europe* (Cambridge: Cambridge University Press, 1987), chaps. 2–3; Max Beloff, *United States and the Unity of Europe* (Washington, DC: Brookings Institution, 1963), chap. 1; Milward, *Reconstruction of Western Europe*, 114–15.

32. Timothy Garton Ash, *In Europe's Name: Germany and the Divided Continent* (New York: Vintage Books, 1994), 217–18. Ash also notes that the post-1945 Polish and German historiographies of the prewar period were like distorted mirror images of each other (220).

33. W. W. Kulski, *Germany and Poland: From War to Peaceful Relations* (Syracuse: Syracuse University Press, 1976), chap. 1.

34. For descriptions of the treaty and how it was perceived in the media at the time, see S. Szechanowski, "The Polish–West German Treaty," *Poland and Germany (East & West)* 14, nos. 3–4 (July–December 1970): 3–9; and "Press Notes: The Polish–West Germany Treaty," *Poland and Germany (East & West)* 14, nos. 3–4 (July–December 1970): 43–63.

35. Jeanne Lavon Jensen, "Cooperation and Conflict in the Normalization of Relations between the People's Republic of Poland and the Federal Republic of Germany" (PhD diss., University of South Carolina, 1985), 125.

36. Ash, *In Europe's Name*, 237–40.

37. Poland insisted that the border issue be resolved before it would agree to German reunification.

38. Randall E. Newnham, *Poland and Germany, 1989–1991: The Role of Economic Factors in Foreign Policy* (Seattle: Henry M. Jackson School of International Studies, University of Washington, 2000), 46–59, 66.

39. See Joanna M. M. Kepka, "The Nysa Euroregion: The First Ten Years," *Eurasian Geography and Economics* 45, no. 3 (2004): 62–189; Stefan Krätke, "Regional Integration or Fragmentation? The German-Polish Border Region in a New Europe," *Regional Studies* 33, no. 7 (August 1999): 631–41. For a detailed description of the various cooperation initiatives, see Patricia A. Davis, *The Art of Economic Persua-*

sion: Positive Incentives and German Economic Diplomacy (Ann Arbor: University of Michigan Press, 1999), chaps. 3–4.

40. This is the central argument of Davis, *Art of Economic Persuasion*, 16–19. Also see Robert Mark Spaulding, *Osthandel and Ostpolitik: German Foreign Trade Policies in Eastern Europe from Bismarck to Adenauer* (Providence, RI: Berghahn Books, 1997), 487.

41. Ash, *In Europe's Name*, 244–45.

42. Laszlo Görgey, *Bonn's Eastern Policy, 1964–1971: Evolution and Limitations* (Hamden, CT: Archon Books, 1972), 19–21.

43. Reinhard Neebe, "German Big Business and the Return to the World Market after World War II," in Volker R. Berghahn ed., *Quest for Economic Empire: European Strategies of German Big Business in the Twentieth Century* (Providence, RI: Berghahn Books, 1996), 117.

44. Görgey, *Bonn's Eastern Policy*, 8–10.

45. For a thorough review of these various strategies, see Newnham, *Poland and Germany*, 20–25

46. Görgey, *Bonn's Eastern Policy*, 8–10.

47. S. Gomulka, "The New Policy for Poland's Industrialization," *Poland and Germany (East & West)* 19, nos. 1–2 (January 1975): 9.

48. Jensen, "Cooperation and Conflict in the Normalization of Relations," 28–69.

49. Newnham, *Poland and Germany*, 12–16.

50. Ash, *In Europe's Name*, 246.

51. Peter J. Katzenstein, "Germany and Mitteleuropa: An Introduction," in Peter J. Katzenstein, ed., *Mitteleuropa: Between Europe and Germany* (Providence, RI: Berghahn Books, 1997), 19.

52. Davis, *Art of Economic Persuasion*, 74–75.

53. Spaulding, *Osthandel and Ostpolitik*, 8–9. On the development of Polish agriculture under Communist rule and after the transition to a market economy and its ongoing crisis, see Silvia Borzutzky and Emmanuel Kranidis, "A Struggle for Survival: The Polish Agricultural Sector from Communism to EU Accession," *East European Politics and Societies* 19, no. 4 (2005): 614–45.

54. On the German reaction to the crisis, see Ash, *In Europe's Name*, 94–96.

55. Davis, *Art of Economic Persuasion*, 37–39, 48–49.

56. Ibid., 71.

57. Randall E. Newnham, "More Flies with Honey: Positive Economic Linkage in German Ostpolitik from Bismark to Kohl," *International Studies Quarterly* 44, no. 1 (March 2000): 84, n. 1.

58. Sulimierski Bronislaw, "Issues in Financial and Investment Relations

between Poland and Germany," *Russian and East European Finance and Trade* 31, no. 4 (July–August 1995): 1–2; Kepka, "Nysa Euroregion," 168, table 2.

59. Wlodzimierz Borodziej, "Consequences of the Treaty between the Republic of Poland and the Federal Republic of Germany on Good Neighborliness, Friendship, and Co-Operation," *Polish Foreign Affairs Digest* 2, no.1 (2002): 175.

60. Newnham, *Poland and Germany*, 64–65.

61. Kepka, "Nysa Euroregion," 174–75. For more on the problems of regional cooperation on the border, see Krätke, "Regional Integration or Fragmentation?," 631–41.

62. See Peter J. Katzenstein, "United Germany in an Integrating Europe," *Current History* 608 (March 1997): 116–23; Simon J. Bulmer, "Shaping the Rules? The Constitutive Politics of the European Union and German Power," in Peter J. Katzenstein, ed., *Tamed Power: Germany in Europe* (Ithaca: Cornell University Press, 1997); and Jeffrey J. Anderson, "Hard Interests, Soft Power, and Germany's Changing Role in Europe," in Peter J. Katzenstein, ed., *Tamed Power: Germany in Europe* (Ithaca: Cornell University Press, 1997).

63. Wayne C. Thompson, "Germany and the East," *Europe-Asia Studies* 53, no. 6 (September 2001): 929, 933.

64. Jerzy Kranz, "Germany, Quo Vadis? A View from Poland," *German Politics* 10 (April 2001): 141–54.

65. Adrian Hyde-Price, "Stable Peace in Mitteleuropa: The German-Polish Hinge," in Arie M. Kacowicz, Yaacov Bar-Siman-Tov, Ole Elgström, and Magnus Jerneck, eds., *Stable Peace Among Nations* (Lanham, MD: Rowman and Littlefield, 2000), 268–70.

66. Marcin Zaborowski, *Germany, Poland, and Europe: Conflict, Co-operation, and Europeanisation* (Manchester: Manchester University Press, 2004), 176.

67. Tytus Jaskułowski, "Poland's Relations with Germany," in *Yearbook of Polish Foreign Policy* (Polish Institute of International Affairs, 2006).

CHAPTER 4

Making Peace with Nonstate Armed Actors

The Role of Economic Incentives

Marie-Joëlle Zahar

How can economic statecraft be used to bring nonstate armed actors to the peace table in the service of ending regional conflicts? Over the past two decades, nonstate armed actors have gained preeminence as an inescapable reality of contemporary conflicts and a key feature in the study of conflict and peace. Nowhere is this more obvious than in the Middle East where such actors have played an important role in civil wars (e.g., in Iraq following the 2003 US invasion), interstate conflicts (as in the summer 2006 war between Israel and Hezbollah), and transnational violence (such as al-Qaeda's involvement in insurgencies, civil wars, and domestic security incidents in several Middle Eastern countries). While there are few examples of nonstate armed actors triggering regional rivalries, several are responsible for deepening rivalries and making conflict resolution seem more remote. Examples include the role played by Hezbollah in Lebanon-Israel relations or that currently played by the Islamic State (formerly the Islamic State in Iraq and Syria, or ISIS) in conflict dynamics inside and between erstwhile regional rivals Syria and Iraq. It is therefore no exaggeration to say that regional transition in the Middle East requires dealing with nonstate armed actors.

However, if the international relations (IR) literature is relatively silent on the economics of peacemaking,[1] it is particularly mute when addressing war-to-peace transitions involving nonstate armed actors. Most of the "standard" IR literature on nonstate armed actors focuses on their role in the production of insecurity.[2] For its part, the literature on civil wars pays more attention to nonstate armed actors.[3] But it also tends to focus on the role of economic incentives at the onset of and during a conflict.[4] Inter alia, this body of work suggests that economic incentives and/or grievances are important in understanding decisions to go to war at both the individual and aggregate group levels.[5] It also suggests that war economies influence the dynamics of civil wars.[6] For some they are a key reason for the protracted nature of civil conflicts.[7] for others they are an important element in understanding the success or failure of international peace-building efforts.[8]

In a disjuncture similar to that of the broader field of IR,[9] there is relatively little on the economics of peacemaking, particularly as regards the manner in which nonstate armed actors, which are identified as key players in war economies, can be induced to come to the negotiating table. This contribution begins to fill that gap. It proceeds in three steps. First, I review the literature on the economics of peace agreements as it relates specifically to nonstate armed actors. Second, I draw on the literature on civil wars to bring out key linkages between varieties of nonstate armed actors and dimensions of the war economies in which they tend to be involved. Third, I discuss the manner in which economic incentives and/or sanctions could facilitate peacemaking. After thus establishing the foundation for examining the political economy of engaging armed nonstate actors in support of regional peacemaking, I then discuss three of the core questions of this volume: (1) which nonstate actors present the most appropriate targets of economic statecraft, (2) what types of economic instruments are most likely to influence these actors, and (3) what is the appropriate timing of economic statecraft designed to influence armed nonstate actors? Although it is more focused on civil wars than regional rivalries per se, the argument is intended to have broader import, and the chapter draws illustrations primarily from the experience of nonstate armed actors in the Middle East, one of the few regions of the world where regional rivalries, whether the Arab-Israeli conflict or Sunni-Shi'a tensions epitomized by the competition between Iran and Saudi Arabia, endure with little prospect of resolution.

The Economics of Peace Agreements

How do economic considerations facilitate peacemaking on the morrow of wars? How can economic instruments convince parties to lay down their weapons? The civil war literature provides two sets of answers. The first highlights the role of economic instruments in affecting the balance of power between protagonists.[10] The second considers their role in affecting the possibility of pork.[11]

Economic instruments can and have been used to manipulate the balance of power in order to bring a civil war to an end. Most common is their use to create the conditions for a negotiated settlement, something the literature describes as a "ripe moment." Ripe moments are said to be created either when one side faces a "precipice" and accepts the principle of negotiations or when both sides fail to prevail militarily and come to a "hurting stalemate."[12] From Angola to Bosnia and Herzegovina and beyond, economic sanctions and embargoes have variously been used to create ripe moments or induce hurting stalemates with varying degrees of success.[13] There are legitimate questions about the ability of sanctions to affect the behavior of nonstate armed actors. Underlying any sanctions regime is the assumption that inflicting pain on a society will lead that society to mobilize and demand a change in the behavior of its leaders. In other words, sanctions are expected to work where accountability mechanisms tie leaders to their populations. In counter-distinction, scholars who study nonstate armed actors stress that such actors often control populations by meting out violence and inducing fear and compliance.[14]

Economic instruments can also be used to help one of the protagonists prevail over its adversaries. While most foreign intervention in civil wars is framed in terms of direct or indirect military assistance, foreign powers can use economic instruments to support one party to a conflict. In Bosnia and Herzegovina, for example, the government of Slobodan Milošević did more than provide military support to the Bosnian Serb Army; most of the top Bosnian Serb officers received salaries from Belgrade. Outside financial assistance can also come from multinationals and for-profit companies through transactions involving illegal access to resources: blood diamonds, Coltan, precious woods, and the like. However, authors who have studied such foreign intervention tend to argue that instead of achieving a speedy resolution of the conflict such foreign support increases its severity and duration.[15]

The second type of argument linking economic instruments to peacemaking revolves around the notion of pork, the fact that "having rents to divide among faction leaders greases the wheels of a negotiation process; if rents can be provided to multiple sides, the argument goes, their adherence will be more reliable."[16] Material incentives are indeed said to help bring nonstate armed actors to the table; in Mozambique, for instance, they have proven essential to securing RENAMO's (the Mozambique National Resistance; in Portuguese,

Resistência Nacional Moçambicana) commitment to peace at key junctures.[17] According to Caroline Hartzell and Matthew Hoddie, economic power sharing is one of four mutually reinforcing dimensions of power sharing that can stabilize a transition from war to peace. This it does by easing the credible commitment problem, which makes transitions from war to peace particularly fragile and fraught with danger, and by preventing the capture of power by one protagonist at the expense of the other. However, as Hartzell and Hoddie note,[18] most peace settlements are not likely to specify rules governing the distribution of wealth and income in a society beyond general formulas. In practice economic power sharing has often been reduced to the distribution of pork to bring elites onboard, as was the case in Sierra Leone, where the Revolutionary United Front's Foday Sankoh demanded and obtained the post of minister of natural resources.[19]

Questions have been raised as to the efficacy of this mechanism for stabilizing the peace. In her article on the recurrence of civil wars,[20] Barbara F. Walter convincingly argues that individual mobilization is an understudied element of the equation. She underlines the fact that individuals, like leaders, expect material and/or political benefits to accrue from their decision to lay down weapons. If and when these do not materialize, the opportunity for renewed recruitment into rebel organizations increases accordingly. Others have questioned whether incentive-based commitments to peace are a lasting way to secure the commitment of protagonists. Drawing on Albert Hirschman's notions of voice and exit, I have argued that incentive-based commitment to peace develops at best an instrumental loyalty to the peace process, which depends on the continued provision of said incentive(s).[21] Others have argued that the luxurious perks that delegates to peace talks receive in return for their participation become an incentive for the prolongation of talks rather than, as intended, an inducement to reach a peace agreement.[22]

In brief, and in spite of the existence of arguments attempting to probe the economics of peacemaking, as Norrin M. Ripsman and Steven E. Lobell observe in the introduction to this volume, these remain in dire need of further refinement and specification. As already mentioned, the scope conditions of some arguments should render them inapplicable to transitions involving nonstate armed actors. Evidence in support of other arguments is at best mixed, at worst merely illustrative. As will be discussed in the next section, the recent turn in the study of civil wars, which focuses on the micropolitics of these conflicts, helps us refine the existing literature.

Nonstate Armed Actors and the Economics of Civil Wars

Not only does the literature reviewed in the preceding section not provide particularly strong arguments linking economic incentives to peacemaking; it also does not ask the specific question "Whether, when, and what incentives are likely to convince nonstate armed actors to lay down their weapons"? Indeed, while much has been written about the connection between nonstate armed actors and war economies, little has been done to investigate the flip side of this coin. The following section begins by summarizing key dimensions of the economics of conflict as these relate specifically to nonstate armed actors. It then identifies three mechanisms that the literature has linked to conflict onset and duration and extends their logic to investigate their potential role in peacemaking.

Much as states come in diverse forms, so do nonstate armed actors. There are those that draw a stark dividing line between the "insurgents" and "guerrillas" of yesteryear and the "warlords," "rebels," and other armed thugs of so-called new wars.[23] Others argue that these differences are neither empirically accurate nor necessarily the most fruitful theoretical lines of inquiry.[24] While this contribution is not the place to catalog the diversity of nonstate armed actors, suffice it to say that these groups are usually described with reference to their mode of operation (e.g., using the term *revolutionary armies* or *guerrillas*), to their relationship with the state (using the terms *militias* or *paramilitaries* to describe pro-state groups and *insurgents* or *rebels* to describe antistate groups), or to the extent to which they further collective or private aims (often using terms like *warlord* or *narco-terrorist* to deny groups collective motivations).[25]

While certain regions of the world and certain historical periods have tended to be associated with specific types of nonstate armed actors, for example, with the rise of insurgencies in the 1960s and 1970s in Latin America, the Middle East is rife with nonstate actors of all types. The Palestine Liberation Organization (PLO) has historically been identified as one of the longer-lasting guerrilla movements, and militias abounded in the course of Lebanon's 15-year-long civil war. After the reunification of the two Yemens in the early 1990s, Houthi rebels engaged in a struggle against the regime of President Ali Abdallah Saleh, until the latter stepped down in 2012, and they have been battling the new Yemeni authorities ever since. Iraq saw a violent Sunni insurgency following the US invasion and the fall of Saddam Hussein, and insurgents emerged in Libya and Syria when the 2011 Arab uprisings spread to those two countries. While the Sudanese state may have called them rebels, the scope and organization of the

Sudan People's Liberation Army warranted its description as a revolutionary army. Likewise, groups such as the Lebanese Hezbollah are often described by their domestic and foreign opponents as terrorists, but their military complexity and stated objective to upset the regional status quo warrants their labeling as revolutionary armies as well.

To be able to sustain themselves, nonstate armed actors require access to two types of resources: fighters and revenue. Both are necessary if a group is to survive to fight another day. Both can also affect the trajectory of nonstate armed actors. Without fighters and revenue, groups cannot sustain themselves for long. Nor can they develop into large and often complex organizations, which, like the Lebanese Hezbollah, not only have an organized military wing but also operate an array of social, educational, political, and sometimes economic institutions to cater to the needs of combatants, their families, and the broader community that the group seeks to represent. While the institutionalization of nonstate armed actors is neither linear nor unidirectional, it is heavily influenced by the means at the disposal of groups.[26]

Both revenue and fighters can be secured in diverse ways. They can be domestically generated, externally garnered, or secured through cooperation, inducement, or force. In the Middle East, for example, al-Qaeda recruits fighters domestically as well as transnationally, as evidenced by the rise to prominence of the likes of al-Qaeda leader Abu Musab al-Zarqawi, a Jordanian national, during the insurgency in Iraq. Other groups, such as the various Palestinian organizations, be they the Fatah, Hamas, or the Popular Front for the Liberation of Palestine, do not seek to recruit outside the community. As regards fighters, Jeremy M. Weinstein's typology draws a useful distinction between groups that attract investors—that is, individuals willing to take risks in the present in return for the promise of rewards in the long run—and groups that attract consumers who seek short-term gains from participation in armed conflict.[27] In earlier work, I showed that nonstate armed actors that fit in Weinstein's investor category are also likely to develop ties to the broader community in the form of the provision of social services.[28] It was this that earned Latin American insurgencies of the 1960s the label *gobierno de arriba* (government of the hills) as opposed to the *gobierno de abajo* (government of the cities), which referred to the state authorities.[29] Similarly, during Ethiopia's civil war, the Eritrean People's Liberation Front was often referred to as a *hukuma*, the Arabic word meaning "government."[30]

Revenue generation can also take a dizzying array of forms. It can range from force-based predatory activities such as extortion, theft of international aid, and revolutionary taxation to productive economic activities.[31] Economic activities can broadly be categorized as divestment- versus investment-oriented and domestically versus externally generated. In Latin America's insurgencies, for example, productive activities typically revolved around the agricultural sector. Insurgents tended to buy supplies from local peasants at prices well above market rates.[32] In Peru, Sendero Luminoso established cooperative forms of agriculture in all areas under its control. Resources can be generated internally, but they can also come from outside through the patronage of foreign powers, the activation of ethnic kin ties, or the participation in transnational economic activities. Much has been made in this respect of Hezbollah's ties with Iran and of the role of diaspora-based Islamic charities in funding Islamist groups throughout the Middle East and beyond.

Focusing on the nature of links between nonstate actors and the broader communities within which they are embedded, R. Thomas Naylor developed a three-pronged typology to classify the economics of civil wars.[33] Predation is a pure-divestment strategy in which armed groups take what they want or need at gunpoint. Parasitism is a divestment-dominant mixed strategy inasmuch as the parasite lives off its host but does provide limited services—typically security in the case of nonstate armed actors. Symbiosis is an investment-dominant mixed strategy in which the revenue-generating activities of nonstate armed actors interface with the real economy. The Lebanese civil war provides an interesting illustration of these categories while highlighting the fact that they need not be fixed. At the outset of the Lebanese civil war, "Militias demanded outright ransoms from industrialists, merchants, or wealthy investors (easily totaling U.S. $500 million since 1975)."[34] When the plunder of Lebanon's (limited) assets proved insufficient, militias turned to predation, imposing taxes on citizens, commercial establishments, and industries in return for the protection they provided against rivals. As for symbiosis, it was masterfully achieved in Lebanon's Christian enclave by the Christian Lebanese Forces (LF). By the mid-1980s, this group had established an elaborate infrastructure to regulate the conduct of its economic activities. This involved customs duties, harbor facilities, a price control commission, and a body of business-law-like regulations, as well as the provision of internal security within the Christian enclave. But the LF also directly engaged in economic activities. It ran its own chain of supermarkets, gas stations, and transportation companies, and it partnered with private investors in opening a banking establishment and a low-cost construction company.[35]

Another important characteristic of the economics of nonstate armed actors is the extent to which they depend on networks. Networks are important to the discussion of peace economics because they can provide points of leverage against a nonstate armed actor or, alternatively, provide the nonstate actor with the means to entrench itself in a position in which it refuses to engage in peace negotiations. The type and extent of a group's networks do not simply derive from the type of economic activity in which it is engaged. For example, we could make the assumption that a nonstate actor that relies on predation to survive does not have extensive networks. This could prove to be utterly wrong, as predation can also be associated with the development of extensive networks in the diaspora. Two illustrations come to mind in this respect: the cases of the Liberation Tigers of Tamil Eelam (LTTE) and the Kosovo Liberation Army (KLA or UCK in Albanian), both of which developed extensive networks, respectively, among Sri Lankan Tamils and Kosovar Albanians in the diaspora. These communities were subjected to revolutionary taxation, which was used to fund the military efforts of the two groups. As far as networks are concerned, these can be community based (as in diasporas and ethnic kin states) or interest based (as in commercial networks involved in the transnational aspect of a divestment war economy, including smuggling networks and multinationals).

In brief the economics of civil war affect nonstate actors in multiple ways. Not only are they key to garnering the resources needed to fight, but they can also have an effect on the organizational structure of groups, their recruitment patterns, and their vulnerability to external shocks. The more resources at a group's disposal, the more likely it will be, all other things being equal, to develop into a complex organization and to attract consumers into its ranks. In turn relations among a nonstate armed actor, its rank-and-file membership, and the broader community can either heighten or lessen the group's vulnerability to external shocks. Groups composed of mostly consumer-type combatants are likely to lose their fighters if and when they fail to dispense economic incentives. Groups that rely on force to subdue the communities in the midst of which they operate are not likely to be responsive to demands from these communities. Finally, groups with dense networks that contribute to their financing and support will have to take account of these networks, which may, under specific conditions, provide points of leverage to bring the nonstate armed actors into peace talks or to keep them in the fold of a transition from war to peace. With these insights as its departure point, the next section sketches a preliminary framework with which to analyze the economics of peacemaking.

The Economics of Peacemaking with Nonstate Armed Actors

Given the importance of economic considerations in influencing the trajectory of nonstate armed actors, it is puzzling that little systematic attention has been paid to the incentive side of the economics of peacemaking when attempting to bring nonstate actors into the fold of a transition from war to peace. Three lines of inquiry seem particularly fruitful in conceptualizing the role that economic incentives can play in inducing nonstate armed actors to negotiate peace agreements: the organizational effects of economic instruments or their impact on the structure of nonstate armed actors; their domestic premium effects—specifically their impact on recruitment (and retention) patterns; and their network effects or the manner in which they tie the nonstate groups to or separate them from other groups in society—the intuition being that denser networks stabilize a transition while sparser ones can cause fragility.[36] While these mechanisms have been studied in relation to conflict onset and duration, they have not been equally probed from the perspective of peace building. What follows is a brief exposition of the manner in which the mechanisms are likely to work with illustrations drawn from Middle Eastern case studies.

The Organizational Effects of Economic Instruments

The link between resources and institutional development or capacity is two sided. A basic endowment of material resources is needed if nonstate armed actors are to survive. At the outset of conflict, nonstate actors are usually weak relative to the governments they are fighting. This fundamental fact about insurgency means that rebels have two options if they are to survive: either continuously hide from government forces or increase their strength.[37] Empirically, rebel strategies include a mix of both. Most insurgencies seek hideouts in remote areas outside the reach of government forces; most also engage in activities intended to increase their manpower and weaponry. In turn, as they develop into complex and multifaceted organizations, nonstate armed actors require sufficient resources to sustain their multiple activities. In other words, policy makers can expect that, other things being equal, material incentives will be more important to those nonstate armed actors that have developed into complex organizations. Indeed, these actors will need more resources to maintain not only their military effort but also an ever growing number of non-military activities.

This suggests that, ceteris paribus, material sanctions are likely to be more effective when wielded against organizationally complex nonstate armed actors. The experience of the PLO and the reasons that drove Yasser Arafat to enter into talks leading to the Oslo Peace Accords provide support for this hypothesis. In the late 1970s, a tremendous increase in infrastructure accompanied the transformation of the PLO from a mere guerrilla movement into a government-in-exile for Palestinian refugee populations.[38] The 1982 invasion of Lebanon underscored the vulnerability of this infrastructure. Israel "sought out and physically destroyed $400 million worth of PLO infrastructure and assets in the form of factories, offices, commercial real estate, hospitals and schools, as well as seizing bank records that might have permitted them to trace financial assets around the world."[39] The organization, which had managed to regroup its forces after severe setbacks in the late 1960s and 1970s, could not reconstitute its fighting potential as easily in the wake of the Lebanon defeat. The next military challenge to Israel did not emanate from PLO camps outside Israel. In December 1987, Arafat watched from Tunis as the first Intifada rocked the West Bank and the Gaza Strip. The center of gravity of Palestinian decision making had just shifted from Tunis to the Occupied Territories. In November 1988, the legislative wing of the PLO, the Palestinian National Council, met in Tunis, and, in an attempt to regain control over the "Palestinian Question," Arafat seized the occasion to proclaim the independence of Palestine, formally recognize all United Nations (UN) resolutions, and demand direct talks with Israel.

The first Intifada weakened the PLO further, but the most severe blow to the organization came when Arab Gulf states suspended their financial support of the organization in 1991 after Yasser Arafat refused to condemn Saddam Hussein's invasion of Kuwait. Having lost its international credibility as a result of this decision, militarily sidelined, and financially strapped, the PLO's survival was seriously at stake. Israel and the United States subsequently refused to allow the organization to participate in the Madrid peace talks of 1991; the leadership of the Intifada, for its part, was ultimately brought into the talks as part of a joint Jordanian-Palestinian delegation. In a stark reversal of events, in September 1993 Arafat reemerged on the international scene following the disclosure of the Oslo Peace Accords. Several analysts argue that the decision to enter into peace talks with the Israeli leadership was prompted by the PLO's survival imperative.[40]

The Domestic Premium Effects of Economic Instruments

What does a review of the literature tell us about the impact of economic incentives on recruitment (and retention) patterns, and how can economic statecraft be manipulated to bring nonstate armed actors to the negotiating table?

Presumed differences between ethnic and ideological conflicts have not held up well under the weight of close scrutiny.[41] But one of the most consistent findings of research on civil wars is that separatist and nonseparatist conflicts differ.[42] This finding seems to hold across several dimensions, including conflict duration and severity.[43] It also ties directly into the issue of recruitment patterns. Separatist wars often involve sons of the soil, whose commitment to asserting their right to a given territory is based on claims to its ownership.[44] Going back to the typology developed by Weinstein, these are investors not consumers. That is, sons of the soil are individuals willing to take risks in the present in return for the promise of rewards in the long run. Compared to consumers, who seek immediate compensation for the risks they take, investors ought to be less sensitive to the use of economic incentives in agreeing to come to the table.

This is not to say that investors are totally impervious to economic instruments; simply, economic instruments alone will not be sufficient to secure a transition involving investors. Discussing the case of Israel-Palestine, Guy Ben-Porat makes a similar point when he shows that dividends of peace initially buttressed the peace process but Palestinian opposition to Oslo increased as the prospects of peace grew more distant.[45] Peace dividends should not be confused with peace.

This lesson is also borne out in the Iraqi experience. The Sunni Awakening Movement, also known as the Sahwa, is a popular committee for self-defense created by the different Sunni tribes of Iraq.[46] At the outset of the US invasion of Iraq, Sahwa members were targets of the American "debaathification" campaign, which sought to uproot Baath Party members from positions in all parts of the state. Sunni males were thus left with little if any alternatives to eke out a living in the immediate aftermath of the fall of Saddam Hussein. Many joined the insurgency. Initially allied with jihadist elements, Sahwa members ultimately balked at the violence and bloodiness of jihadist insurgency methods. Some are said to have also been "bought off" by American forces.[47] The Sahwa dealt a severe blow to al-Qaeda in Iraq through military attacks and massive defection among the Sunni tribes previously affiliated with the organization.[48] According to Gen. Joseph Fil Jr., a US troop commander in Baghdad, al-Qaeda's retreat from the Iraqi capital was explicitly linked to the recruitment and arming of 67,000 Sunni militiamen across the country.[49] The decision of Sahwa members to switch sides may have had to do with disagreement between the Sunni tribes and al-Qaeda over the methods used in the course of the insurgency; they were definitely encouraged by the prospect of reintegration in the Sunni armed forces and the police.

The limits of economic incentives started to appear when in October 2008 the United States agreed to hand over responsibility for the Sahwa committees to the majority Shia Iraqi government. Under the terms of the deal, the government not only had to pay the salaries of Sahwa militiamen; it also had to commit to reintegrate 20 percent of them into the armed forces and local police. This commitment had difficulties materializing; salaries were often late or unpaid, and reintegration proceeded at a much slower pace than planned. By September 2008, only 3,400, or a mere 6.5 percent, of Sahwa troops had been reintegrated.[50] Further, a number of high-ranking government officials publicly expressed doubts about the commitment of Sahwa fighters to the new Iraq, wondering about the wisdom of reintegrating Sunnis into the institutions of the state. In March 2009, a brief rebellion in Sahwa ranks illustrated the tension between the movement and the Nouri al-Maliki government. In 2014, concerns were expressed in many quarters that disgruntled Sahwa fighters might be supporting ISIS and contributing to the group's rapid ascendancy.

The Iraqi case highlights the connections among resources, recruitment patterns, and violence, as well as the potential connection between economic instruments of statecraft and peace. After the US Transitional Administration disbanded the Iraqi army and banned all Baath Party members from obtaining positions in the new Iraqi state, fighters used the one skill they had—using weapons to extract resources from their environment. Prevented from accessing the only two stable sources of gainful employment, conscripts turned into bandits and endangered the transition by contributing to the general insecurity in the country.[51] This accounts in part for the breadth of the Sunni insurgency and for its decision to ally itself with al-Qaeda. The manipulation of economic incentives, including the prospect of gainful employment, was key to the emergence of the Sahwa and to the decision of Sunni tribes to shift alliances and side with the United States. Last, but not least, the troubles between Sahwa fighters and the Maliki government illustrate both the importance of including economic incentives in security sector reform schemes to buy support for the transition and the limited impact of economic instruments when these are not accompanied by political gains.[52]

The Network Effects of Economic Instruments

Economic statecraft can be deployed to bring nonstate actors into the fold of a transition from war to peace. However, different economic instruments will need to be leveraged, depending on the type of networks in which nonstate actors are embedded. Earlier I identified two types of networks: community based and interest based. Networks will sometimes covary with the nature of the war economy; divestment-based war economies are mainly supported by interest-based transnational networks. If and when nonstate armed actors develop divestment-oriented war economies, as was partly the case in Iraq with the smuggling of oil, the deployment of economic statecraft needs to be targeted not simply at the nonstate armed actors but also at the networks that stand to lose from the disruption of black market activities. This conclusion proceeds from the recognition that war (and peace) economies often have a regional dimension and that policies developed to address only the national dimension of these economies are doomed to fail.[53] It must be said, however, that this type of network (and of war economy) is more prevalent in Africa than it is in the Middle East, in part because of the lack of easily accessible and tradable natural resources in the theaters where nonstate armed actors have operated—Lebanon, the Palestinian Territories, Yemen, and South Sudan—Iraq of course being the partial exception to the trend.

The other type of network that one must consider is community based. Community-based networks can be external, as with diasporas and ethnic kin. They can also be national, in which case they often covary with investment-oriented war economies. In such instances, nonstate armed actors engage in all kinds of nonmilitary activities that embed them further in the community. The tight relationship between the community and the nonstate actor must then be taken into account when deciding on the use of specific instruments of economic statecraft. The impact of western assistance to the reconstruction of Lebanon on the morrow of the Israel-Hezbollah war in 2006 is a telling illustration. In this instance, the manipulation of economic statecraft contributed to deepening the rift between Hezbollah and other Lebanese political factions, ushering in a serious crisis of political governance that ultimately led to the first outburst of armed violence between Lebanese factions since the end of the civil war in 1991.

In areas under its control (the southern suburbs of Beirut, the Biqa' Valley and South Lebanon), Hezbollah has embedded itself in the community. The cornerstone of this effort and the key to its remarkable efficacy is Hezbollah's own nongovernmental organization (NGO), Jihad Al Bina, which was established to "provide medical, financial and practical support to Hezbollah members and its mainly Shiite supporters."[54] The extent to which the party has interfaced with society makes it unlikely that Hezbollah's infrastructure can be dismantled without seriously affecting the livelihoods of the most vulnerable in the Shia community. That was amply demonstrated by the Israel-Hezbollah war of 2006, during which Israeli air strikes leveled not only Hezbollah offices but entire buildings and sometimes neighborhoods. Following the war, western powers deployed material incentives to rebuild Lebanon and strengthen the Lebanese state. Western donors gave to an Emergency Flash Appeal, but several "exerted pressures on UN agencies and NGOs not to meet or provide assistance to Hezbollah."[55] This "very political reconstruction" contributed to deepening the political divide between the Shia and their Lebanese political opponents.[56] In turn Hezbollah deployed symbols that resonated with its supporters and set it apart from the western powers and their Lebanese allies and supporters. The party indicated its disinterest in liberal democracy, western style, and snubbed liberal approaches to the economy in favor of "an integrated and holistic policy network, disseminating the values of resistance while constructing a collective identity derived from the notion of hala al-islamiyya, or 'Islamic sphere.'"[57] In 2008 political tensions boiled over, and the protagonists faced off in an episode that rekindled fears of descent into civil war.

The decision by the United States, France, and their allies to provide material incentives to the Lebanese government and regions controlled by friendly political forces had two perverse consequences: it solidified Hezbollah's base of support and deepened the cleavages between the group and its detractors. There are those who argue that a similar conclusion can be reached in the Palestinian case in connection with the impact of foreign aid on the relationship between Fatah and Hamas post-2006.[58]

Bringing Nonstate Armed Actors to the Negotiating Table: Implications for Practice

Although it is preliminary and perforce sketchy, the preceding discussion of the manner in which economic statecraft can be wielded to bring nonstate armed actors to the negotiating table holds several implications for policy makers. I conclude this chapter by discussing three sets of implications: identifying the right targets (*who* the nonstate armed actors most likely to be sensitive to the use of economic statecraft are), identifying the right incentives (*what* economic instruments are most likely to work in which context), and identifying the right time (*when* the manipulation of economic statecraft is likely to have the most impact).

Identifying the Right Targets

It is often argued that the assumption of *Homo economicus* is one of the key limitations of economic instruments of peacemaking. People and states embroiled in protracted conflicts may value other goods, especially territory imbued with national or religious importance, over the prospects of economic gains or the avoidance of economic losses. As a result, manipulating the economic context may not be able to overcome the entrenched nationalist, religious, or ideological hostility that underpins a conflict. This argument has often been made in reference to nonstate armed actors, specifically in the Middle East where several such actors have variously been labeled extremists, fanatics, or terrorists. The civil war literature has even developed the notion of "total spoilers" to describe groups that have "total" objectives over which they are not willing to compromise and which are impervious to calculations of cost and risk.[59] But, as this chapter has made clear, there is a danger in ascribing labels to groups and excluding them de facto from efforts at securing a transition. The PLO, which was considered a total spoiler until the late 1980s, became a linchpin of the Oslo Accords in the 1990s. It was again demonized after the start of the second Intifada, only to be "redeemed" after the 2006 Palestinian elections, which saw the victory of Hamas. This chapter suggests that there might be ways to identify nonstate armed actors that are more likely to be sensitive to the manipulation of economic sanctions or incentives. Preliminary conclusions suggest that complex organizations, the likes of the PLO or the Lebanese Forces, have a survival imperative and that, under certain conditions, economic sanctions might edge them toward the negotiating table. However, the case study of the PLO suggests that economic sanctions alone are not enough. It was the convergence of economic sanctions, military reversals, and political marginalization that brought the leadership of the organization to a "precipice" and prompted it to enter into talks with the Israeli leadership. Still, the complexity of the organization meant that to survive it required more resources than smaller groups would need, and it was ultimately that survival imperative that led Arafat to Oslo.

Identifying the Right Incentives

As was touched on earlier in this chapter, if nonstate armed actors and war economies vary, then the appropriate incentives to ensure a transition must also vary accordingly. In this regard, preliminary evidence suggests that a nonstate actor's recruitment patterns (investor or consumer) need to be taken into consideration. Sons-of-the-soil dynamics indicate that investors are likely to be less susceptible than consumers to economic incentives. But the discussion of the Sahwa movement in Iraq has also shown that things can be more complex and the lines between investors and consumers are not always as clear-cut as they may seem. Indeed, the Iraqi case study raises the interesting possibility that there might be a principal-agent problem at work here. Sahwa members acted as consumers in relation to the US forces in Iraq; however, when dealing with fellow Iraqis, they tended to act as investors as well. Whereas economic incentives were sufficient to persuade Sahwa militiamen to switch sides, there is reason to believe that, irrespective of the Maliki government's respect for its economic commitments, Sahwa members would not have been satisfied with mere economic advantages and that in their dealings with their fellow Iraqis the issue of the political reintegration of the Sunni community was paramount.

Another aspect to consider when calibrating incentives is their impact on the formation and transformation of networks. Stable transitions require the establishment of bridging rather than bonding networks,[60] that is, the creation of ties between the various protagonists and the communities they represent. Instead, too often, the material incentives create ties only at the level of elites. Although they represent a first step, these networks have proven vulnerable to the vagaries of politics, something that the history of the rise and demise of the Oslo Peace Accords underlines only too well.

Identifying the Right Moment

This raises the issue of the ripe moment for the use of economic instruments. It is usually the case that economic support for transition is slow to take off, peaks within the first year, and often fades as violence abates.[61] Again, the disbursement of funds and other economic incentives are often functions of the politics of donor states rather than the timeline of conflict. Yet there are good reasons to expect that the effectiveness of economic instruments will vary depending on the moment at which they are applied.

As Ripsman and Lobell note in the introduction to this volume, applying economic incentives too early in the process runs the risk of diverting actors' interests away from signing the peace. This was observed by Tieku in connection with the negotiations in the Sudan. However, economic incentives might help create a ripe moment, especially where nonstate armed actors face a military situation in which they have already lost or stand to lose the gains they had achieved in the course of the conflict. This is particularly the case where groups have multiple competing interests. In the Israel-Palestine case, the political threat to PLO leader Yasser Arafat from the leadership of the first Intifada, combined with his organization's weakened capacity following its ousting from Lebanon in 1982 at the hands of the Israeli army, contributed, alongside the expected material incentives, to bringing the PLO to the negotiating table. The combined impact of these factors was necessary, yet the ouster from Lebanon happened in 1982, the first Intifada began in 1987, and the loss of financial support followed the second Gulf War in 1991. Had the PLO been offered the same incentives in 1982 or 1987, it is likely that they would not have had the same impact.

Other considerations revolve around the nature of the nonstate armed actors. Consumers will often expect rapid rewards whereas investors may be more patient in the short term. However, in the long run, investors will expect the peace to translate into an improvement in their circumstances, particularly where economic marginalization was bound up with political grievances. If and when such improvements fail to materialize, investors will be easily mobilized for violence. Again the Palestinian case is instructive in this regard.

Conclusion

This chapter has sought to address a gaping hole in the literature, the potential of using economic incentives for peacemaking where nonstate armed actors are involved. Whereas economic factors are front and center in the literature on civil wars, there has been no sustained attempt to theorize the potential impact of economic statecraft on the willingness of nonstate armed actors to accept the principle of negotiations and to commit to a transition from war to peace.

Drawing on the literature on civil wars, I have identified three ways in which economic factors affect nonstate actors. First, resources have a direct impact on the trajectory and institutional development of nonstate armed actors. Second, they affect recruitment patterns. Third, they affect the kind of networks in which nonstate actors are embedded. Each and every one of these sets of linkages can provide entry points into the use of economic statecraft for peacemaking. Institutionalization increases the complexity but also the dependence of nonstate actors on resources for their survival. Recruitment patterns provide us with a rough perspective through which to assess the importance of economics to the decision making of the nonstate actors and their individual combatant members. Last but not least, networks can either shield nonstate actors from or provide leverage for and increase the impact of economic policies and instruments.

In regions where nonstate armed actors are legion, their presence can complicate the resolution of regional rivalries. Although preliminary, this discussion suggests that, although it is complicated by the presence of nonstate armed actors, the use of economic tools for peacemaking still holds the potential to contribute to the resolution of both civil wars and, by extension, regional rivalries. The insights and hypotheses developed in this chapter should help identify the most vulnerable actors, the appropriate tools and incentives, and the most likely moment at which to intervene if one is to give peace a chance.

NOTES

1. See the introduction to this volume.

2. Daphné Josselin and William Wallace, eds., *Non-state Actors in World Politics* (Basingstoke: Palgrave Macmillan, 2001); Mats Berdal and Monica Serrano, *Transnational Organized Crime and International Security: Business as Usual?* (Boulder: Lynne Rienner, 2002).

3. Pablo Policzer, "Democracy and Non-state Armed Groups," in Michaelene Cox, ed., *State of Corruption, State of Chaos: The Terror of Political Malfeasance* (Lanham, MD: Rowman and Littlefield, 2008), 35–51; Jeremy M. Weinstein, *Inside Rebellion: The Politics of Insurgent Violence* (Cambridge: Cambridge University Press, 2007); Macartan Humphries and Jeremy M. Weinstein, "Who Fights: The Determinants of Participation in Civil War," *American Journal of Political Science* 52, no. 2 (April 2008): 436–55; Elizabeth Jean Wood, *Insurgent Collective Action and Civil War in El Salvador* (Cambridge: Cambridge University Press, 2003); Jorn

Gravingholt, Claudia Hofman, and Stephen Klingebiel, "Development Cooperation and Non-state Armed Groups," working paper, German Development Institute, Bonn, 2006.

4. Mats Berdal and David Malone, eds., *Greed and Grievance: Economic Agendas in Civil Wars* (Boulder: Lynne Rienner, 2000); Paul Collier and Anke Hoeffler, *Greed and Grievance in Civil War* (Washington, DC: World Bank Development Group, 2000).

5. On decisions at the individual level, see Mats Berdal and David Keen, "Violence and Economic Agendas in Civil Wars: Some Policy Implications," *Millennium: Journal of International Studies* 26, no. 3 (1997): 795–818; Paul Collier, "Rebellion as a Quasi-Criminal Activity," *Journal of Conflict Resolution* 44, no. 6 (2000): 839–53; Mary Kaldor, *New and Old Wars: Organized Violence in a Global Era* (Stanford, CA: Stanford University Press, 1999). On decisions at the aggregate level, see Mansoob Murshed, "Inequality, Indivisibility, and Insecurity," in Stephen M. Saideman and Marie-Joëlle Zahar, eds., *Intra-state Conflict, Governments, and Security: Dilemmas of Deterrence and Assurance* (London: Routledge, 2008).

6. Karen Ballentine and Jake Sherman, eds., *The Political Economy of Armed Conflict: Beyond Greed and Grievance* (Boulder: Lynne Rienner, 2003).

7. See Berdal and Keen, "Violence and Economic Agendas in Civil Wars."

8. Michael Pugh and Neil Cooper, with Jonathan Goodhand, *War Economies in Regional Context: The Challenges of Transformation,* A project of the International Peace Academy (Boulder: Lynne Rienner, 2003).

9. See the introduction to this volume.

10. I. William Zartman, "Ripeness: The Hurting Stalemate and Beyond," in Paul Stern and Daniel Druckman, eds., *International Conflict Resolution after the Cold War* (Washington, DC: National Academy Press, 2000), 240–65.

11. Pierre Englebert and James Ron, "Primary Commodities and War: Congo-Brazzaville's Ambivalent Resource Curse," *Comparative Politics* 37, no. 1 (2004): 61–81.

12. I. William Zartman, "The Timing of Peace Initiatives: Hurting Stalemates and Ripe Moments," *Global Review of Ethnopolitics* 1, no. 1 (2001): 8–18.

13. David Cortright and George A. Lopez, eds., *Smart Sanctions: Targeting Economic Statecraft* (Lanham, MD: Rowman and Littlefield, 2002); David Cortright and George A. Lopez, *The Sanctions Decade: Assessing UN Strategies in the 1990s,* A project of the International Peace Academy (Boulder: Lynne Rienner, 2000).

14. Stathis N. Kalyvas, *The Logic of Violence in Civil War* (Cambridge: Cambridge University Press, 2006).

15. Bethany Lacina, "Explaining the Severity of Civil Wars," *Journal of Conflict Resolution* 50, no. 2 (2006): 276–89; Patrick Regan, "Third-Party Interventions and the Duration of Intrastate Conflicts," *Journal of Conflict Resolution* 46, no. 1 (2002):

55–73; Patrick Regan, *Civil Wars and Foreign Powers: Outside Intervention in Intrastate Conflict* (Ann Arbor: University of Michigan Press, 2002). Regan finds that, when it comes to bringing conflicts to a speedy end, biased interventions, whether in favor of governments or rebels, tend to be more effective than impartial ones.

16. Macartan Humphreys, "Natural Resources, Conflict, and Conflict Resolution: Uncovering the Mechanisms," *Journal of Conflict Resolution* 49, no. 4 (2005): 515.

17. Carrie L. Manning, *The Politics of Peace in Mozambique: Post-conflict Democratization, 1992–2000* (Westport, CT: Praeger, 2002).

18. Caroline Hartzell and Matthew Hoddie, *Crafting Peace: Power-Sharing Institutions and the Negotiated Settlement of Civil Wars* (University Park: Pennsylvania State University Press, 2007), 36.

19. Chandra Lekha Sriram and Marie-Joëlle Zahar, "The Perils of Power-Sharing: Africa and Beyond," *Africa Spectrum* 44, no. 3 (2009): 11–39.

20. Barbara F. Walter, "Does Conflict Beget Conflict? Explaining Recurring Civil War," *Journal of Peace Research* 41, no. 3 (2004): 371–88.

21. Albert O. Hirschman, *Exit, Voice, and Loyalty: Responses to Decline in Firms, Organizations, and States* (Cambridge, MA: Harvard University Press, 1970); Marie-Joëlle Zahar, "Political Violence in Peace Processes: Voice, Exit, and Loyalty in the Post-accord Period," in John Darby, ed., *Violence and Reconstruction*, vol. 1, Research Initiative on the Resolution of Ethnic Conflict Series (South Bend, IN: Notre Dame University Press, 2006), 33–51; "Understanding the Violence of Insiders: Loyalty, Custodians of Peace, and the Sustainability of Conflict Settlement," in Edward Newman and Oliver Richmond, eds., *Challenges to Peacebuilding: Managing Spoilers during Conflict Resolution* (Tokyo: United Nations University Press, 2006), 40–58.

22. Thomas Tieku, "How Perks for Delegates Can Influence Peace Process Outcomes," Discussion Papers, no. 3, Centre for International Governance Innovation, Africa Initiative, 2012.

23. These "new wars" are waged by new groups driven by particularistic motives. Especially prone to violence, they are absolutely nonrepresentative of the communities in the name of which they claim to fight. See Kaldor, *New and Old Wars*.

24. Stathis Kalyvas, "'New' and 'Old' Civil Wars: A Valid Distinction?," *World Politics* 54, no. 1 (2001): 99–118; Stathis Kalyvas, "The Ontology of 'Political Violence': Action and Identity in Civil Wars," *Perspectives on Politics* 1, no. 3 (2003): 475–94.

25. *Guerrillas* refers to small bands of irregulars that engage in hit-and-run operations. See Walter Laqueur, *Guerrilla Warfare: A Historical and Critical Study* (New York: Transaction, 1976). *Militia* is loosely used to describe the private armies of pro-regime strongmen. Paramilitaries usually organize in parallel with regular

armed forces, with which they often have informal (though sometimes formal) connections. On warlordism, see William Reno, *Warlord Politics and African States* (Boulder: Lynne Rienner, 1999). Warlords sometimes mobilize followers along tribal or family lines, as was the case in Somalia.

26. On the institutional development of nonstate armed actors, see Marie-Joëlle Zahar, "Handling Spoilers: External Actors, Mediation, and the Prospect of Violence," in I. William Zartman and Mark Anstey, eds., *The Slippery Slope to Genocide: Reducing Identity Conflict and Preventing Mass Murder* (Oxford: Oxford University Press, 2012), 173–93.

27. Jeremy M. Weinstein, "Resources and the Information Problem in Rebel Recruitment," *Journal of Conflict Resolution* 49, no. 4 (2005): 598–624. See also Macartan Humphreys and Jeremy M. Weinstein, "Demobilization and Reintegration," *Journal of Conflict Resolution* 51, no. 4 (2007): 531–67.

28. Zahar, "Handling Spoilers."

29. Norman Gall, "Venezuela and the Continental Revolution," *New Leader* 48 (April 12, 1965), cited in Timothy P. Wickham-Crowley, *Guerrillas and Revolution in Latin America: A Comparative Study of Insurgents and Regimes since 1956* (Princeton: Princeton University Press, 1993), 39.

30. Christopher Clapham, ed., *African Guerrillas* (Oxford: James Currey, 1988).

31. Extortion is a common source of revenue for nonstate armed actors. They often use their weapons to engage in theft, looting, kidnapping, and the like. This predatory attitude feeds on the population's fear and helplessness. Although extortion can generate substantial revenues, the supply side is not inexhaustible unless the predatory activities involve the plunder of natural resources and their sale on international markets. A common feature of civil wars, the theft of international aid has been particularly discussed with reference to Somalia. Aid taxation can be imposed on the aid recipients, at distribution sites, or at the source. Aid can be hijacked and sold for profit. A protection cost can also be imposed to secure its delivery. Nonstate armed actors can and often do impose fees on individuals and merchandise entering or exiting their zones of territorial control. For more on aid in conflict, see John Prendergast, *Frontline Diplomacy: Humanitarian Aid and Conflict in Africa* (Boulder: Lynne Rienner, 1996).

32. Wickham-Crowley, *Guerillas and Revolution in Latin America*, 40.

33. R. Thomas Naylor, "The Insurgent Economy: Black Market Operations of Guerrilla Organizations," *Crime, Law, and Social Change* 20, no. 1 (1993): 13–51.

34. Georges Corm, "The War System: Militia Hegemony and the Reestablishment of the State," in Deirdre Collings, ed., *Peace for Lebanon? From War to Reconstruction* (Boulder: Lynne Rienner, 1994), 217.

35. Marie-Joëlle Zahar, "Is All the News Bad News for Peace? Economic Agendas in the Lebanese Civil War," *International Journal* 56, no. 1 (2000): 115–28.

36. Humphreys, "Natural Resources, Conflict, and Conflict Resolution."

37. This fundamental fact was first identified by Fearon and Laitin in James D. Fearon and David D. Laitin, "Ethnicity, Insurgency, and Civil War," *American Political Science Review* 97, no. 1 (2003): 75–90.

38. For a detailed description of this infrastructure, see Rex Brynen, *Sanctuary and Survival: The PLO in Lebanon* (Boulder: Westview Press, 1990).

39. Naylor, "Insurgent Economy," 43.

40. D. G. Pruitt, "Ripeness Theory and the Oslo Talks," *International Negotiation* 2, no. 2 (1997): 237–50; Daniel Lieberfeld, "Secrecy and 'Two-Level Games' in The Oslo Accord: What the Primary Sources Tell Us," *International Negotiation* 13, no. 1 (2008): 133–46; Marie-Joëlle Zahar, "Arafat: Le passé, le présent et les options futures," *Études Internationales* 34, no. 4 (2003): 631–38.

41. Chaim Kaufman, "Possible and Impossible Solutions to Ethnic Civil Wars," *International Security* 20, no. 4 (1996): 136–75; Nicholas Sambanis, "Do Ethnic and Nonethnic Civil Wars Have the Same Causes? A Theoretical and Empirical Inquiry (Part 1)," *Journal of Conflict Resolution* 45, no. 3 (2001): 259–82.

42. James D. Fearon, "Why Do Some Civil Wars Last So Much Longer Than Others?," *Journal of Peace Research* 41, no. 3 (2004): 275–301.

43. It is also compatible with findings about the territorial dimension of ethnic war according to which if an ethnic group is concentrated and its claim cannot be used as a precedent by other groups, the state will be more likely to settle and even allow for the autonomy or full separation of the territory in question. Monica Duffy Toft, *The Geography of Ethnic Violence: Identity, Interests, and the Indivisibility of Territory* (Princeton: Princeton University Press, 2010).

44. Fearon, "Why Do Some Civil Wars Last So Much Longer Than Others?"

45. Guy Ben-Porat, "Grounds for Peace: Territoriality and Conflict Resolution," *Geopolitics* 10, no. 1 (2005): 147–66. See also Guy Ben-Porat, "Between Power and Hegemony: Business Communities in Peace Processes," *Review of International Studies* 31, no. 2 (2005): 325–48.

46. It is estimated that Sahwa members are 82 percent Sunni.

47. Patrice Claude, "En Irak, al-Qaeda aurait subi des pertes sévères," *Le Monde,* February 12, 2008, 1.

48. Patrice Claude, "Reportage: En Irak, al-Qaeda aurait subi des pertes sévères; les Etats-Unis rendent publics des documents pris sur des djihadistes," *Le Monde,* February 12, 2008, 1.

49. Patrice Claude, "En Irak, al-Qaeda ne contrôle plus aucun quartier de Bagdad," *Le Monde,* November 19, 2007, 5.

50. Patrice Claude, "Irak: Les autorités irakiennes rechignent à intégrer les supplétifs sunnites dans leur armée," *Le Monde,* November 5, 2008, 8.

51. Christopher Parker and Pete Moore, "The War Economy in Iraq," *Middle East Report* 37, no. 2 (2007): 6–15.

52. Greg Bruno, "Finding a Place for the 'Sons of Iraq,'" Council on Foreign Relations, January 9, 2009, http://www.cfr.org/iraq/finding-place-sons-iraq/p16088.

53. Pugh, Cooper, and Goodhand, *War Economies in Regional Context*.

54. David Sharer and Francine Pickup, "Dilemmas for Aid Policy in Lebanon and the Occupied Palestinian Territories," *Humanitarian Exchange*, March 2007, 4–6, www.odihpn.org/report.asp?id=2871.

55. Roger Mac Ginty, "Reconstructing Post-war Lebanon: A Challenge to the Liberal Peace?," *Conflict, Security, and Development* 7, no. 3 (2007): 470.

56. See Christine Sylva Hamieh and Roger Mac Ginty, "A Very Political Reconstruction: Governance and Reconstruction in Lebanon after the 2006 War," *Disasters: The Journal of Disaster Studies, Policy, and Management* 33, no. 1 (2009): 103–23.

57. Mona Harb and Reinoud Leenders, "Know Thy Enemy: Hizbullah, 'Terrorism,' and the Politics of Perception," *Third World Quarterly* 26, no. 1 (2005): 192. See also Roger Mac Ginty and Christine Sylva Hamieh, "'Made in Lebanon': Local Participation and Indigenous Responses to Development and Post-war Reconstruction," *Civil Wars* 12, nos. 1–2 (2010): 47–64.

58. Steven Stotsky, "Does Foreign Aid Fuel Palestinian Violence?," *Middle East Quarterly* 15, no. 3 (2008): 23–30. See also Anne Le More, "The Dilemma of Aid to the PA after the Victory of Hamas," *The International Spectator: Italian Journal of International Affairs* 41, no. 2 (2006): 87–94.

59. Stephen John Stedman, "Spoiler Problems in Peace Processes," *International Security* 22, no. 2 (1997): 5–53.

60. Robert D. Putnam, *Bowling Alone: The Collapse and Revival of American Community* (New York: Simon and Schuster, 2001).

61. Shepard Forman and Stewart Patrick, eds., *Good Intentions: Pledges of Aid for Postconflict Recovery* (Boulder: Lynne Rienner, 2000).

CHAPTER 5

Economic Incentives, Rivalry Deescalation, and Regional Transformation

William R. Thompson

Regions are like neighborhoods. Some are crowded and noisy, while others are peaceful and sedate. Some are bad places to be in late at night, while others are oases of calm. But neither regions nor neighborhoods are static. They all have the potential to become more or less orderly. The question is how they do so. One critical component of the regional process has been the deescalation, and in some cases the termination, of key and long-standing strategic rivalries between and among major regional actors. In Western Europe, the termination of the Franco-German rivalry was vitally important to the emergence of the European Union (EU). In the Middle East, the deescalation of the Egyptian-Israeli rivalry was essential to the consequently reduced probability of a resumption of Arab-Israeli warfare. In South America, the termination of the Argentine-Brazilian rivalry accelerated the tendency toward greater interstate cooperation in the Southern Cone leading ultimately to Mercosur (Mercado Comun del Sur).

It would help theoretically if these three events represented a class of phenomena that could be generalized as a process toward reduced conflict. They certainly do constitute a category of stepping stones toward less conflict, but, at the same time, their causes have little in common. The initiation of the Franco-German process was a fallback on a plan B after the French failed to gain support for dismembering Germany. The Egyptian-Israeli process is a basically triangular affair, with the United States as the linchpin and financier of the extent to which that conflict is deescalated. The Argentine-Brazilian process, initially, seemed to be more about domestic coup proofing than the advantages of inter-state cooperation per se. It became something else as developments proceeded beyond the initial motivation.

But, whatever the idiosyncratic causation, there is a common denominator in the forward-looking nature of the rivalry deescalation processes. Zartman captures backward- and forward-looking tension in negotiations in the following way. Backward-looking outcomes that only halt the hostilities that preceded them are merely cease-fires if they do not deal with deeper causes that remain untended and are susceptible to producing future hostilities. To be fully effective, negotiations also need to provide forward-looking outcomes that put in place regimes that can establish a new political order and handle future outbreaks of conflict.

> Backward-looking negotiations are those that seek to end the previous violence, that try to resolve a confrontation of rights and status, and that seek accountability for past actions in the conflict. Forward-looking negotiations look for mechanisms to prevent future violence, seek outcomes that reach beyond the conflict to opportunities for cooperation and problems solving, and try to prevent the resurgence of the old conflict in a new, later form by resolving its underlying causes.[1]

Thus, it might not matter much whether the negotiators fully realize what they are up to in their bargaining. The question is whether some mechanism emerges that reduces the incentives for conflict in the future as opposed to negotiations that merely lead to temporary cease-fires. Moreover, for regional transformation to be maximized, the emergent mechanism(s) need to catch on and diffuse throughout the region. This outcome definitely occurred in Europe. It has proceeded to some extent in South America. It has not worked much in the Middle East, presumably because the Egyptian-Israeli mechanism is very different from the European and South American mechanisms. In the Middle East, a third party funds the deescalation. Remove or decrease the funding and the deescalation is apt to become less likely to survive. It may also end if one or both parties decide that they can do without the external aid. In Europe and South America, the main mechanism is economic integration, which can proceed on its own in evolutionary spasms or fits and starts of greater cooperation as circumstances encourage.

This chapter has two somewhat related foci. One is to examine more closely the motivations underlying the interest in emphasizing forward over backward looking in negotiations concerning rivalry deescalation. Why were they present in the Franco-German, Egyptian-Israeli, and Argentine-Brazilian cases? The second is to consider where economic inducements figure in rivalry termination processes. Answers to the first question should help us answer the second and vice versa.

Rivalries and Termination

Discussions of rivalries and rivalry termination require some agreement on, or at least specification of, basic terms. Rivalries are seen as hostile relationships between states that view each other as competitive and threatening enemies.[2] If one accepts this definition of *rivalry*, rivalry termination means that the former adversaries no longer view each other as competitive—that is, in the same league. Usually this means that one side has lost its ability to continue in the rivalry through either a devastating defeat in war or noncoercively acknowledging its inferiority. In some cases, both sides become too exhausted to continue as adversaries. Or the two states might no longer view each other as threatening enemies. This type of change can come about because one or both sides alter their strategic priorities (as in elevating economic development over other concerns); select new domestic leaders, especially if the new decision makers have foreign policy reorientations in mind; engage in regime change that redefines which groups are considered to be friends or enemies; or enter into negotiations to reduce tensions and hostilities. Of course, it is most likely that some mixture of changes in priorities, leadership, regimes, and negotiations are likely to emerge as packages.

The two paths to termination are roughly equally common in history. A bit less than half (45 percent) of the rivalry termination cases since 1815 have ended with one side acknowledging defeat and some form of subordination. Fifty-five percent have pursued the alternative path involving changes in how the adversary is perceived. Keep in mind that changing expectations about an adversary does not imply that opponents renounce their negative images of the other. It only means that for various reasons opponents come to be seen as less threatening or something less than full-fledged enemies, thereby creating opportunities for negotiating some level of deescalation.

But how do rivalries end? How and when do economic factors enter into the process—if they do? Who is most responsible for peacemaking—decision makers, elites, or society at large? What is the relationship between rivalry termination and regional peace? These are all important questions.[3] Their answers are also closely interrelated, which is to say that how one answers them will hinge on how protracted conflict processes are viewed. One perspective focuses on negotiated treaty making between two former adversaries. The main issue then becomes one of what sort of bargains are struck or not attained, and for what reasons. This type of approach can be used with both rivalry termination tracks. Negotiations and treaties tend to ensue whether or not one of the parties was defeated in combat.

Another approach is more useful for the first type of rivalry termination: that involving changes in perceptions of competitiveness or enemy threat perception. It focuses primarily on changes that precede any negotiations and assumes that the success or failure of the consequent negotiations is predicated on whether certain preconditions have been met. In particular, decision makers need to alter their interpretations of the adversary. This is not a matter of suddenly learning to love one's enemies. That rarely happens. But circumstances and contexts can change in ways that encourage revised expectations about the capabilities or intentions of opponents. When these expectations change—not necessarily for all the decision makers involved but for some of those who have the most clout (and the cast of most significant decision makers can change as well)—successful negotiations become more probable. In their absence, negotiations are less likely to bring about a substantial deescalation of hostility. Treaties, if concluded, are more likely to become dead letters.

One model of rivalry termination that pursues this interpretation track envisions an ensemble of four to six factors as being most responsible for explaining successful outcomes.[4] Shocks facilitate the revision of decision-maker expectations. Policy entrepreneurs and third-party intervention may be necessary, but not always. More critical is a combination of reciprocity—decision makers need to be responsive to overtures from their adversary—and, once a deescalation process is under way, it needs to be reinforced continuously.

The ensemble of factors appears to be capable of accounting for rivalry terminations. If the model is useful, economic factors are most likely to enter in the shocks, the third-party intervention, reciprocity, and reinforcement. Shocks are important because decision makers and their perceptions of their adversaries acquire inertia over time. Something needs to happen to disturb the inertia.

Most shocks, of course, have little real impact, but a few do. One category of shocks that often qualify is economic deterioration or decline. One or both sides are experiencing (or decision makers anticipate experiencing) some significant loss in economic capability. A loss in economic capability, in turn, can encourage some policy makers to rethink what their state can hope to accomplish. Alternatively, they may perceive a declining adversary as less threatening than before.

Third parties use carrots and sticks, some of which are economic in nature, to cajole their targets into doing whatever it is that the third parties prefer. The problem is that these carrots and sticks may or may not be sufficient to achieve some changes in behavior, but, in and of themselves, they are unlikely to influence expectational changes. If so, the changed behavior becomes contingent on the continued application of the carrots and sticks. Take away the carrots and sticks and the protracted conflict problem is capable of returning in full force.

Overtures to adversaries that attempt to signal a preference or possibility of deescalation can often take the form of economic activity. Relaxing restrictions on trade or movement of people across borders, for instance, is not difficult. Nor is it difficult to respond in kind or to reciprocate at fairly low levels. Offering to negotiate over contested territory with substantial economic resources may be something for which it is harder to generate support among domestic veto players, but it still possible as long as it is clear that nothing will be given away without extracting an appropriate price. Whether or not decision makers are prepared to reciprocate on offers such as these is another matter entirely. Too often one side is prepared to contemplate deescalation while the other is not. It takes two sides to tango, especially when it comes to following up on the initial reciprocation. Extremely critical to an ultimately peaceful outcome is the issue of reinforcement. It may be at this phase of the process that economic interactions are most critical. Increased economic integration can be an excellent agent of reinforcement for pacification processes. Former adversaries become enmeshed in a network of linkages and exchanges that make it increasingly costly to return to old habits of conflict. Given time, the increased interactions should, or at least can, also work to break down perceptions of threat without anyone really working at it all that explicitly.

As chapter 1 in this volume, by Norrin M. Ripsman, suggests, decision-maker expectations are the initial target for beginning the process.[5] Ultimately, elites and society need to be persuaded by the reciprocity and reinforcement processes. Again, increased economic integration appears to be the best vehicle, especially if we are concerned about regional pacification—as opposed to simply dyadic deescalation. Increased economic integration literally offers something for everyone. That is, all levels of society are likely to become participants in the enmeshment/deescalation process in due course.

Not directly related to the model per se but implicit in this discussion is the observation that, from a rivalry perspective, the main link between rivalry termination and regional peace is a matter of focusing on deescalating the most central rivalries in a region. Most regions encompass a set of rivalries that possess variable significance to questions of war and peace within them.[6] For instance, deescalating the rivalry between Afghanistan and Pakistan will not necessarily influence Indo-Pakistani relations but an end to the Indo-Pakistani rivalry would probably have important reverberations for the Afghan-Pakistani relationship. Similarly, a deescalation of, say, Saudi-Yemeni conflict is most unlikely to affect relations between Arab states and Israel. Deescalating the Egyptian-Israeli rivalry, however, would make it very difficult for Arab states to go to war with Israel without Egyptian participation. Variable forms of regional peace in South Asia and the Middle East, as well as elsewhere, thus hinge on first reducing hostilities in the region's key rivalries.[7]

Reducing hostilities in the region's key rivalries is critical, but it is only an initial part of the pacification process. Some combination of shocks, expectation revision, policy entrepreneurs, third-party intervention, and reciprocity may bring about the onset of rivalry deescalation and termination. Reinforcement, on the other hand, takes time. If key rivalry deescalation is to be translated into regional pacification, it must involve other actors beyond those involved in the key rivalry or rivalries. To show how this works, we can move on to a discussion of the three cases of key rivalries in three different regions. I date the Franco-German rivalry as lasting from 1756 to 1955. The Argentine-Brazilian rivalry is dated as lasting from 1817 to 1985. The Egyptian-Israeli rivalry began in 1948 and has yet to terminate.

The Franco-German Rivalry

Concerning the question of Franco-German relations, the end of World War II, in some respects, was similar to the end of World War I. France was a member of the victorious coalition and sought to ensure its security against a future revival of German power. The French problem was compounded by economic weaknesses. France needed German coal, but it also needed the coal at a lower price than was likely if the market for interstate coal transfers was allowed to operate. Otherwise, German steel producers would have access to cheaper raw materials and could be expected to regain their superior market position. France would be faced with the reemergence of German economic centrality in Europe and its own economic subordination. As representatives of a defeated state, German decision makers sought to regain some semblance of their prewar position, at least in terms of sovereignty and autonomy. Yet sovereignty and autonomy, other things being equal, implied a likely return to German preeminence and a continuation of the Franco-German rivalry over leadership in the European region.

What to do? France's plans for dealing with its German problem(s) after 1945 varied considerably. There was strong popular sentiment within France for punishing Germany in such a way that it could never again become a primary source of threat. Not coincidentally, French economic and military centrality to postwar Europe would also be assured. Some plans envisioned dismembering what remained of Germany after eastern Germany seemed lost behind the iron curtain. France would gain the Saar and Rhineland either permanently or via some internationalization of the territory critical to coal deposits and steel production. Other plans involved restricting the German economy to the production of textiles and light industry or having French firms purchase key German industries.

French decision makers never seemed to coalesce around any of these schemes for any length of time. They agreed only on the necessity of handicapping Germany's likely reemergence to European centrality. One might describe the prevailing French sentiment as forward looking solely in terms of probable threat while at the same time emphasizing looking backward in terms of getting even for past transgressions. The situation was complicated by the emergence of the Cold War, which led to the United States and Britain developing a strong preference for rebuilding Germany—as opposed to dismembering it. France could not act without US and British concurrence. If its allies would not support radical approaches to resolving the German problem, some other approach was necessary.

Victor G. Munte describes the emergence of a plan developed by Jean Monnet in the following way.[8] As head of the General Commissariat for the Modernization and Equipping of the French Economy, Monnet's charge was to reinvigorate the French economy and put it on a path that would reinforce

France's claim to great power status. French steel and coal, central to the task of rebuilding the French economy, could not compete with German steel and coal. If France was not to be allowed by its allies to control German steel and coal production directly through outright occupation of the Saar and Rhineland, some more indirect approach was desirable.[9]

The general solution was preventing Germany from managing its own coal resources. If the postwar occupation of Germany was coming to an end,

> why not pass on the role to a European authority dedicated to managing not only the German resources but those of all the states wanting to participate, an authority working for the benefit of all. . . . As part of this new authority, France—although it would lose its capacity to manage its coal and steel resources unilaterally—would be liberated from the German commercial practices that were damaging to its industry. This reasoning gave birth to the Schuman Declaration of May 9, 1950, which would develop into the European Coal and Steel Community (ECSC), the first institution of the new European community. It had been given the task of managing the Franco-German production of coal and steel under a European High Authority. Four other states joined the initiative: Italy, Belgium, Luxembourg, and the Netherlands.[10]

Munte goes on to note that the Schuman Declaration framed the new initiative as a way to avoid future war via the federation of Europe, with the ECSC as the initial step. Yet the primary motivation was to solve France's lack of competitiveness in steel and coal. What would happen with European federation remained a fairly open question in 1950, but there was some strong likelihood that whatever did happen would proceed under French leadership. If nothing more happened, which Munte believes was the French government's expectation, this dimension of the immediate French industrial competitiveness problem would still be resolved. From Konrad Adenauer's perspective, the plan appealed as a way to accelerate the resumption of German autonomy and equality in other spheres. If a traditional national approach was likely to be blocked or constrained, an international approach promised a way out of pariah status.

Things do not always proceed as planned. Subsequent developments led to greater European integration, though hardly on a linear schedule and however unintended. If European integration had halted in 1950, it seems unlikely that the Franco-German rivalry would have continued to deescalate and eventually terminate. Integration did not solve French industrial problems. Nor did it thwart the reemergence of German economic centrality in Europe. What it did was gradually reduce the strictly interstate nature of French and German competition by transferring much of it to the venue of expanding regional institutions. The two states have continued to compete for leadership in European affairs but not like they did prior to the creation of the EU. There have been numerous opportunities for institutionalized, Franco-German cooperation in EU leadership. Moreover, EU leadership does not involve the same kind of seemingly zero-sum stakes inherent in regional strategic hegemony.

It is possible to push the ultimate nature of this shift even farther. Gisela Hendriks and Annette Morgan stipulate that

> the new and radical phenomenon released by the Schuman Plan is not that the French and German governments no longer perceive their respective national interests as antagonistic, but that they perceive them as complementary. In the final analysis, it is not possible for either Bonn or Paris to overlook the other's interests in the EU. No effective reform or new venture can be agreed upon until these two calculate that visible disharmony is more dysfunctional than relinquishing sovereignty in areas where in the short term loss of status, and possibly of earnings at the national level is a very real deterrent to supranational decision-making.
>
> The basis of the Franco-German axis is a shared objective, i.e., a strong and united Europe: both countries feel that their respective fortunes are tied up with and safeguarded by the Union. The success of the Franco-German axis does not depend on spontaneous empathy, but on the actors' political will to reconcile divergent positions for the sake of their common objective. It is this shared vision which allows no compromise. In identifying it, both France and Germany accepted their interlocking needs, arising out of geographical proximity, a shared painful history, and a common future. . . . Both countries have needed European integration: France because it wanted to secure a place as a global player in the multi-polar international system, Germany because it perceived the EU as a legitimate vehicle for the articulation of national interests.[11]

The authors go on to say that this shift in both interests and tactics means that the process is irreversible. That conclusion goes too far. The axis is not and never has been irreversible, but, beginning from a humble French policy solution to economic noncompetitiveness in coal and steel that was forced on both the French and the Germans to varying extents, the two states' interests and preferences have both shifted and converged on making regional integration work. It did not start this way, but it did evolve in this direction. The Schuman Plan did "release" a process that took several decades to evolve into an explicit Franco-German partnership and to erase gradually the old animosities and fears.

Can the shift in focus from traditional interstate competition to constrained competition and cooperation within regional institutions account for European regional transformation singularly? The answer is of course not. The shift itself took place within a specific context. The preponderance of the United States, its involvement in European affairs, and its support of European regional integration were important factors and cannot be taken for granted. The absence of any of these three factors probably would have changed the likelihood of the shift being made in the first place. Perhaps equally important was the Soviet threat. In the absence of a Soviet threat, the incentives to cooperate by ancient enemies in Europe would have been fewer.[12] Then there is the defeat of Germany in World War II. Devastating war defeats are often sufficient to end rivalries and, quite possibly, to transform regional settings. While the World War II outcome did end a number of rivalries, it did not suffice to terminate the Franco-German rivalry. The French regional integration scheme was helped by the German need to end its military occupation, regain its independence, and shed its guilt for Nazi atrocities. Yet German politicians and politics might have been less accommodating than the pro-integrationist Adenauer regime proved to be. Hendriks and Morgan instead contend that French regional leadership provided good cover through the 1950s and 1960s for a German effort to reestablish itself as a major player in international politics.[13] Once the cover was no longer needed in the 1970s, German preferences became more likely to deviate from the French line. An early, recalcitrant but prospering Germany presumably would have led to an entirely different trajectory for European regional integration. Much the same can be said about France if it had been relatively stronger in the late 1940s and early 1950s.

The Argentine-Brazilian Rivalry

Argentina and Brazil were longtime rivals, dating back to independence and even before to Spanish-Portuguese rivalry in the New World. Quite abruptly, two of the more powerful states in South America began negotiating closer economic ties in the mid-1980s—negotiations that led to attempts to make the two states' economies more interdependent and ultimately to a wider set of integrative efforts culminating in Mercosur, which linked Argentina, Brazil, Paraguay, and Uruguay in 1991, and Venezuela in 2012, with other neighbors adopting affiliate status. Previous efforts to integrate South American markets had been made, but the most recent and successful advance seemed to have literally sprung out of nowhere and was somehow connected to the movement away from military regimes in the Southern Cone.

Several sources converge on linking regional integration between Argentina and Brazil from the mid-1980s on to democratization processes.[14] However, it is not always spelled out just how democratization enters the picture other than to note the acceleration in integration negotiations once both sides' political systems had become democratic. Gian Luca Gardini is the most specific on this conjunction of separate but linked processes that are described as proceeding differently in the two states.[15]

Both Argentina (1976–83) and Brazil (1964–85) were exiting periods of military rule in the early to mid-1980s. In Argentina military rule had virtually collapsed after the debacle of the Malvinas/Falklands War. In Brazil military rule was in a gradual transition back to civilian rule. Both states, despite their traditional rivalry, had increased their cooperative gestures while under military rule, but no discussion of economic integration had been broached. Instead, negotiations had focused on boundaries, water sources, and wartime support. The new Argentine civilian decision makers seized the initiative even before Brazil's political transition had begun by proposing negotiations on lowering tariffs with Brazil. The underlying motivation appears to have been primarily political. Argentine decision makers argued that they needed to create a more pacific external environment in order to prevent a future return to military rule in Argentina. A more benign regional environment would undercut the military mission and its claims on state resources and prestige. Some movement toward closer economic interaction should work toward negating some 165 years of interstate rivalry. It also helped that Brazil was an attractive market for Argentine exports, which needed more buyers.

Brazil's situation was different. Not only was the military still in power when the Argentines launched their regional peace initiative, but the rulers were also uneasy about Argentine efforts to punish military officers for their human rights transgressions during the "Dirty War." In Brazil the military was allowed to withdraw from politics with immunity from subsequent prosecution. But, as noted, the transition to civilian rule was proceeding slowly, and the Argentine initiative appeared attractive to the emerging civilian regime for political purposes. Argentine imports were not regarded as all that important, but the campaign to make the Southern Cone less conflictual did appeal. If nothing else, it would bolster the cooperative and democratic image of the new Brazilian civilian regime in a region in which Brazil's standing could use some improvement. Brazilian civilians had less to fear from their military returning to the political arena, but the argument for making the military less prominent for national security reasons held some attraction as well.

Jeffrey W. Cason quotes a Brazilian diplomat's 1988 description of the motivation for economic integration in the mid-1980s.

> With the economic integration program between Brazil and Argentina there is both an internal and external political strategy . . . the political objectives are, to summarize, to substitute cooperation for competition between the two countries and thus reduce tensions in the region and eliminate any possibility of an arms race, including a nuclear arms race. There is no doubt that, given the [history of military] interference in the political systems in the region, and particularly in the Southern Cone, that the reciprocal political support between the two democratic regimes has contributed to the strengthening of each.[16]

It is not so much democratization per se that explains the abrupt movement toward economic integration, then, but rather the democratizers' desire, especially in Argentina but apparently also in Brazil, to protect their political flanks from the possibility of renewed military intervention in domestic politics. Economic integration was one possible tool for creating a more pacific external threat environment, which was expected to have domestic political dividends, in addition to some immediate economic payoffs, at least for Argentine producers.

The Argentine-Brazilian Economic Integration Program (ABEIP) emerged from these negotiations in 1986. The initial agreement was restricted to lowering tariffs, but the leaders of each country were also required to meet twice a year to find ways to expand the initial agreement. The immediate impact was to increase trade between the two states but only temporarily. Neither state was prepared initially to use trade as a significant engine of growth. Neither state's economy could be described initially as flourishing. In 1990, ABEIP was discarded and almost immediately replaced with Mercosur in 1991.[17] Mercosur can hardly be described as a runaway economic success either, but it has survived.[18] Equally important, the regional political environment appears to have been transformed considerably. David Pion-Berlin writes:

> Three decades ago, realists would have felt thoroughly vindicated by the security environment in the Southern Cone and Brazil. "Beware of thy neighbor" was the motto for defense and security precautions. . . .
>
> Today, realists would be on the defensive in the case of the Southern Cone. In a change as dramatic as it is recent, the Southern Cone states have developed cooperative security relations predicated on intense diplomacy followed by increased military-to-military contacts, forewarning, disclosures, and transparency.[19]

Pion-Berlin goes on to note that Mercosur presidents agreed in 1996 that a military coup could result in the expulsion of the offending country from the market.[20] In 1998 they declared their region a zone of peace, which was operationalized in terms of an absence of weapons of mass destruction, military consultation on security issues, and transparency in military budgeting matters. While no one contends that security competition has been abandoned altogether, it would appear that gains in rivalry deescalation have outpaced gains in economic interdependence and democratization. This outcome is not quite the liberal anticipation of democratization, economic interdependence, and then reduced interstate conflict. The causal dynamics are almost entirely reversed. But perhaps it does not matter which comes first in transforming regions. Different mixes of similar ingredients can lead to the same outcome.

The Egyptian-Israeli Rivalry

Janice Gross Stein divides Arab-Israeli conflict into two epochs.[21] From 1948 to 1973, intermittent warfare was followed by largely backward-looking attempts to negotiate cease-fires and prevent the renewal of combat. Negotiators talked about how best to conclude the fighting and what rules needed to be established to prevent the recurrence of war. Most important, few assumed that an end to the fighting meant an end to the conflict. Another war could be anticipated. The immediate concern, however, was how best to deal with the ongoing combat. From 1974 to 2000, warfare was largely absent, but the emphasis was placed more on a mixture of backward- and forward-looking outcomes. Egypt led the way in seeking genuine conflict resolution. Another war was no longer certain. Attempts were made to accelerate negotiations over settling the conflict issues as opposed to merely preventing a return to the battlefield.

Stein argues that the reason for the two different periods is a learning process about the costs of warfare and the failure of exclusively backward-looking approaches to resolution. Decision makers learned through trial and error that more forward-looking approaches would work better to deter future warfare. She also rejects the contention that it suffices that the weaker parties in a conflict learn that they can no longer sustain the costs of warfare and must prepare to accommodate the stronger party in a rivalry. Both sides must learn that the costs are too great to continue the old process of intermittent warfare. The rivals do not have to like or trust each other, but they must be prepared to try something different to preclude a return to old ways of dealing with each other.

Stein's emphasis on the need for learning on both sides is supported by the disinclination of Israeli decision makers to negotiate with Anwar Sadat after the death of Gamal Abdel Nasser in 1970. Israeli decision makers needed the shock of the 1973 war to be prepared to contemplate the need for genuine negotiations, as opposed to perpetuating the war and peace cycle. But even then the initial emphasis was backward-looking and restricted to disengagement rules. The focus then shifted to agreements about the nonuse of force, supported by sophisticated detection technology, US involvement, and the return of United Nations peacekeeping forces. This focus was still primarily backward looking, but it contained some potential for forward looking as long as the participants came to believe that the system would work and they could observe their opponents not seeking to do them harm.

Still these preliminary outcomes were insufficient to resolve Egyptian-Israeli antagonisms. The negotiations had to switch from multilateral to bilateral, domestic economic distress had to increase on both sides, Egypt had to threaten to abandon the peace talks more than once, and, in particular, US mediation and financial support had to increase in order to obtain an agreement. But this is where Stein's argument inadvertently goes astray.

The triadic structure of the bargaining process, where Egypt and Israel each bargained with the United States rather than directly with each other, reflected the importance of the United States to each and maximized American leverage. This was so, in large part, because of the special role of the United States as monitor, guarantor, insurer, and financier of any agreement that would emerge from Camp David. It was American economic aid, investment, and technology that were critical to the reshaping of the Egyptian economy and the stabilization of the Israeli economy. In this context, Israel and Egypt, again bargaining through the United States at Camp David, were able to reach an agreement exchanging full normalization of relations for the complete return of Sinai to Egyptian sovereignty. Their peace treaty mixed ongoing backward-looking outcomes with forward-looking agreements that together resolved their conflict.[22]

The problem is that Egypt and Israel did not resolve their conflict at Camp David. Their rivalry was deescalated to be sure. As long as the United States guaranteed (and paid for) the negotiated outcome, Egypt and Israel were unlikely to return to the battlefield. However, the rivalry did not end. What was attained is often described as a "cold peace." The two sides stopped short of revising their views of the other side's ultimately hostile intentions. Apparently, the infusion of forward-looking elements into the negotiation was insufficient to bring about an outcome similar to the Franco-German and Argentine-Brazilian outcomes.

One clear difference in the three cases is the strong US mediation in the Egyptian-Israeli case. In the Franco-German and Argentine-Brazilian cases, the rivals had to negotiate with each other and do so indefinitely. That is, they agreed, whatever the individual motivations, to continue negotiating about economic integration into the future. The neofunctional explanation of integration success is that learning occurs when negotiators find that they can achieve some success on a case-by-case basis.[23] What is learned is that what worked last time might work again the next time. In the process, the range of behaviors subject to integration expands. Not part of the neofunctional explanation is the corollary that former rivals learn to view their opponents differently. Former enemies are transformed into competitors but also partners in selective enterprises and endeavors. This transformation in expectations about opponents went only so far in the Egyptian-Israeli negotiations. It stopped short of changing enemies into neighboring competitors and also failed to create ongoing partnership discussions. Where the integrative institutions became too costly to abandon in the European and possibly the South American cases, there are no integrative institutions at work in the Egyptian-Israeli case other than massive amounts of third-party assistance and investment. American aid may or may not prove to be too costly to abandon, but it cannot be expected to work in the same fashion as gradual economic integration schemes to genuinely normalize the relations between former rivals.

It follows, therefore, that the presence of elements of forward-looking negotiations do not suffice to differentiate rivalry termination successes from more limited deescalations or failures to end rivalries. What is needed in these cases of negotiated settlements is continuous reinforcement. This component can be supplied by successful integration schemes, which provide ongoing incentives to cooperate. It is not clear, at least from the three cases examined, that economic integration is the only path to continuous reinforcement. Yet it should be reasonably clear that cold peaces do not have and cannot be expected to have the same effect.

Where does that leave the role of economic incentives in terminating rivalries? Assessing economic incentives depends very much on how one views rivalry termination processes. Figure 5.1 sketches the perspective on negotiated rivalry termination that has undergirded this examination. Basically, shocks can sometimes lead to revisions in how rivals perceive their opponents. However, only some types of shocks are effective and, even so, most go nowhere. Third-party mediators and a change in policy entrepreneurs may be involved but are not absolutely necessary to this process. More necessary is reciprocation between the antagonists as they send deescalating signals, engage in exchanges of cooperation, and eliminate outstanding grievances (often concerning but certainly not limited to the possession of contested territory). Equally necessary is reinforcement of the initial negotiated gains. It does no good to agree to something at time X only to fall back into the old conflict groove a few years later because cooperation ceased once the negotiations were concluded. Nonetheless, Karen Rasler, William R. Thompson, and Sumit Ganguly find that it is a combination of shock, expectation revision, reciprocity, and reinforcement that is crucial to negotiated rivalry settlements. In the cases examined, all four were present when a rivalry was terminated successfully.[24] In situations in which all four model components did not appear, some deescalation might have taken place but rivalry termination did not occur.

A consideration of the three cases suggests that it is principally in the reinforcement category that economic incentives enter the rivalry termination picture.[25] In the case of economic integration efforts, they serve primarily as ongoing reinforcement of situations that are already deescalated in the short term. The reinforcement helps turn the short-term deescalation into a long-term deescalation. Yet all economic incentives do not have the same

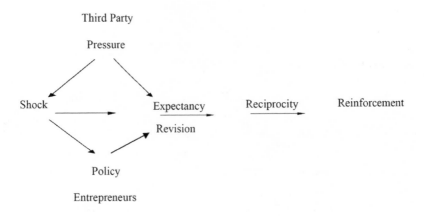

Fig. 5.1. An expectancy model for rivalry deescalation and termination. The number of arrows shown are considered the minimal number required to maintain simplicity. Arrows might easily be drawn linking entrepreneurial consolidation and reciprocity/reinforcement. Double-headed arrows, no doubt, should be drawn in the connections among expectancy revision, reciprocity, and reinforcement. Third-party pressures might also be manifested in terms of entrepreneurial consolidation, reciprocity, and reinforcement.

yield. Third-party financial aid can make it very costly to revert to old forms of conflict. What it does not do is provide incentives to create the new forms of forward-looking relationships embodied in integration pacts. In the absence of the appropriate incentives, older relationships tend to persist. Rivalries can be deescalated as long as the economic incentives continue to flow and are deemed to be crucial to economic survival. Yet forward looking focused on a third-party source of economic gain does not work the same way as forward looking focused on a former adversary. It does not and cannot be expected to have the same behavioral impact. Given the right type of changes, it is also something that parties can decide to do without, leading them to return to traditional modes of conflict as if no intervention had ever taken place.

There is a difference, then, between regions that are transformed by rivalry terminations on the part of major regional actors and ones that are frozen in place as long as third-party economic incentives continue to flow. The former are genuinely transformed. The transformation of the latter is likely to be both artificial and temporary. Forward-looking negotiations that do not address or lead to the resolution of more fundamental causes of conflict can also lead to temporary cease-fires.[26]

Conclusion

Economic incentives do seem to play some role in rivalry terminations. Just how often they occur remains to be seen. It is unlikely that they are found in every case. Nor are they likely to be either necessary to or sufficient for rivalry termination. However, where they fit into the deescalation process most prominently appears to be a matter of reinforcement of deescalation processes already under way. In other words, as Lobell and Ripsman suggest in their introduction to this volume, economic incentives do not drive regional peacemaking, but they can facilitate the process by helping to make and entrench agreements reached for other reasons. Economic incentives can encourage former rivals to remain former rivals. It is less clear that economic incentives can persuade rivals to become former rivals. Other things are needed. In the rivalry termination model relied on in this examination, some combination of shocks, expectational revision, policy entrepreneurs, third parties, and reciprocity must precede reinforcement.

Economic incentives can bolster forward looking in negotiations, which is probably important to successful rivalry termination. However, the European and South American cases suggest that it is not always economic incentives per se that make the rivalry termination come about. In two rather significant cases for regional transformation purposes, the initial motivations for engaging in economic integration were not purely about the advantages of integration. France and Argentina's motivations were partially about economic concerns. But France's goals were also very much about relative power and security. Argentine decision makers were most worried about their own military's propensity for domestic political intervention. German and Brazilian decision makers were most concerned about improving their regional standings.

What seems more important is not so much the initial motivations, but rather the need to engage in near-continuous negotiations over integration details contributes substantially to reinforcing the initial deescalation of conflict. Neofunctionalists call this attitudinal spillover with success in one sphere, suggesting that other issues can also be dealt with internationally and successfully. Of course, it also helps if the ongoing integration efforts are reasonably successful.

Economic integration does not exhaust the inventory of possible economic incentives. But integration negotiations may be exceptional in their ability to back up rivalry deescalations. The Egyptian-Israeli case suggests, if nothing else, that economic incentives per se—even rather ample economic incentives—need not lead to full rivalry deescalation and termination.

Finally, economic incentives are but one factor among many. Various contextual developments were probably critical to the emergence of European and Latin American economic integration and the cold peace in the Middle East. It helped immensely that Germany, France, and Argentina had been defeated in war. Israel was not defeated in the 1973 war, but it probably was shaken by a possible near defeat. In the European and Middle Eastern cases, US support was important. In the South American case, US distraction may have been important as well. Some of the policy entrepreneurs that were involved (Monnet, Adenauer, Alfonsin, Sadat) were at the very least highly facilitative of the stances states developed at critical junctures. Moreover, the Soviet threat to Western Europe and the world economic climate of the 1970s and 1980s encouraged the search for collective cooperation. Did the absence of some sense of mutual threat restrict cooperation in the Egyptian-Israeli case? Somewhat paradoxically, Argentine acceptance of being eclipsed by Brazil and the European, especially French, reluctance to accept being eclipsed as great powers also played some role in their respective regions—as did Soviet-US limitations on the extent of the Egyptian defeat in 1973. In spite of our attempts to create simplified models, negotiated rivalry terminations and regional transformations are rarely simple matters. At the same time, they are not inexplicable phenomenon.

NOTES

1. William Zartman, "Negotiating Forward- and Backward-Looking Outcomes," in I. William Zartman and Victor Kremenyuk, eds., *Peace versus Justice: Negotiating Forward- and Backward-Looking Outcomes* (Lanham, MD: Rowman and Littlefield, 2005).

2. William R. Thompson and David R. Dreyer, *Handbook of International Rivalries, 1494–2010* (Washington, DC: Congressional Quarterly Press, 2011).

3. See Norrin M. Ripsman and Steven E. Lobell's introduction to this volume.

4. Karen Rasler, William R. Thompson, and Sumit Ganguly, *How Rivalries*

End: Shocks, Expectations, Reciprocity, and Reinforcement (Philadelphia: University of Pennsylvania Press, 2013).

5. See Norrin M. Ripsman, "Two Stages of Transition from a Region of War to a Region of Peace: Realist Transition and Liberal Endurance," *International Studies Quarterly* 49, no. 4 (December 2005): 669–93; and "Top-Down Peacemaking: Why Peace Begins with States and Not Societies," in T. V. Paul, ed., *International Relations Theory and Regional Transformation* (Cambridge: Cambridge University Press, 2012). On this point, I agree with Ripsman that rivalry terminations begin as top-down actions taken by government decision makers but not because domestic pressures demand it. On the contrary, elites and masses are likely to oppose such activity at the outset, and their opposition is often a barrier to successful outcomes.

6. At any given time, it is conceivable that the central rivalries will have been terminated. For example, the Anglo-American rivalry was once the central rivalry in North America, but it was terminated more than a century ago. There may also be periods of time in which no single rivalry looms as preeminent, as in Central America in the nineteenth century.

7. There is no assumption here that each region possesses only one key rivalry. That is the case in South Asia but not in the Middle East, which, moreover, is further complicated by encompassing three different regional subsystems (the Maghreb, the Gulf, and the Mashriq). The Egyptian-Israeli rivalry has been one of the key adversarial relationships in the Middle East overall, but its significance is greater for the Mashriq than it is for the Maghreb and the Gulf. For instance, the key rivalry relationship in the Gulf is the rivalry triangle involving Iran, Saudi Arabia, and Iraq, which is another way of saying that there are three key rivalries in the Gulf. In the Maghreb, the strongest candidate for key rivalry status, largely by default, is the Algerian-Moroccan rivalry.

8. Victor G. Munte, "A New Framework for Franco-German Relations through European Institutions, 1950 to 1954," in Carine Germond and Henning Turk, eds., *A History of Franco-German Relations in Europe: From "Hereditary Enemies" to Partners* (New York: Palgrave Macmillan, 2008).

9. See John Gillingham, *Coal, Steel, and the Rebirth of Europe, 1945–1955: The Germans and French From Ruhr Conflict to Economic Community* (Cambridge: Cambridge University Press, 1991), 149–57. Gillingham has an amusing passage about how this shift in policy came about. He notes that if one reads Monnet's autobiography the policy shift is described in Moses-like terms—a hike in the Swiss wilderness, a return with a tablet of new commandments, a gathering of tribal elders, and a proclamation to the assembled tribes. Gillingham's interpretation is that Monnet and others had formulated a plan as early as 1943–45 to avoid the deindustrialization and/or permanent military occupation of Germany as counter-

productive and too expensive. Instead the plan was to take away German control of the Ruhr until either France was sufficiently strong to compete without access to German coal or the Germans had learned to mend their ways. Exactly what entity was to supervise Ruhr production seems to have been left open-ended as long as it wasn't German in nationality. Gillingham goes on to argue that French decision makers were not in a position to promote this approach prior to very late in the 1940s and were inclined to push strong and radical proposals to deal with the German problem until they had a better bargaining position and more sympathetic ears for their plan to internationalize Ruhr production. Of course, a rival hypothesis is that French decision makers were not united on how to deal with Germany initially and an approach conceived earlier could have led to the Schuman Plan only when the policy setting was more receptive.

10. Munte, "New Framework for Franco-German Relations," 167–68.

11. Gisela Hendriks and Annette Morgan, *The Franco-German Axis in European Integration* (Cheltenham: Edward Elgar, 2001), 14–15.

12. For a view that exaggerates the role of the Soviet threat and balancing in response to it as an explanation for European regional integration, see Sebastian Rosati, *Europe United: Power Politics and the Making of the European Community* (Ithaca: Cornell University Press, 2011). The Soviet threat was certainly a factor, but it was not the only factor that mattered.

13. Hendriks and Morgan, *Franco-German Axis in European Integration*, 5.

14. Riordan Roett, "Introduction," in Riordan Roett, ed., *Mercosur: Regional Integration, World Markets* (Boulder: Lynn Rienner, 1999); Gian Luca Gardini, *The Origins of Mercosur: Democracy and Regionalization in South America* (New York: Palgrave Macmillan, 2010); Jeffrey W. Cason, *The Political Economy of Integration: The Experience of Mercosur* (London: Routledge, 2011).

15. Gardini, *Origins of Mercosur*.

16. Cason, *Political Economy of Integration*, 39.

17. European integration efforts were not always successful either.

18. See Lia Valls Pereira, "Toward the Common Market of the South: Mercosur's Origins, Evolution, and Challenges," in Riordan Roett, ed., *Mercosur: Regional Integration, World Markets* (Boulder: Lynne Rienner, 1999); and Juan Carlos M. Beltramino, "The Building of Mercosur: A Continuous Negotiation Process," in I. William Zartman and Victor Kremenyuk, eds., *Peace versus Justice: Negotiating Forward- and Backward-Looking Outcomes* (Lanham, MD: Rowman and Littlefield, 2005).

19. David Pion-Berlin, "Sub-regional Cooperation, Hemispheric Threat: Security in the Southern Cone," in Louise Fawcett and Monica Serrano, eds., *Regionalism and Governance in the Americas: Continental Drift* (New York: Palgrave Macmillan, 2005), 211–12.

20. Ibid., 212–13.

21. Janice Gross Stein, "Loss and Learning: From Backward-Looking to Forward-Looking Outcomes in the Egypt-Israel Rivalry," in I. William Zartman and Victor Kremenyuk, eds., *Peace versus Justice: Negotiating Forward- and Backward-Looking Outcomes* (Lanham, MD: Rowman and Littlefield, 2005).

22. Ibid., 154.

23. Technically, neofunctionalists focus on state bureaucrats' learning while the cases we are examining are more about state decision makers.

24. Rasler, Thompson, and Ganguly, *How Rivalries End*.

25. However, the three cases selected did not exist in vacuums. Any examination of the termination of the Argentine-Brazilian rivalry has implications for the termination of the Argentine-Chilean rivalry, which was part of the same Argentine initiative to pacify its regional external environment. Any examination of the deescalation of the Egyptian-Israeli rivalry has implications for the termination of the Israeli-Jordanian rivalry and the failure to deescalate the Israeli-Syrian rivalry. In particular, the Israeli-Jordanian rivalry was sold to the Jordanian public in part based on the economic benefits that would be forthcoming once a peace with Israel was formally arranged. The benefits have so far been disappointing, which suggests that a lack of reinforcement, not solely due to the relative absence of economic benefits, could at some future point contribute to the negation of the 1994 rivalry termination. See, for instance, Dona Stewart, *Good Neighbourly Relations: Jordan, Israel, and the 1994–2004 Peace Process* (London: I. B. Tauris, 2007).

26. Imagine what might have taken place if all of the money spent on Israeli and Egyptian aid since Camp David had been spent instead on a Marshall Plan for the Middle East. Of course, the easy retort is that Middle Easterners were not and still are not ready for such a radical undertaking. But that only reinforces the need for revising rivalry expectations. One might also imagine the Marshall Plan as a US-controlled mechanism that paid France and Germany for not going to war with one another and involved little in the way of direct negotiations between French and German decision makers.

CHAPTER 6

The Political Economy of Sino-Japanese Ties

The Limits and Risks of Economic Statecraft

Jean-Marc F. Blanchard

This chapter focuses on Sino-Japanese relations in order to address three questions raised in Norrin M. Ripsman and Steven E. Lobell's introduction to this volume. Specifically, I address the different types of economic statecraft that many thought would help bring about a warm peace between China and Japan, including trade, foreign aid, low-interest loans, and foreign direct investment (FDI). With a critical eye toward commercial liberal theory, I also discuss the limitations and risks associated with economic statecraft and economic interdependence as a means of promoting bilateral peace agreements and regional peacemaking. In the conclusion I address briefly how economic statecraft can be used to move from a bilateral peace agreement to regional peace. I find that frictions between China and Japan have hindered regional peace building because they have led each country to pursue regional arrangements that exclude, balance, or constrain the other.

Since the mid-1990s, the Sino-Japanese relationship has been tense. Among other sources of strife, there have been heated frictions over history, anti-China diatribes by Japanese conservatives and mass anti-Japanese demonstrations in China, repeated low-level clashes around the Diaoyu or Senkaku Islands (hereafter "the Islands"), air and naval encounters in the East China Sea (ECS), and military balancing.[1] Relations are so fragile that some commentators speculate whether there will be militarized conflict between these two protagonists.[2] Yet, according to various lines of commercial liberal thought, Sino-Japanese relations should not be so fractious and cold.[3] After all, Beijing and Tokyo interact within a milieu of extensive economic interdependence. As will be detailed, the two countries have very high trade relations, extensive FDI ties, and manifold other economic links.

Numerous analysts take the position that economic interdependence has had a positive effect on the political relationship.[4] More extreme variants go so far as to argue, "When forced to choose, Chinese and Japanese leaders tend to pursue economic gains at the expense of their nationalist credentials."[5] Studies in this vein often conflate correlation with causation, exaggerate the pacifying effects of economic ties, or ignore alternative explanations. The majority of studies of Sino-Japanese relations, though, focus on the factors that mediate the positive spillover of their economic ties. For example, there are abundant analyses of the two countries' territorial and maritime disputes.[6] In addition, there are a plethora of studies of the Sino-Japanese competition for influence in Southeast Asia.[7] As well, analysts have probed tensions related to Taiwan.[8] The shortcoming of this strain of the literature is that it cannot explain why massive trade ties and multiple realms of economic cooperation do not surmount these frictions but produce a relationship the Chinese depict as "economics hot, politics cold."

Understanding the limitations of economic statecraft and the short reach of economic interdependence in the China-Japan case is important for both theoretical and policy reasons. In the case of the former, the unimpressive results of employing economic links to constrain conflict and promote warmer relations, despite a favorable milieu, call into question the power of commercial liberal arguments. They also encourage us to think more deeply about the conditions under which the weaving of broad and deep economic ties can be used to promote bilateral and regional peace or ease the path to it.

Regarding regionwide peacemaking, the state of Sino-Japanese relations has great ramifications for the Asia-Pacific Region (APR), issues such as the South China Sea (SCS) conflict, and the regional and global economic situation. Moreover, militarized conflict between these two East Asian protagonists would cast a huge pall over the entire region. Thus, it is critical to investigate mechanisms for preventing bilateral conflict, as well as stabilizing and warming their relations.

Similar to other studies of Sino-Japanese relations, this analysis highlights a large number of conflicts that complicate the ability of extensive bilateral economic ties to foster warm bilateral political relations between Beijing and Tokyo. Different from other studies, it finds that it is not these frictions per se that matter, although it certainly accepts that they matter. Instead, the problem is that economic interactions take place within a relationship characterized by power relations and a security dilemma, which constrains their positive externalities. Moreover, there are aspects of the economic relationship, ranging from the way it is viewed on the Chinese side to the inability of Japanese constituencies to promote better political relations, that limit what economic interdependence can do. This chapter thus sheds light directly on the fourth central question— "What are the limits of and risks associated with economic statecraft?"—posed in the introduction to this volume, although *statecraft* here pertains to massive bilateral economic ties rather than targeted economic sanctions or incentives.

The next section reviews various arguments about how economic ties facilitate peacemaking. The second supplies background information on Sino-Japanese economic ties. The third describes a number of political factors that engender frictions between Beijing and Tokyo and limit the positive political spillover of economic links. The fourth makes several arguments about why extensive economic interdependence neither pacifies nor warms the relationship as some might expect. The final section addresses some potential critiques and expounds on the chapter's theoretical and policy ramifications.

The Peacemaking Potential of Economic Interdependence

The crux of commercial liberalism is the notion that interstate economic ties promote good political relations, as embodied in Montesquieu's classic quote, "[T]he natural effect of commerce is to lead to peace."[9] Essentially, economic ties are believed to remove the causes of war (the "neutralizing" view), to constrain states from going to war even though a casus belli exists (the "binding" view), and/or to facilitate cooperation and perhaps even shared identities and interests, all of which logically would build an environment quite conducive to peace building and peacemaking.[10] This section provides an overview of these arguments about the positive political spillover of economic interdependence before concluding with brief highlights of some critiques of them.

The neutralizing view takes the stance that economic interdependence obviates the need for states to engage in war since states can obtain through trade, investment, and borrowing what they otherwise obtained through plunder. Others in this mind-set also believe economic interdependence can eliminate the chauvinistic behaviors that fuel conflict. A third group sees economic interdependence as reducing the causes of war because economic linkages fuel development and, in turn, democracy, which promotes peace because democracies do not fight one another. A fourth group believes that economic interdependence, if nested in certain structures, can help prevent war, since these structures facilitate bargaining and negotiation.[11]

The binding view argues that economic interdependence restrains states that are otherwise inclined to engage in conflict. After all, war damages trade, investment, and other economic ties and is quite costly. Consequently, policy makers facing such costs pull back from the brink. In addition, economic interdependence fuels the creation of constituencies with a vested interest in promoting international economic links. Not only does it give birth to such groups, but it also enriches them and thereby gives them the wherewithal to fight aggressive government behaviors.[12] Many students of Sino-Japanese political relations have advanced these kinds of arguments.[13]

Economic interdependence is believed to improve the ideational environment, too. First, it facilitates interaction by decision makers and officials, which aids in the development of habits of cooperation and problem solving. Second, it is supposed to promote communication, mutual understanding, and less prejudice among those involved in exchange. Third, it putatively can promote shared interests and a sense of community.[14]

Aside from what they see as a lack of empirical support for many of these schools of thought, skeptics also highlight what they see as their logical deficiencies. Some believe economics simply cannot trump politics. Others believe interstate economic linkages actually may fuel conflict by creating frictions or prompting states to take action to sever the bonds that create political dependencies. Other individuals posit that economic interdependence changes the distribution of power relations, which in turn can be destabilizing. Yet others observe that by constraining higher levels of conflict economic interdependence might promote lower levels of conflict. Finally, some point out that any link between economic interdependence and peace most likely is a spurious correlation reflective of other factors such as alliances or territorial contiguity.[15]

A Primer on Sino-Japanese Economic Ties

Sino-Japanese economic statecraft is multifaceted, encompassing trade, FDI, foreign aid, and low-interest loans. Bilateral trade has deep roots and multiple drivers.[16] Starting in the 1970s, it expanded throughout the 1980s and 1990s. Whereas bilateral trade was $4.8 billion in 1978, it hit $10 billion in 1983 and reached $16.8 billion in 1990.[17] Five years later it totaled an astounding $57.8 billion.[18] Table 6.1 provides statistics for the past 10 years on Chinese exports to Japan, Chinese imports from Japan, and total trade between the two countries.

The table shows some interesting trade trends. First, except for the year following the outbreak of the 2008 Great Recession, Chinese exports to Japan, Japanese exports to China, and total trade have continuously increased. Second, the growth rate of trade has been impressive with more than a doubling of trade between 2002 and 2007 and a near doubling between 2007 and 2012. Not only are absolute trade figures quite high, but each country constitutes the other's first or second most important trade partner.[19]

A second type of economic statecraft is FDI. Prior to the mid-1990s, the amount of Japanese outward foreign direct investment (JOFDI) in China was relatively small, totaling only $3.4 billion in 1992.[20] By 1996, however, JOFDI in China had reached $13 billion.[21] China's accession to the World Trade Organization (WTO) in 2001 and the APR's recovery from the Asian financial crisis provided a newfound impetus for Japanese companies to invest in China. In 2001, annual JOFDI in China ran at $2.16 billion with the total stock of FDI hitting $10.043 billion. Five years later, the annual amount reached $6.17 billion, with the total stock of JOFDI in China reaching $30.316 billion. As of 2010, annual JOFDI into China was approximately $7.25 billion, and total JOFDI had topped $66.478 billion.[22] For various reasons, Chinese outward foreign direct

TABLE 6.1. Sino-Japanese Trade Flows, 2000–2010 ($US hundreds of millions)

	China's Exports to Japan	Chinese Imports from Japan	Total Merchandise Trade with Japan (Exports + Imports)
2000	44.3	41.5	85.80
2001	49.0	42.8	91.80
2002	55.3	53.5	108.80
2003	70.8	74.1	144.90
2004	89.6	94.3	183.90
2005	102.4	100.4	202.80
2006	112.0	115.7	227.70
2007	124.9	134.0	258.90
2008	138.7	150.6	289.30
2009	118.0	130.9	248.90
2010	148.3	176.7	325.00

Source: World Trade Organization, "Merchandise Trade by Region and Selected Economy, 2000–2010," table A14 (https://www.wto.org/english/res_e/statis_e/its2011_e/its11_appendix_e.htm).

investment (COFDI) in Japan has been piddling, to say the least. One factor was the much later start of the internalization of Chinese companies. Another was the unreceptive attitude of Japanese companies, the Japanese government, and the Japanese public toward Chinese investment in Japan. Yet another was Japan's lack of natural resources, a major driver of investment overseas by Chinese firms.[23] Illustrating this, in 2002, COFDI in Japan was a meager ¥300 million.[24] By 2007, the cumulative stock hit only $558 million. Three years later it was a lowly $1.1 billion.[25] While these numbers are unimpressive, the evidence, as shown by some recent transactions, predicts that Chinese firms will pour increasing (albeit not huge) sums of money into Japan over the coming years.[26] Table 6.2 provides statistics for the past 10 years on JOFDI in China and COFDI in Japan.

A third type of economic statecraft is foreign aid.[27] In 1979, Japan began to give aid in the form of low-interest loans to China. Over the next 10 years, the total amount of low-interest loans provided to China reached the significant sum of $17 billion.[28] By 1982, China had become the largest recipient of Japanese official development assistance (ODA), comprised largely of preferential loans, and through much of the 1980s Japan was China's major bilateral aid provider.[29] Tokyo froze ODA and other assistance programs (grants and technical assistance) in the wake of the 1989 Tiananmen crackdown, but measures undertaken by Beijing to warm relations with Japan led to a resumption

TABLE 6.2. Sino-Japanese Outward/Inward FDI Flows, 2000–2011 ($US millions)

	Annual Inward FDI from Japan	Japan's Total FDI Stock in China	Annual Inward FDI from China	China's Total FDI Stock in Japan
2000	934	8,699	0	—
2001	2,158	10,043	2	—
2002	2,622	12,408	1	—
2003	3,980	15,296	−2	—
2004	5,863	20,208	−9	139
2005	6,575	24,655	11	151
2006	6,169	30,316	12	224
2007	6,218	37,797	15	558
2008	6,496	49,002	37	510
2009	6,899	55,045	−137	693
2010	7,252	66,478	314	1,106
2011	12,649	83,379	109	N/A

Source: Japan External Trade Organization (JETRO), "Japan's Outward FDI by Country," "Japan's Inward FDI by Country/Region," and "Japan's Total Outward FDI by Country/Region," http://www.jetro.go.jp/en/reports/statistics/; MOFCOM, "2010 Statistical Bulletin of China's Outward Foreign Direct Investment."

of these programs. Despite friction over the Taiwan issue and Chinese nuclear testing, Tokyo agreed to supply Beijing with several billion dollars in loans in the second half of the 1990s.[30] After 2001, though, Japan began to cut ODA steadily and significantly due to inter alia Japan's economic woes, China's economic and military modernization, Tokyo's disillusionment with the lack of Chinese gratitude, public opposition, and the passing from the scene of Japanese heavyweights who had supported ODA.[31]

The preceding discussion reveals the depths of Sino-Japanese commercial liberal statecraft. Both trade and FDI links are very large, albeit in regard to Japanese FDI in China rather than the reverse. Finally, economic relations in terms of Japanese aid and assistance to China are quite extensive. It should not be overlooked that layered on top of bilateral trade, FDI, and aid links are joint participation in myriad regional integration activities, rising monetary cooperation, and millions of tourists. Furthermore, there are tens of thousands of students involved in exchange programs, dozens of ongoing cultural, sporting, and sister city interactions, and numerous scientific and technical delegations. Last, there are numerous ministerial and sub-cabinet-level economic dialogues and meetings, many regular, to deal with trade, environmental, and investment issues.[32]

Sources of Bilateral Political Friction

Over the past 40 years, the Sino-Japanese political relationship has been replete with positives. For instance, Beijing and Tokyo have worked collaboratively to address political issues ranging from the termination of the Cambodian Civil War to tackling North Korean proliferation. The two countries also have participated in regional efforts to manage problems related to fisheries, pollution, and disaster relief. Yet the relationship also is replete with diverse conflicts, surveyed below, which often have far greater visibility than the collaborations. Analysts often highlight these frictions as reasons why Sino-Japanese economic interdependence has not yielded a warm peace.

Security

Between 1972 and the early 1980s, security was the basis of a warming Sino-Japanese relationship as both countries confronted a common enemy, the Soviet Union. However, from the early 1980s to the end of the decade, the glue provided by the Soviet threat declined with the warming of Sino-Soviet relations and the subsequent demise of the Soviet empire and the Soviet Union itself.[33] Concurrently, Japanese military modernization posed an increasing threat to China. A turning point was Japan's 1987 defense budget, which exceeded its long-standing defense budget threshold of 1 percent of its gross domestic product (GDP). For Japan the Chinese threat began to emerge in the 1990s due to China's economic growth, military modernization and nuclear tests, and the 1995–96 Taiwan Straits crisis, which showed China's willingness to use force.[34]

China began to view Japan's military modernization as an even greater threat after the 1996 Joint Declaration on the U.S.-Japan Security Alliance (hereafter "1996 Joint Declaration") and the 1997 Revised U.S.-Japan Defense Cooperation Guidelines (hereafter "1997 Guidelines"). Beijing viewed these two documents, which called for Japan to involve itself in areas in its vicinity and to provide "noncombat" support, as easing Taiwan's path to independence and signs of a US-Japan plan to contain China.[35] China also was alarmed about US-Japanese cooperation on missile defense. Japanese missile defense was directed at North Korea but obviously had the potential to degrade China's ability to strike Japan, US forces in Japan, and the United States.[36] Also worrisome to Beijing was Japan's growing activism in the post–Cold War period, with Tokyo deploying forces, in various capacities, in Cambodia, Afghanistan, and Iraq.

Disaggregating the security issue, the main problem is that the two countries are maneuvering to become or maintain their status as great powers.[37] Another problem is that the two countries threaten each other's interests with respect to a slew of concrete issues, noted below. Yet another problem is the clash between the two countries' identities. Chinese view themselves as victims (particularly of Japanese aggression) and see Japan as an adversarial "other" or state. For its part, Japan sees itself as a liberal democracy and China as anything but one![38]

Territorial and Maritime Issues

Sino-Japanese territorial friction pertains to competing ownership claims to the Islands while maritime friction is linked to incompatible positions on the exclusive economic zone (EEZ) boundary in the ECS that separates China and Japan. One reason the Islands and ECS EEZ are important is because they raise issues of sovereignty and territorial integrity. Another is because the waters around the Islands and ECS EEZ are believed to possess precious hydrocarbon resources and minerals and contain rich fisheries. Yet another reason is their strategic location between China and Japan and proximity to the Chinese coast.[39]

A United Nations (UN) report in 1968, which estimated that there were vast resources in the ECS and around the Islands, sparked the contemporary era of tension, Although Beijing and Tokyo kept a lid on their territorial and maritime disputes for most of the 1970s and 1980s in order to promote their partnership against the Soviet Union and to bolster economic ties. For various reasons, the situation deteriorated after 1992. Both capitals began to make strong assertions of sovereignty while denigrating the claims of the other. In addition, the two countries moved to shore up their positions by deploying coast guard vessels and engaging in resource survey and exploitation activities in disputed areas. Furthermore, the two sides took steps to defend their interests militarily, with, for instance, Japan planning how it might repel a Chinese invasion of the Islands and increasing the number of its troops in the area.[40]

Serious clashes over the Islands and ECS EEZ continue to occur. In September 2010, near the Islands, a Chinese fishing boat intentionally rammed a Japanese coast guard vessel. This incident produced strong rhetoric and protests, the suspension of diplomatic exchanges and cancellation of thousands of tourist trips, and what one might deem more conventional economic statecraft in the form of a Chinese cutoff of rare earth exports to Japan.[41] In September 2012, the Islands once again sparked a crisis, with the Japanese central government's decision to purchase them from their private owners serving as the catalyst. Aside from diplomatic protests and strong rhetoric from Beijing, political, cultural, and educational interactions slid into a deep freeze.[42] Japan suffered a multitude of economic sanctions: consumer boycotts of Japanese products, canceled tourist trips, rare earth export reductions, customs processing delays, the dumping of Japanese assets, and violence against Japanese firms in China.[43] Japan's action also led to increased Chinese efforts to assert sovereignty in the form of military (air and naval) and coast guard patrols, surveys, and public diplomacy, which elicited tit-for-tat responses from Japan.[44] China's reaction fueled growing support in Japan for a major buildup of its military and coast guard capabilities.[45]

History

Among other things, controversies over history relate to the way Japanese textbooks treat (or fail to treat) Japan's invasion and occupation of China in the 1930s and 1940s, especially the horrendous Nanjing massacre.[46] Relatedly, they pertain to the way Japanese politicians and military officials acknowledge or deny these events.[47] They are also tied to the controversial visits of Japanese leaders, Diet members, and Cabinet members to the Yasukuni Shrine, which commemorates Japanese World War II "heroes"—an obvious afront to China. Examples include Prime Minister Koizumi Junichiro's visits there every year between 2001 and 2005 and the hundreds of Japanese Diet members who have gone to Yasukuni over the past three decades. Other historical issues include a Japanese apology for the suffering it inflicted during the 1930s and 1940s, the disposition of Japanese chemical weapons left in China, and the issue of reparations.[48] The "soft" issue of history has led to massive anti-Japanese protests, worsened bilateral relations, ensconced antagonistic perceptions among Chinese and Japanese, obstructed government interactions, and spurred diplomatic protests.[49]

Competition for Influence

The Sino-Japanese competition for influence manifests itself most visibly in places such as Southeast Asia and the Pacific islands. China and Japan compete hard for the loyalties of countries in these areas to promote their diverse national interests. For example, China seeks partners in these regions in order to isolate Taiwan, to secure resources and vital sea lines of communication (SLOCs) in the SCS, and to gain friends in a multipolar world. For its part, Japan seeks partners in the APR in order to promote its economic interests, to contain or engage China, and to advance diverse nonsecurity goals such as democratic values and whaling rights. In pursuing friends in the APR, both countries seek not only to enhance their power and prestige but to dilute the power and prestige of the other. They further compete to dominate regional free trade agreements and economic institutions such as the East Asian Summit.[50]

This competition has generated considerable diplomatic heat as China and Japan jockey to influence the membership of APR bodies, the location of meetings, and their economic and financial obligations. As well, it has resulted in the competitive expenditure of billions of dollars in loans, debt relief, and technical assistance. To illustrate, between 2000 and 2010, Beijing struck deals with diverse Pacific island nations involving hundreds of millions of dollars in loans, debt relief, and investment. Japan responded with hundreds of millions of dollars for ODA, development projects, and so on.[51] In Southeast Asia, the two countries have inter alia advanced rival free trade agreements and research institutes; spent millions to support cooperation in science and technology, counterterrorism, anti–drug trafficking, the environment, and human resources; and engaged in a dance of dueling meetings and summits.[52]

Competition for Energy

The competition for energy is a fairly new source of controversy. Its roots can be traced to 1993 when China became a net oil importer for the first time.[53] Afterward China increasingly sought to nurture relationships with foreign suppliers. Related measures include government support for COFDI in places such as Angola, Russia, and Sudan; massive energy deals with hydrocarbon-rich countries such as Iran, Saudi Arabia, and Venezuela; and huge policy loans to support the construction of roads, ports, and pipelines. In addition, Beijing has sought to enhance direct political and military ties with energy-supplying countries, as well as championing the agendas of selected energy suppliers in forums such as the UN.[54] In tandem, Japan, which is a major energy consumer but energy poor, has been competing to sustain or expand its relationships with similar countries, to provide money and technology to facilitate energy conservation, investment, and production; and to develop a global energy infrastructure geared toward Japan.[55]

The competition has fueled some anxieties on both sides. It also has led both countries to pay increasing attention to the security of SLOCs in places such as the Indian Ocean, the SCS, and the Straits of Malacca. On the one hand, this has produced cooperation on marine safety and antipiracy.[56] On the other, it has driven them to strengthen their naval capabilities and their relationships with regional players that can increase their policy options (e.g., Japan has a close partnership with Australia, while China has close relations with Russia).[57] Aside from these ramifications, it has, as noted, contributed to the sparring over the ownership of the Islands and the delimitation of the ECS, as well as each country's unilateral measures to assert its sovereignty.

Taiwan

Although Tokyo severed diplomatic relations with Taipei in 1972, it has never fully abandoned Taiwan, its former colony. Since then, Japanese economic links with Taiwan have continued to grow, with bilateral trade reaching $70 billion in 2010 and JOFDI hitting $10.35 billion that same year. In addition, cultural links, educational exchanges, and tourism have remained strong. Moreover, nonofficial political and military links have persisted, as shown by retired Japanese military officials traveling to Taiwan to provide advice and training and Tokyo's support of Taiwanese membership in the UN World Health Organization. Japan's close relationship with Taiwan is a function, among other things, of history, balancing against China, the desire to protect SLOCs, public support in Japan for an independent Taiwan, and economic interests.[58]

From China's vantage point, the problem is that Japan continues to strengthen its ties with Taiwan despite Japan's longtime recognition of Beijing.[59] After 1995, Japanese-Taiwanese relations injected an increasing amount of tension into Sino-Japanese relations because US-Japanese security relations evolved in a direction that implied Japan would assist the United States in the event of a cross-strait clash. First, as noted, the 1996 Joint Declaration and the 1997 Guidelines seem to obligate Japan to involve itself in conflicts in areas surrounding it. Second, a February 2005 US-Japan declaration described the peaceful settlement of the Taiwan conflict as a common security issue.[60] In the twenty-first century, there have been various Sino-Japanese frictions pertaining to the Taiwan issue. To illustrate, in May 2009, Japan's top representative to Taiwan infuriated Beijing when he remarked that the status of Taiwan was unclear.[61]

The preceding narrative highlights a large number of issues that engender bilateral tensions and hinder progress in regional peacemaking. Among them are beliefs that the other side presents a security threat, territorial and maritime conflicts, disputes over Taiwan, controversies over history, and competition for power and prestige.[62] These political frictions both contribute to and are exacerbated by the growth of nationalistic politics in both countries.[63] Nationalists play up such tensions, make it difficult for their leaders to pursue compromise, and obstruct cooperation in these areas. In any event, it is logical that the problems enumerated in this section limit the positive political spillover of Sino-Japanese economic ties. But it remains unclear why such active economic statecraft and the interdependence that flows from it cannot surmount these frictions. It is to this issue that we now turn.

Assessing the Limitations of Economic Statecraft

A plausible reason why Sino-Japanese economic interdependence may not have overcome political tensions is that many of the matters discussed in the previous section are power relations and security issues. Examples include territorial and maritime disputes, the issue of Taiwan, and the two sides' military modernization programs. But there is no reason to believe that security issues per se are immune from the pacifying effects of economic links. Germany used economic incentives strategically to persuade the Soviet Union to accept German reunification and reunified Germany's membership in the North Atlantic Treaty Organization (NATO).[64] Economic mechanisms have been used to promote nuclear disarmament in the case of Ukraine.[65] Economic arrangements in the form of free trade agreements seem to have eased the settlement of territorial and maritime problems among the member states of Mercosur and the Association of Southeast Asian Nations (ASEAN).[66] As Norrin M. Ripsman and Steven E. Lobell discuss in chapters 1 and 2 of this volume, the United States has used economic statecraft with both Israel and Jordan.

The real issue in regard to political limitations to a positive spillover from economic interdependence is that the two countries view each other as adversaries.[67] Indeed, one leading analyst describes them as being locked in a classic security dilemma with each side bolstering its military with quantitative or qualitative improvements, each side making moves to enhance its naval reach and capabilities, and each side striving to garner an increasing number of allies.[68] In such a context, relative gains become more important, and thus economic ties are more likely to raise fears than warm hearts. Each side will think more about how economic links constrain it while empowering the other side.[69] Moreover, given frictions over history and strongly negative attitudes toward the other side, there are signs that the public in both countries will want "payback" from the other side, magnifying the pernicious consequences of the hunt for relative gains.[70]

Another limitation to the ability of economic statecraft to produce a warm bilateral peace is the fact they often have negative externalities (real and perceived) that can mitigate or undermine their positive spillovers. For instance, in the case of China and Japan, trade deficits have raised issues such as the exhaustion of foreign currency reserves (China) and the hollowing out of manufacturing (Japan). Trade in agricultural commodities or high-technology products has created, respectively, friction over issues such as dumping or intellectual property rights violations. Further, it has engendered anxieties about product quality and safety.[71] Acquisition by the People's Bank of China (China's central bank) of Japanese government bonds has provoked anxieties about Chinese motives and Japanese dependence while Chinese purchases of Japanese land have led to fears of Chinese "buying up the Japanese homeland."[72] Finally, it should be recognized that the Islands and ECS EEZ disputes, which both have economic components, actually are *causes* of conflict.

Even if bilateral economic interactions are purely positive, there is reason to question the positive political externalities that will flow from them. One reason is that the brutality of Japan's invasion and occupation of China in the 1930s and 1940s, coupled with the absence of a Japanese requirement to pay reparations, seems to have created an entitlement mentality. In other words, many Chinese apparently consider ODA, technology transfers, economic concessions, educational and scientific exchanges, and the like not as manifestations of Japanese generosity or goodwill (even if self-interested) but as something Japan *owes* to China. If so, the political spillover resulting from the growth and jobs, technology upgrading, and infrastructure produced by China's economic dealings with Japan will be quite tempered.[73] Beyond this, economic ties may serve as lightning rods for critics or rallying points for nationalists rather than sources of cooperation. To illustrate, Chinese have critiqued Japanese firms operating in China for contributing less to the Chinese economy than they should.

A fourth factor hampering the ability of economics to deliver a warm peace is each side's doubts that its "good behavior" can induce "good behavior" in the other. To illustrate, the Japanese are highly suspicious that a cessation of visits to Yasukuni, the cleaning up of textbooks, or cooperative measures on territorial problems would lead China to stop bullying Japan, shunning self-righteous behaviors, or accommodating Japan's interests in regional structures.[74] The Chinese are distrustful, too, as I know from interviews I conducted in China in 2005 and 2007, about Japan's pursuit of a UN Security Council seat. They doubt the Japanese will meaningfully reciprocate their positive gestures if they were to support a Japanese UNSC seat.

A fifth constraint on the ability of economic mechanisms to sweeten politics is the domestic context.[75] Beijing and Tokyo certainly have internationalist-oriented leaderships, and there are groups in both countries that favor stable relations that support trade, facilitate FDI, and undergird continued exchange. On the Chinese side, these interests are opaque but likely to include exporters, China's northeastern provinces, and those in partnership with Japanese firms.[76] On the Japanese side, the existence of China-oriented economic constituencies is more evident. These constituencies supported continuing ODA to China, have spoken out against the visits of Japanese leaders to the Yasukuni Shrine, and have backed a broadening of political relations. However, these constituencies have had limited success. First, they are divided (with not all favoring friendlier stances toward China) and/or politically weak, and leaders responsive to their sentiments have often lacked "stateness."[77] Second, security considerations have drowned out their voices. For instance, Japanese economic minister Seiji Maehara stated, "I cannot sympathize with comments that put priority on economic issues because our sovereignty is the basis of the nation on which economic activities depend."[78]

This section has highlighted diverse factors that impede the ability of economic statecraft emphasizing massive economic links to create a warm peace between China and Japan. Beyond acknowledging the sheer number of serious political frictions and the fact that a number of them are security issues, it emphasizes that fact that economic interdependence takes place within the context of a security rivalry, as well as that economic spillovers are neither always positive nor always translated into the political process even if they are.

Conclusion

In the early 1990s, there were hopes that China and Japan might move toward a regional security community.[79] Indeed, one China-Japan specialist commented in 1994 that "the relationship is now better than at any time in well over a century."[80] Twenty years later it is obvious that China and Japan have not formed anything approximating a community, much less a security community. It is indisputable that they have shared interests and that economic interaction in the form of trade, FDI, foreign aid, and loans is significant. Yet they have many conflicting interests and few shared values, and force is not off the table as a policy option. Many wonder about "the apparent asymmetry between the economic interdependence of the two nations . . . and their simmering strategic rivalry."[81] The traditional answer is that the two countries have a large number of political frictions that get in the way. My analysis shows, though, that there is more to it. The security rivalry between China and Japan plays a critical role, as do the intrinsic limits of economics within the context of the relationship.

Commercial liberals are likely to contend that, although economic ties may have not resolved problems or created a warm peace, they have stabilized the relationship, especially during periods of high tension, or made it better than it otherwise would be. Given repeated statements by Chinese and Japanese elites about the importance of bilateral economic links, we should not dismiss this possibility. However, one problem with embracing such arguments is that they often fail to consider the fact that political variables (e.g., the military balance of power or political imperatives) may be the actual factors driving moderation or tempering conflict escalation.[82] Importantly, the United States frequently has pushed both sides to temper the frictions.[83] Regarding political imperatives, the 2008 Sino-Japanese joint exploitation deal for the ECS EEZ may have been linked to China's desire to undermine the China threat theory, to create a good atmosphere for the 2008 Olympics, and to give it space to focus on domestic challenges.[84] China also may have taken a quiescent stance toward the Islands in the immediate post-Tiananmen period to ensure a visit by the Japanese emperor in 1992, which, in turn, helped China escape its post-1989 isolation.[85]

In terms of theoretical contributions, the finding of this chapter is not that realist logics trump commercial liberal ones. It is that bilateral economic statecraft is likely to have positive political effects given a particular constellation of international and domestic variables. To elaborate, when the security dilemma is serious, it is not likely to sweeten politics much. As well, economic tools are not likely to transform political relations if domestic economic constituencies do not have a political voice.[86] From a policy vantage point, this analysis directs us to think about what might be done to create a better context in which economics can spill positively into the political realm. One step is to keep the United States involved as a guarantor of the peace in the region as this mitigates the severity of the Sino-Japanese security dilemma.[87] Another step is to take steps to mitigate the negative externalities of economic links. A third step is to continuously address history issues since this can help reduce security anxieties, improve perceptions, and cause economic interactions to be viewed in a more positive way.

This chapter also speaks to the fifth central question enumerated in this volume's introduction: "How can economic statecraft be used to move from a bilateral peace agreement to regional peace?" On one level, frictions between China and Japan have hindered regional peace building because they have led each country to pursue regional arrangements that exclude or constrain the other. Given that such arrangements often stunt regional cooperation, it seems to follow that anything that advances Sino-Japanese relations will aid the cause of regional peace building. However, things are not so simple. The reason is that bilateral frictions have led Beijing and Tokyo to play a key role in supporting regional institution building in order to balance or engage the other. In short, bilateral frictions hurt *and* help regional peace building.[88] Also worth noting is that Sino-Japanese peace building at the regional level has spurred bilateral insecurities. Thus, regional peace building is not just a matter of addressing bilateral frictions but of creating regional arrangements that support "peace" from below.

Ming Wan, a longtime student of Sino-Japanese ties, observes that the relationship "can be described . . . as dispute-prone, cyclical, and downward trending, but manageable politically; as troubled and uncertain militarily; as integrating economically; and as closer in people-to-people contact yet more distant psychologically."[89] This is not encouraging given that "it has rarely ever been the case that China and Japan have been dominant powers at the same time."[90] We must give more attention to stabilizing one of the world's most important bilateral relationships.

NOTES

1. Reinhard Drifte, *Japan's Security Relations with China since 1989: From Balancing to Bandwagoning?* (London: RoutledgeCurzon, 2003); Caroline Rose, *Sino-Japanese Relations: Facing the Past, Looking to the Future?* (London: Routledge, 2005); Ming Wan, *Sino-Japanese Relations: Interaction, Logic, and Transformation* (Stanford, CA: Woodrow Wilson Center Press, 2006).

2. See, for example, Guang Wu, *The Third Sino-Japanese War: Dream of Pacific Empire* (Hauppauge: Nova Science Publishers, 2012).

3. This is also observed by Michael Yahuda in "The Limits of Economic Interdependence: Sino-Japanese Relations," in Alastair Iain Johnston and Robert S. Ross, eds., *New Directions in the Study of China's Foreign Policy* (Stanford, CA: Stanford University Press, 2006), 162.

4. Ming Zhang, *Major Powers at a Crossroads: Economic Interdependence and an Asia Pacific Security Community* (Boulder: Lynn Rienner, 1995); Erica Strecker Downs and Phillip C. Saunders, "Legitimacy and the Limits of Nationalism: China and the Diaoyu Islands," *International Security* 23, no. 3 (Winter 1998–99): 114–46; Ming Wan, "Economic Interdependence and Economic Cooperation: Mitigating Conflict and Transforming Security Order in Asia," in Muthiah Alagappa, ed., *Asian Security Order: Instrumental and Normative Features* (Stanford, CA: Stanford University Press, 2003); Wan, *Sino-Japanese Relations*; Min Gyo Koo, "The Senkaku/Diaoyu Dispute and Sino-Japanese Political-Economic Relations: Cold Politics and Hot Economics?," *Pacific Review* 22, no. 2 (May 2009): 205–32.

5. Koo, "Senkaku/Diaoyu Dispute," 211.

6. Jean-Marc F. Blanchard, "China's Peaceful Rise and Sino-Japanese Territo-

rial and Maritime Tensions," in Sujian Guo, ed., *China's "Peaceful Rise" in the 21st Century: Domestic and International Conditions* (Aldershot: Ashgate, 2006), 211–36; Janet Xuanli Liao, "Sino-Japanese Energy Security and Regional Stability: The Case of the East China Sea Gas Exploration," *East Asia* 25, no. 1 (April 2008): 57–78; James Manicom, "Sino-Japanese Cooperation in the East China Sea: Limitations and Prospects," *Contemporary Southeast Asia* 30, no. 3 (2008): 455–78.

7. See, for example, Lai Foon Wong, "China-ASEAN and Japan-ASEAN Relations during the Post–Cold War Era," *Chinese Journal of International Politics* 1, no. 3 (Summer 2007): 373–404.

8. Jing Sun, "Japan-Taiwan Relations: Unofficial in Name Only," *Asian Survey* 47, no. 5 (September–October 2007): 790–810; Jason J. Blazevic, "The Taiwan Dilemma: China, Japan, and the Strait Dynamic," *Journal of Current Chinese Affairs* 39, no. 4 (2010): 143–73.

9. Montesquieu is quoted in Jean-Marc F. Blanchard, Norrin M. Ripsman, and Edward D. Mansfield, "The Political Economy of National Security: Economic Statecraft, Interdependence, and International Conflict," in Jean-Marc F. Blanchard, Norrin M. Ripsman, and Edward D. Mansfield, eds., *Power and the Purse: Economic Statecraft, Interdependence, and National Security* (London: Frank Cass, 2000), 8.

10. Arthur A. Stein, "Governments, Economic Interdependence, and International Cooperation," in Philip E. Tetlock et al., *Behavior, Society, and International Conflict*, vol. 3 (New York: Oxford University Press, 1993); Blanchard, Ripsman, and Mansfield, "Political Economy of National Security," 1–14; Edward D. Mansfield and Brian M. Pollins, "Interdependence and Conflict: An Introduction," in Edward D. Mansfield and Brian M. Pollins, eds., *Economic Interdependence and International Conflict: New Perspectives on an Enduring Debate* (Ann Arbor: University of Michigan Press, 2003). The terms *neutralizing* and *binding* come from Stein.

11. Blanchard, Ripsman, and Mansfield, "Political Economy of National Security," 8; Edward D. Mansfield, Jon C. Pevehouse, and David H. Bearce, "Preferential Trading Arrangements and Military Disputes," in Jean-Marc F. Blanchard, Edward D. Mansfield, and Norrin M. Ripsman, eds., *Power and the Purse: Economic Statecraft, Interdependence, and National Security* (London: Frank Cass, 2000), 92–118.

12. Stein, "Governments, Economic Interdependence, and International Cooperation," 253–54; Paul A. Papayoanou and Scott L. Kastner, "Sleeping with the (Potential) Enemy: Assessing the U.S. Policy of Engagement with China," in Jean-Marc F. Blanchard, Edward D. Mansfield, and Norrin M. Ripsman, eds., *Power and the Purse: Economic Statecraft, Interdependence, and National Security* (London: Frank Cass, 2000), 157–87; Jack S. Levy, "Economic Interdependence, Opportunity Costs, and Peace," in Edward D. Mansfield and Brian M. Pollins, eds., *Economic*

Interdependence and International Conflict: New Perspectives on an Enduring Debate (Ann Arbor: University of Michigan Press, 2003), 128–34.

13. Zhang, *Major Powers at a Crossroads*, 60–62; Wan, "Economic Interdependence and Economic Cooperation," 280–305; Wan, *Sino-Japanese Relations*, 213–29.

14. Stein, "Governments, Economic Interdependence, and International Cooperation," 249–52; Mansfield and Pollins, "Interdependence and Conflict," 3; Levy, "Economic Interdependence, Opportunity Costs, and Peace," 128.

15. Mansfield and Pollins, "Interdependence and Conflict," 3–4; Levy, "Economic Interdependence, Opportunity Costs, and Peace," 130–34; Hyung Min Kim and David L. Rousseau, "The Classical Liberals Were Half Right (or Half Wrong): New Tests of the 'Liberal Peace,' 1960–88," *Journal of Peace Research* 42, no. 5 (September 2005): 523–44.

16. For a discussion, see Donald W. Klein, "China and the Second World," in Samuel S. Kim, ed., *China and the World: New Directions in Chinese Foreign Relations* (Boulder: Westview Press, 1989), 138; Zhang, *Major Powers at a Crossroads*, 60; and Chu-yuan Cheng, "Sino-Japanese Economic Relations: Interdependence and Conflict," in James C. Hsiung, ed., *China and Japan at Odds: Deciphering the Perpetual Conflict* (Houndmills: Palgrave Macmillan, 2007), 82–83.

17. Zhang, *Major Powers at a Crossroads*, 165, app. A, table A.5.

18. Donald W. Klein, "Japan and Europe in Chinese Foreign Relations," in Samuel S. Kim, ed., *China and the World: Chinese Foreign Policy Faces the New Millennium*, 4th ed. (Boulder: Westview Press, 1998), 139.

19. Klein, "Japan and Europe in Chinese Foreign Relations," 138; Wan, *Sino-Japanese Relations*, 47–48; Claes G. Alvstam, Patrik Strom, and Naoyu Yoshino, "On the Economic Interdependence between China and Japan: Challenges and Possibilities," *Asia Pacific Viewpoint* 50, no. 2 (August 2009): 206–7.

20. Klein, "Japan and Europe in Chinese Foreign Relations" (1994), 121–22.

21. Klein, "Japan and Europe in Chinese Foreign Relations" (1998), 140.

22. See the sources provided for table 6.1.

23. For a discussion of the history of COFDI and its drivers, see Jean-Marc F. Blanchard, "Chinese MNCs as China's New Long March: A Review and Critique of the Western Literature," *Journal of Chinese Political Science* 16, no. 1 (March 2011): 91–108.

24. Wan, *Sino-Japanese Relations*, 53.

25. MOFCOM [People's Republic of China, Ministry of Commerce], "2010 Statistical Bulletin of China's Outward Foreign Direct Investment," accessed October 18, 2011, http://english.mofcom.gov.cn/article/statistic/foreigninvestment/201109/20110907742320.shtml.

26. Michiyo Nakamoto, "Chinese Textile Maker Set to Control Renown," *Financial Times*, May 25, 2010; Michiyo Nakamoto, "Japanese Businesses Bow to Need for Cash," *Financial Times*, July 5, 2010; Jonathan Soble, "Corporate Japan Warms to Chinese Investment," *Financial Times*, July 31, 2011.

27. There was no explicit quid pro quo, but Japan expected that its aid would enhance relations with China.

28. Andrew J. Nathan and Robert S. Ross, *The Great Wall and the Empty Fortress: China's Search for Security* (New York: W. W. Norton, 1997), 86.

29. Klein, "China and the Second World," 139; Klein, "Japan and Europe in Chinese Foreign Relations" (1994), 121; Wan, *Sino-Japanese Relations*, 264.

30. Nathan and Ross, *Great Wall and the Empty Fortress*, 89–90, 92.

31. Reinhard Drifte, "The Ending of Japan's ODA Loan Programs to China: All's Well That Ends Well?," *Asia-Pacific Review* 13, no. 1 (2006): 94–117; Wan, *Sino-Japanese Relations*, 51–52, 262–86.

32. Yahuda, "Limits of Economic Interdependence," 165; Wan, *Sino-Japanese Relations*, 52, 64–65; Jin Qiu, "The Politics of History and Historical Memory in China-Japan Relations," *Journal of Chinese Political Science* 2, no. 1 (Spring 2006): 25–53.

33. Wan, *Sino-Japanese Relations*, 202–3.

34. Michael J. Green and Benjamin L. Self, "Japan's Changing China Policy: From Commercial Liberalism to Reluctant Realism," *Survival* 38, no. 2 (1996): 35–58; Wu Xinbo, "The Security Dimension of Sino-Japanese Relations: Warily Watching One Another," *Asian Survey* 40, no. 2 (March 2000): 304–5; June Teufel Dryer, "Sino-Japanese Relations," *Journal of Contemporary China* 10, no. 28 (August 2001): 376–77.

35. Wu, "Security Dimension of Sino-Japanese Relations," 302–3; Paul Midford, "China Views the Revised US-Japan Defense Guidelines: Popping the Cork?," *International Relations of the Asia-Pacific* 4, no. 1 (2004): 124–32; Tomonori Sasaki, "China Eyes the Japanese Military: China's Threat Perceptions of Japan since the 1980's," *China Quarterly* 203 (September 2010): 572–79.

36. Kori J. Urayama, "Chinese Perspectives on Theater Missile Defense: Policy Implications for Japan," *Asian Survey* 40, no. 4 (July–August 2000): 599–621.

37. Wan, *Sino-Japanese Relations*, 2.

38. Akira Chiba and Lanxin Xiang, "Traumatic Legacies in China and Japan: An Exchange," *Survival* 47, no. 2 (June 2005): 228; Wan, *Sino-Japanese Relations*, 158–65; Shogo Suzuki, "The Importance of 'Othering' in China's National Identity: Sino-Japanese Relations as a Stage of Identity Conflict," *Pacific Review* 20, no. 1 (March 2007): 23–47.

39. For background, see Jean-Marc F. Blanchard, "The U.S. Role in the Sino-

Japanese Dispute over the Diaoyu (Senkaku) Islands, 1945–1971," *China Quarterly* 161 (March 2000): 95–123; Jean-Marc F. Blanchard, "China's Peaceful Rise and Sino-Japanese Territorial and Maritime Tensions," 211–36; and Linus Hagström, "Quiet Power: Japan's China Policy in Regard to the Pinnacle Islands," *Pacific Review* 18, no. 2 (June 2005): 159–88.

40. Blanchard, "China's Peaceful Rise and Sino-Japanese Territorial and Maritime Tensions," 211–36; Jean-Marc F. Blanchard, "Economics and Asia-Pacific Region Territorial and Maritime Disputes: Understanding the Political Limits to Economic Solutions," *Asian Politics and Policy* 1, no. 4 (October–December 2009): 686–91; "Troops on Nansei Islands May Double to 4,000," *Japan Times*, November 22, 2010, accessed November 22, 2010, http://www.japantimes.co.jp/text/nn20101122a1.html.

41. Martin Fackler and Ian Johnson, "Arrest in Disputed Seas Riles China and Japan," *New York Times*, September 19, 2010, accessed September 22, 2010, http://www.nytimes.com/2010/09/20/world/asia/20chinajapan.html; "China Halts Top-Level Ties with Japan over Boat Dispute," *BBC News*, September 19, 2010, accessed October 9, 2010, http://www.bbc.co.uk/news/world-asia-pacific-11363024; Keith Bradsher, "Amid Tension, China Blocks Vital Exports to Japan," *New York Times*, September 23, 2010, accessed September 23, 2010, http://www.nytimes.com/2010/09/24/business/global/24rare.html.

42. Li Xiaokun and Zhang Yunbi, "PLA Pledges Support," *China Daily*, September 12, 2012, accessed September 12, 2012, http://usa.chinadaily.com.cn/china/2012-09/12/content_15751329.htm; Zhang Yunbi, Zhou Wa, and Cang Wei, "Tokyo Must Come Back 'from the Brink,'" *China Daily*, September 13, 2012, accessed September 13, 2012, http://usa.chinadaily.com.cn/china/2012-09/13/content_15754042.htm; "China Tells Diet Members, Ex-Lawmakers to Drop Visit Amid Island Row," *Japan Times*, September 13, 2012, accessed September 13, 2012, http://www.japantimes.co.jp/print/nn20120913a5.html.

43. Jun Hongo, "Japanese Companies Become Protest Targets in China," *Japan Times*, September 19, 2012, accessed September 19, 2012, http://www.japantimes.co.jp/print/nb20120919a1.html; "China Delays Approval of Working Visas," *Japan Times*, September 23, 2012, accessed September 29, 2012, http://www.japantimes.co.jp/print/nn20120923a1.html; Yuri Kageyama, "Japan Inc. Pays Dearly as Isle Row Gets China's Goat," *Japan Times*, October 11, 2012, accessed October 11, 2012, http://www.japantimes.co.jp/print/nb20121011a7.html; "China Boycott Ups Firm's Bond Risk," *Japan Times*, October 13, 2012, accessed October 13, 2012, http://www.japantimes.co.jp/print/nb20121013n3.html; Kayo Mimizuka, "Senkakus Backlash Slashes Carmakers' Earnings Outlook," *Japan Times*, November 10, 2012, accessed November 10, 2012, http://www.japantimes.co.jp/print/nb20121110a1.html.

44. Reiji Yoshida, "Senkaku Intrusions Seen as Testing Abe," *Japan Times*, January 9, 2013, accessed January 9, 2013, http://www.japantimes.co.jp/print/nn20130109a3.html; Zhang Yunbi and Zhao Shengnan, "Japanese Jets 'Disturb Routine Patrols,'" *China Daily*, January 12, 2013, accessed January 12, 2013, http://usa.chinadaily.com.cn/world/2013-01/12/content_16107411.htm; "China 'to Survey Disputed East China Sea Islands,'" *BBC News*, January 15, 2013, accessed January 15, 2013, http://www.bbc.co.uk/news/world-asia-21022459.

45. Mure Dickie, "Senkaku Spat Reinforces Military Rethink," *Financial Times*, September 25, 2012.

46. For an extensive treatment, see Jin, "Politics of History and Historical Memory in China-Japan Relations," 25–53.

47. Wang Chenyan, "History 'Must Not Damage Our Links,'" *China Daily*, March 20, 2012, accessed March 20, 2012, http://www.chinadaily.com.cn/cndy/2012-03/20/content_14867818.htm.

48. Klein, "China and the Second World," 139; Wan, *Sino-Japanese Relations*, 235–61; Yung-deh Richard Chu, "Historical and Contemporary Roots of Sino-Japanese Conflicts," in James C. Hsiung, ed., *China and Japan at Odds: Deciphering the Perpetual Conflict* (Houndmills: Palgrave Macmillan, 2007), 31–33.

49. Wan, *Sino-Japanese Relations*, 22–31, 128–33; Chu, "Historical and Contemporary Roots of Sino-Japanese Conflicts," 33; James Reilly, "Harmonious World and Public Opinion in China's Japan Policy," in Sujian Guo and Jean-Marc F. Blanchard, eds., *"Harmonious World" and China's New Foreign Policy* (Lanham, MD: Lexington Books, 2008), 189–223.

50. You Ji, "East Asian Community: A New Platform for Sino-Japanese Cooperation and Contention," *Japanese Studies* 26, no. 1 (May 2006): 19–28; Takashi Terada, "Forming an East Asian Community: A Site for Japan-China Power Struggles," *Japanese Studies* 26, no. 1 (May 2006): 5–17; Wong, "China-ASEAN and Japan-ASEAN Relations during the Post–Cold War Era," 373–404; Chien-peng Chung, "China's Multidimensional Diplomacy towards the Pacific Islands," in Simon Shen and Jean-Marc F. Blanchard, eds., *Multidimensional Diplomacy of Contemporary China* (Lanham, MD: Lexington Books, 2010), 272–77; Benny Cheng Guan, "Japan-China Rivalry: What Role Does the East Asia Summit Play?," *Asia Pacific Viewpoints* 52, no. 3 (December 2011): 347–60.

51. Chung, "China's Multidimensional Diplomacy towards the Pacific Islands," 270–72.

52. Wong, "China-ASEAN and Japan-ASEAN Relations during the Post Cold War Era," 373–404; Christopher W. Hughes, "Japan's Response to China's Rise: Regional Engagement, Global Containment, and Dangers of Collision," *International Affairs* 85, no. 4 (2009): 846–48; Guan, "Japan-China Rivalry," 347–60.

53. Pak K. Lee, "China's Quest for Oil Security: Oil (Wars) in the Pipeline?" *Pacific Review* 18, no. 2 (June 2005): 265–301; Kent E. Calder, "Coping with Energy Insecurity: China's Response in Global Perspective," *East Asia* 23, no. 3 (Fall 2006): 49–66; Xuanli Liao, "The Petroleum Factor in Sino-Japanese Relations: Beyond Energy Cooperation," *International Relations of the Asia-Pacific* 7, no. 1 (March 2006): 23–46.

54. Lyle Goldstein and Vitaly Kozyrev, "China, Japan, and the Scramble for Siberia," *Survival* 48, no. 1 (Spring 2006): 163–78; Tim Niblock, "China's Growing Involvement in the Gulf: The Geopolitical Significance," in Simon Shen and Jean-Marc F. Blanchard, eds., *Multidimensional Diplomacy of Contemporary China* (Lanham, MD: Lexington Books, 2010), 207–31; Ian Taylor, "China's Rise in Africa," in Simon Shen and Jean-Marc F. Blanchard, eds., *Multidimensional Diplomacy of Contemporary China*, (Lanham, MD: Lexington Books, 2010), 253–65.

55. Goldstein and Kozyrev, "China, Japan, and the Scramble for Siberia," 163–78; Shoichi Itoh, "China's Surging Energy Demand: Trigger for Conflict or Cooperation with Japan?," *East Asia* 25, no. 1 (April 2008): 85–86; Vlado Vivoda, "Oil Import Diversification in Northeast Asia: A Comparison between China and Japan," *Journal of East Asian Studies* 11, no. 2 (May–August 2011): 223–54.

56. Sheng Hongsheng, "Protecting the Waters: All Regional States Should Work Together to Keep the South China Sea Safe," *Beijing Review*, February 27, 2012, accessed May 4, 2012, http://www.bjreview.com/world/txt/2012–02/27/content_427987.htm.

57. Goldstein and Kozyrev, "China, Japan, and the Scramble for Siberia," 163–78; Mahmud Ali, "New 'Strategic Partnership' against China," *BBC News*, September 3, 2007, accessed June 9, 2008, http://news.bbc.co.uk/go/pr/fr/-/2/hi/south_asia/6968412.stm; Hughes, "Japan's Response to China's Rise," 849–51.

58. Jason Chen, "Japan's Policies towards Taiwan," *Stanford Journal of East Asian Affairs* 6, no. 1 (Winter 2006): 53–61; Sun, "Japan-Taiwan Relations"; Max Hirsch, "China's Taipei Envoy Pick Said Potential Tokyo Foil," *Japan Times*, June 11, 2008, accessed June 29, 2008, http://search.japantimes.co.jp/mail/nn20080611f2.html; Reinhard Drifte, "The Future of the Japanese-Chinese Relationship: The Case for a Grand Political Bargain," *Asia-Pacific Review* 16, no. 2 (November 2009): 58–60; Blazevic, "Taiwan Dilemma."

59. For a discussion of Taiwan's importance to China, see Jean-Marc F. Blanchard and Dennis V. Hickey, "More Than Two 'Sides' to Every Story: An Introduction to *New Thinking about the Taiwan Issue*," in Jean-Marc F. Blanchard and Dennis V. Hickey, eds., *New Thinking about the Taiwan Issue: Theoretical Insights into Its Origins, Dynamics, and Prospects* (London: Routledge, 2012), 2–5.

60. J. Sean Curtin, "The Dragon Roars over US-Japan Accord," *Asia Times*

Online, February 23, 2005, accessed May 31, 2009, http://atimes01.atimes.com/atimes/Japan/GB23Dh01.html.

61. "Taiwan Remarks Retracted," *Japan Times*, May 3, 2009, accessed May 31, 2009, http://www.japantimes.co.jp/text/nn20090503a4.html.

62. Another important source of Sino-Japanese friction, which is not covered herein due to space constraints, is North Korea. Useful background sources include Christopher W. Hughes, "'Super-Sizing' the DPRK Threat: Japan's Evolving Military Posture and North Korea," *Asian Survey* 49, no. 2 (March–April 2009): 291–311; Linus Hagström, "Normalizing Japan: Supporter, Nuisance, or Wielder of Power in the North Korean Nuclear Talks?," *Asian Survey* 49, no. 5 (September–October 2009): 831–51; and Mong Cheung, "Japan Eyes the North Korean Nuclear Crisis (2006–2009)," *Journal of Comparative Asian Development* 10, no. 2 (2011): 305–26.

63. Peter Hays Gries, "China's 'New Thinking' on Japan," *China Quarterly* 184 (2005): 831–50; Yahuda, "Limits of Economic Interdependence," 168–69; Gregory J. Moore, "History, Nationalism, and Face in Sino-Japanese Relations," *Journal of Chinese Political Science* 15, no. 3 (2010): 283–306.

64. Randall Newnham, *Deutsche Mark Diplomacy: Positive Economic Sanctions in German-Russian Relations* (University Park: Pennsylvania State University Press, 2002).

65. Virginia I. Foran and Leonard S. Spector, "The Application of Incentives to Nuclear Proliferation," in David Cortright, ed., *The Price of Peace: Incentives and International Conflict Prevention* (Lanham, MD: Rowman and Littlefield, 1997), 21–54.

66. Mansfield, Pevehouse, and Bearce, "Preferential Trading Arrangements and Military Disputes," 101–3.

67. In regard to Japan, see Martin Fackler, "Japan Announces Defense Policy to Counter China," *New York Times*, December 16, 2010, accessed December 17, 2010, http://www.nytimes.com/2010/12/17/world/asia/17japan.html; and "SDF Spending Targeted to Rise in Fiscal 2013," *Japan Times*, January 7, 2013, accessed January 7, 2013, http://www.japantimes.co.jp/news/2013/01/07/news/sdf-spending-targeted-to-rise-in-fiscal-2013. In regard to China, see "Chinese Back More Steps over Senkakus," *Japan Times*, September 18, 2012, accessed September 29, 2012, http://www.japantimes.co.jp/print/nn20120918b3.html.

68. Michael Yahuda, "Sino-Japanese Relations: Partners and Rivals?," *Korean Journal of Defense Analysis* 21, no. 4 (2009): 371–73.

69. Drezner discusses why states view economic options vis-à-vis adversary states differently than allies. Daniel W. Drezner, "The Trouble with Carrots: Transactions Costs, Conflict Expectations, and Economic Inducements," in Jean-Marc F. Blanchard, Edward D. Mansfield, and Norrin M. Ripsman, eds., *Power and the*

Purse: Economic Statecraft, Interdependence, and National Security (London: Frank Cass, 2000), 199–203.

70. Yinan He, "History, Chinese Nationalism, and the Emerging Sino-Japanese Conflict," *Journal of Contemporary China* 16, no. 50 (February 2007): 21.

71. Green and Self, "Japan's Changing China Policy," 50; Joseph Y. S. Cheng, "Sino-Japanese Relations in the Twenty-First Century," *Journal of Contemporary Asia* 33, no. 2 (2003): 266–267; Wan, *Sino-Japanese Relations*; Cal Clark, "The Evolving Global and Regional Economic Roles of China and Japan: Competitive and Complementary Forces," in James C. Hsiung, ed., *China and Japan at Odds: Deciphering the Perpetual Conflict* (Houndmills: Palgrave Macmillan, 2007), 72–75.

72. Michiyo Nakamoto, "Japan Alarm over China's JGB Purchases," *Financial Times*, September 9, 2010; Hiroko Tabuchi, "Chinese Developers Tap into Japanese Insecurity," *New York Times*, September 29, 2010, accessed October 6, 2010, http://www.nytimes.com/2010/09/30/business/global/30spree.html.

73. Drifte, "The Ending of Japan's ODA Loan Programs to China," 98; He, "History, Chinese Nationalism, and the Emerging Sino-Japanese Conflict," 10–12.

74. Chiba and Xiang, "Traumatic Legacies in China and Japan," 215–32.

75. Unless otherwise noted, this paragraph is based on Drifte, "Ending of Japan's ODA Loan Programs to China," 96; Yahuda, "Limits of Economic Interdependence," 165, 181; and Linus Hagström and Bjorn Jerden, "Understanding Fluctuations in Sino-Japanese Relations to Politicize or to De-politicize the Chinese Issue in the Japanese Diet," *Pacific Affairs* 83, no. 4 (December 2012): 719–39.

76. See, for example, Carol Huang, "Dalian's Japan Ties Kept Riots at Bay," *Japan Times*, January 16, 2013, accessed January 16, 2013, http://www.japantimes.co.jp/print/nn20130116f1.html.

77. I benefited here from Hughes, "Japan's Response to China's Rise," and discussions with Professor Thomas Berger. For a discussion of "stateness," see Jean-Marc F. Blanchard and Norrin M. Ripsman, "A Political Theory of Economic Statecraft," *Foreign Policy Analysis* 4, no. 4 (October 2008): 371–98.

78. Michiyo Nakamoto, "Tokyo Stands Firm over Disputed Islands," *Financial Times*, October 11, 2012.

79. Zhang, *Major Powers at a Crossroads*, 1–2.

80. Klein, "Japan and Europe in Chinese Foreign Relations" (1994), 120. Four years later Klein offered the same assessment in "Japan and Europe in Chinese Foreign Relations" (1998), 138.

81. Chiba and Xiang, "Traumatic Legacies in China and Japan," 215.

82. For an argument claiming that China is deterred from using force because of Japan's military capacity, see, for example, comments by Kunihiko Miyake, interviewed in Dickie, "Senkaku Spat Reinforces Military Rethink."

83. "Clinton Urges Dialogue, Calm over Senkaku Row," *Japan Times*, January 10, 2013, accessed January 10, 2013, http://www.japantimes.co.jp/print/nn20130110a7.html; "U.S. Warns China to Steer Clear of Senkakus," *Japan Times*, January 20, 2013, accessed January 20, 2013, http://www.japantimes.co.jp/print/nn20130120a6.html.

84. Blanchard, "Economics and Asia-Pacific Region Territorial and Maritime Disputes," 682–708.

85. Hagstrom, "Quiet Power," 173–81.

86. For a related point focusing on China-Taiwan relations, see Steve Chan, "Unbalanced Threat or Rising Integration? Explaining Relations across the Taiwan Strait," in Jean-Marc F. Blanchard and Dennis V. Hickey, eds., *New Thinking about the Taiwan Issue: Theoretical Insights into Its Origins, Dynamics, and Prospects* (London: Routledge, 2012), 92–115. For a more general treatment, see Beth Simmons, "Pax Mercatoria and the Theory of the State," in Edward D. Mansfield and Brian M. Pollins, eds., *Economic Interdependence and International Conflict: New Perspectives on an Enduring Debate* (Ann Arbor: University of Michigan Press, 2003), 31–43.

87. Yahuda, "Sino-Japanese Relations," 373. Manicom and O'Neil also show that deterrence is an important foundation for containing Sino-Japanese frictions. James Manicom and Andrew O'Neil "Sino-Japanese Strategic Relations: Will Rivalry Lead to Confrontation?," *Australian Journal of International Affairs* 63, no. 2 (June 2009): 213–32.

88. The relevant data and citations are in the subsection "Competition for Influence."

89. Wan, *Sino-Japanese Relations*, 2.

90. James C. Hsiung, "Introduction: Theory and the Long-Running Tussle," in James C. Hsiung, ed., *China and Japan at Odds: Deciphering the Perpetual Conflict* (Houndmills: Palgrave Macmillan, 2007), 14.

CHAPTER 7

Winning Hearts and Minds?

On the Sources and Efficacy of Economic Engagement Policies in US-China and China-Taiwan Relations

Scott L. Kastner and Margaret M. Pearson

National governments often use economic instruments to influence policy choices in rival countries. While economic sanctions have received a great deal of attention in the scholarly literature, somewhat less studied are what might be termed engagement policies, in which governments promote increased economic exchange with a target country in the hopes of influencing policy there and promoting more stable relations. The People's Republic of China (PRC), for instance, has pushed for deeper economic integration with Taiwan, and Chinese officials have argued that the economic benefits Taiwan will reap will help to facilitate national unification by "winning hearts and minds" on the island. During the late 1990s, South Korea launched its "Sunshine Policy," which aimed (among other things) to increase economic exchange with North Korea in the hopes that this would lead to less belligerent behavior by its northern neighbor. And in the 1990s the administration of American president Bill Clinton argued that efforts to integrate China more fully into the global economy would also make it more likely that China would adhere to international norms. In this chapter, we are motivated by two broad questions concerning economic engagement policies toward rival states. As we detail below, these questions tie directly into several of the major themes of this volume.

First, why do countries sometimes choose engagement over alternative approaches for dealing with adversaries? Clinton, for instance, had initially articulated a conditional approach, linking the continuation of China's most-favored-nation trading status to meaningful improvement in its human rights record. But in 1994 his administration shifted gears and began to argue that unconditional economic exchange would best promote change in China. South Korean policy toward North Korea has also changed over time. For example, President Lee Myong-bak (2008–13) backed away from the Sunshine Policy advocated by his two predecessors. And in the early 2000s China at times threatened to sanction Taiwanese businesspeople operating in China who favored independence; more recently, it seems more intent on wooing such constituencies than threatening them. The willingness of leaders in the Asia-Pacific region to embrace engagement has likely contributed to the region's tremendous economic dynamism despite numerous simmering political rivalries. In many cases (such as US-China, Japan-China, and Taiwan-China relations), economic ties have burgeoned despite persistent political tension.

Our second question concerns the effectiveness of engagement policies: do these policies actually lead to changes in target country behavior?[1] In the cases noted above, the policies seem to have had, at best, limited success. South Korea's Sunshine Policy did not, ultimately, have a transformative impact on tense North-South relations; by the time it was abandoned by Lee, it was hard to view the policy as even a partial success. It is far from clear, meanwhile, that China has succeeded in winning Taiwanese hearts and minds with its generous economic policies toward the island; support for unification among Taiwanese remains extremely limited and, if anything, has declined in recent years. Even as China became ever more integrated into global markets—a process that included entering the World Trade Organization (WTO) in 2001—there has been little change in the country's human rights policies. Yet, as we will argue, rigorous testing of the effectiveness of engagement policies is fraught with difficulties, so it is hard to draw sweeping conclusions from these apparent failures.

In the pages that follow, we begin with a very brief overview of some existing work on engagement policies, focusing in particular on (1) when and why states might pursue such strategies and (2) when and how such strategies are likely to prove effective. We then develop two lines of argument, each culminating in a working hypothesis. First, we suggest that explicitly highlighting the potential political or security benefits of increased economic exchange with an adversary (or potential adversary) makes it easier for national leaders in sending countries to rally public support behind liberal economic policies toward that adversary—something that, for reasons we will discuss, might otherwise be unpopular. For instance, by suggesting that increased trade with China would make it more likely that China would conform to international human rights norms, the Clinton administration could more easily gain support for such a policy in the US Congress and among Americans more broadly. One upshot of this argument is that, because explicit engagement policies may serve as a useful frame for preferred economic policies, their articulation and implementation may at times be more a reflection of a domestic political logic than a strategy of influence directed at other states.

Second, we suggest that when a leader in the sending country explicitly highlights the political or security benefits of an engagement policy, he or she may also potentially undermine the effectiveness of such a policy in the target country. Rather than "winning hearts and minds," such policies may increase suspicions and decrease trust. Governments in target countries may be less enthusiastic about economic agreements reached with the sender because they perceive a costly political quid pro quo. Moreover, some research in social psychology suggests that the introduction of monetary incentives in social market interactions can backfire. We believe that explicit economic engagement strategies can backfire for similar reasons. In Taiwan, for instance, PRC economic engagement policies might essentially help reorient Taiwanese thinking from normative and social considerations (Am I Chinese? Do I identify with China?) to cost-benefit, market-based considerations (How much will I gain if Taiwan unifies with China?). Thus, in terms of the fourth question posed by Norrin M. Ripsman and Steven E. Lobell in the introduction to this volume, there are clear risks to or could be unintended negative consequences from an overt strategy of economic statecraft as a means of stabilizing relations between rivals.

Taken together, our hypotheses (if they were to be confirmed) have potentially troubling implications for efforts to gauge the effectiveness of engagement policies more generally. Specifically, not all announced engagement policies are motivated by the desire to effect policy change in the target state, and the most effective engagement policies are likely to be those that are not explicitly framed as having political goals, that is, they are likely to be those that are not framed as engagement policies at all.

After developing our hypotheses in more detail, we probe their plausibility in the context of two cases just mentioned: the Clinton administration's engagement policy toward China and the PRC's effort to win Taiwanese hearts and minds via special economic incentives. It remains critically important for the future of peace and stability in the Asia-Pacific region that these two relationships—US-China and China-Taiwan—be managed carefully. The relationship across the Taiwan Strait has historically been viewed as one of the region's most dangerous potential flashpoints, although relations have become considerably less tense since 2008. Still, stability in this dyad remains fraught: détente has not been institutionalized via a cross-Strait peace agreement, and the issue at the core of the rivalry—Taiwan's sovereign status—remains unresolved. The relationship between the United States and China, meanwhile, is unquestionably the most important bilateral relationship in the region. To the extent that the relationship is stable and cooperative, the two countries have the potential to work together to manage some of the region's difficult challenges—such as North Korea's nuclear weapons program. But tensions in the US-China relationship make such cooperative endeavors less likely, and indeed hostile relations could exacerbate regional disputes between US allies and the PRC—such as the Diaoyu/Senkaku island dispute between Japan and China.

In our study of these two critically important Asia-Pacific cases, we address four of the five questions posed by Ripsman and Lobell in the introduction to this volume. First, our analysis ties into the types of statecraft interested parties might pursue to advance regional peacemaking (question 1). Ours is a study of the efficacy of economic inducements in particular. In both cases that we address, we analyze the context in which the sending governments (the United States and China) came to use economic inducements as a primary tool of statecraft. Second, our discussion relates to the targets of economic incentives (question 2). Especially in the Taiwanese case, but also in the US-China case, we show that economic incentives targeted at societal groups that are skeptical of reconciliation with the sending country have the potential to backfire. While our conclusions are tentative, they nonetheless offer a cautionary tale regarding these types of "second-face" engagement strategies. Our chapter also touches on questions of timing (question 3). Although the timing issue is largely irrelevant in the US-China case, in the cross-Strait case economic engagement strategies have clearly preceded any significant progress on thorny political issues. Firm conclusions are impossible here (a peace agreement remains elusive yet still possible, especially in the medium to long term), but we comment in the conclusion on some implications of allowing economic integration to precede political reconciliation in this case. Finally, as both our cases show how and why economic engagement strategies can backfire, they directly relate to the fourth question, on the limits and risks of economic statecraft.

Engagement Policies: Motivations and Efficacy

A large literature considers whether and when states are able to influence policy choices in other countries through the deliberate manipulation of cross-border economic ties. Much of this literature focuses on coercive economic statecraft, as when states threaten or impose economic sanctions to compel or deter policy changes in other states. The utility of economic sanctions as a policy instrument remains the subject of considerable controversy, and efforts to study the efficacy of sanctions empirically are plagued by daunting methodological obstacles. Indeed, it can be hard to know with precision how frequently states might actually utilize economic sanctions; as Daniel W. Drezner writes, economic coercion is often hidden.[2] Threats to use economic sanctions, for example, may be implicit or communicated in private.[3]

Somewhat less studied in the literature is what we have termed economic engagement, in which a country deliberately expands economic ties with a target in order to alter the target's behavior.[4] Existing studies have drawn a distinction between conditional and unconditional engagement policies.[5] Conditional (or linkage) strategies tie increased economic links to changed political behavior in the target state. Unconditional policies, on the other hand, do not impose an explicit quid pro quo; rather, the hope is that increased economic ties will act as a constraint on target state behavior or will lead to a transformation in the target state's foreign policy goals. Such a transformative effect would most likely occur through the second face of security; deepening economic ties could enhance the political clout of internationalist economic interests in the target state, perhaps leading to a change in the ruling coalition.[6]

Empirically, in contrast to the large number of quantitative studies of coercive economic statecraft, studies of economic engagement have relied heavily on case studies. As Mastanduno notes, no comprehensive database of economic engagement attempts exists.[7] One problem here is that the scope of policies that fall under the umbrella of "engagement" is actually quite broad. Engagement can mean straightforward linkage politics (which occur largely through the first face of security) or a more subtle effort to change cost-benefit calculations or even the makeup of governing coalitions in target countries (a second-face effect). It can be used against allies or adversaries. But, even if we were to restrict the domain of engagement to the sorts of cases touched on above—unconditional policies designed to alter the behavior of an adversary or potential adversary—the barriers to the construction of a comprehensive database are still quite daunting for at least three reasons. First, and most obviously, any national decision to pursue trade with an adversary may be undertaken for reasons having little to do with statecraft; leaders may simply hope, for instance, to reap the efficiency gains that trade generates. As such, it is clearly necessary to have a sense of the motivations behind the decision to liberalize trade vis-à-vis an adversary. But, second, leaders who expand trade with adversaries for reasons that are not related to broader political or security goals may nonetheless have reason to invoke these sorts of goals as a way to build domestic political support for their preferred economic policies. Finally, publically articulating the political and security motivations of an unconditional engagement policy could undermine the effectiveness of the policy by raising suspicions in the target country. As such, leaders truly motivated by political and security objectives in seeking increased trade with an adversary may have reason, instead, to frame engagement as a policy driven by purely economic goals. In the following subsections, we develop the last two points in greater detail.

Engagement as a Framing Mechanism

Trade policy can be controversial, and Michael J. Hiscox shows that the way in which trade is framed as an issue can have a sizable impact on individual views toward it.[8] Meanwhile, a recent study by Edward D. Mansfield and Diana C. Mutz finds that sociotropic perceptions of trade's effects—that is, how trade affects the country as a whole—are more important predictors of individual support for trade than economic self-interest is. The authors also find that individuals with ethnocentric attitudes are less likely to support free trade.[9] Taken together, these findings suggest that maintaining liberal trade policies vis-à-vis an adversary or potential adversary can be a dicey proposition. In these cases, when framing the issue, not only can opponents of trade emphasize economic harms, but they can also play up national interest concerns surrounding trading with an enemy. Trade, for instance, can be framed as making an enemy both richer and stronger. It is also possible that the effects of ethnocentrism may be especially salient in the context of trade with an adversary, as these sorts of negative frames—centered on benefits accruing to an enemy—may resonate especially strongly among individuals with ethnocentric attitudes. In short it should be easier for opponents of trade to frame interstate commerce in a negative light when that trade is conducted in the context of an adversarial relationship.

Consider, for instance, US debates concerning trade policy toward China.

Opponents of that trade often invoke US national security concerns when making their arguments. For example, the prominent protectionist and isolationist Patrick Buchanan noted in 1998, as the US and China started to move closer on an agreement over permanent normal trading relations with China, "Beijing does not practice free trade; it conducts 'strategic trade' to strengthen itself for the coming clash."[10] More recently, one organization focused on promoting the interests of US manufacturing (which has obvious economic reasons to oppose trade with China) has emphasized on its webpage, "America's record $273 billion deficit with China last year has certainly helped Beijing to fuel its military expansion."[11]

We suspect, however, that the rhetoric of engagement can help supporters of trade counter efforts by opponents to frame trade with an adversary in a negative light. Just as negative frames centered on the job loss consequences of trade can be offset by positive frames casting trade more favorably, we suspect that a convincing articulation of an engagement strategy can neutralize (at least to some extent) the argument that trade makes an enemy stronger and more threatening. Our first hypothesis is thus as follows.

> **H1:** The articulation of an engagement policy by the government in country A toward an adversary (or potential adversary), country B, increases support among individuals in country A for liberal trade policies vis-à-vis country B.

This is not to say that we believe all articulated engagement policies are insincere or even cynical efforts to mobilize public support behind liberal trade policies sought by pro-trade economic interests. To the contrary, we suspect engagement will be an effective framing device only if it is a plausible—and potentially effective—policy tool. But, to the extent we are right that engagement is an effective frame, governments seeking to expand trade with adversaries have good reason to utilize this frame—whether or not they sincerely hope for or seek the advertised political or security benefits of engagement.

Why Engagement Can Backfire

We further suspect that when a government in country A publicly articulates an engagement policy toward country B by explicitly highlighting the political or security benefits of trade with B for A, it potentially undermines the effectiveness of such a policy in the target country. Rather than winning hearts and minds, such policies increase suspicion and decrease trust, an effect that can unfold in both the first and second faces of security.

With regard to the first face of security, it seems obvious that governments in target countries will be resistant to and skeptical of policies premised on a desire to change their behavior, especially when the sending country is an adversary. When China, for instance, describes increased economic exchange across the Taiwan Strait as something that will help promote long-term goals of national unification, this must raise red flags in Taiwan—especially when governments averse to unification are in power there. Target governments, in turn, are more likely to resist trade in such cases, viewing it as a potential Trojan horse that could have a significant political or national security downside.

Explicit second-face engagement policies designed to change the calculus of specific constituencies in the target country can even backfire at the individual level. For instance, some research suggests that the introduction of monetary incentives in social market interactions can backfire and lead to reduced effort.[12] Indeed, the mere mention of monetary compensation, even absent provision of compensation, is sufficient to corrode participation in a social market.[13] We believe that explicit second-face engagement strategies can backfire for similar reasons when engagement policies highlight "winning" over new constituencies in the target. Consider again the case of China-Taiwan relations. When the PRC emphasizes that increased trade with Taiwan can help it win Taiwanese hearts and minds, the implications are clear: the economic benefits of cross-Strait economic interaction will lead individuals in Taiwan to reject a Taiwancentric identity. Officials of the PRC are effectively suggesting that identity has a price. Rather than gratitude, individuals may feel insulted by such policies since one's identity is not normally something an individual considers as being for sale. We suspect that this sort of a dynamic might extend to any situation in which engagement is framed as helping to reorient the views of a target constituency on what constitutes the national interest.

Our views in this section can be summarized in a hypothesis and two subhypotheses.

> **H2:** Economic engagement policies directed at adversaries are less effective when the sending state explicitly describes the policies as seeking to achieve political or security goals.

The policies are less effective because the target country government will be more suspicious and hence less inclined to go along with trade liberalization (an effect that occurs within the first face of security).

> **H2a:** When a sending country explicitly frames trade with an adversary as advancing political or security goals, the target is more likely to resist trade.

And trade that does occur between adversaries is less likely to have its intended effects among target constituencies (an effect that occurs within the second face of security).

> **H2b:** When a sending country explicitly frames trade with an adversary as transforming the views of constituencies reaping the gains from trade in the target state, it makes it less likely than would otherwise be the case that those views will actually be transformed.

The next two sections explore, in very preliminary fashion, the plausibility of our hypotheses in the context of two case studies: the US policy of engagement with China articulated during the Clinton administration and PRC efforts to win Taiwanese hearts and minds through expanded economic integration across the Taiwan Strait.

Clinton's Engagement Policy toward China

When President Clinton came to office in January 1993, he oversaw the linking the US Congress's annual approval of China's most-favored-nation trading status to improvements in China's record on human rights.[14] This was consistent with Clinton's election campaign position, responding to popular US sentiment about the events at Tiananmen in 1989. In an October 1992 preelection debate with incumbent president George H. W. Bush, Clinton asserted about policy in China, "I would be firm." The United States should tell China, he said, to "observe human rights. . . . If we can stand up for our economics, we ought to be able to preserve the democratic interests of the people of China." He subsequently referred to Chinese leaders as the "butchers of Beijing" and criticized the Bush view "that we should give Most Favored Nation Status to

Chinese communists who deny their people's basic rights."[15] Clinton's remarks, of course, were designed to tar Bush with appeasing Beijing following Tiananmen, despite the Bush administration's levying of sanctions.

Within a year, Clinton had changed his tactic from "linkage politics" to unconditional engagement, as marked most prominently by the move to grant China permanent most-favored-nation (PMFN) status (now "permanent normal-trade-relation," or PNTR, status).[16] Throughout the Clinton presidency, Robert Sutter argues:

> U.S. leaders from the president on down emphasized that U.S. policy of engagement with China was premised on the belief that firm and constructive interaction with the Chinese leadership would steer the Chinese government away from possible assertive and disruptive policy leanings . . . toward policies of accommodation and cooperation with the United States and the prevailing international order.[17]

Engagement and its posited counterstrategy, containment, had long been seen as the dominant choices for US policy toward the PRC. Even in 1949–50, a strand of the US policy debate over "who lost China?" to communism reflected that, by attempting to isolate China through containment, the United States had created a greater enemy than if it had tried to cooperate with, and, implicitly, co-opt, the communists. But prior to the 1990s, while engagement had its supporters—particularly within the US Left but also among those in President Jimmy Carter's administration who advocated normalization—it failed to gain great traction or popular support. At the same time, many analysts believed that US actions actually *could* shape PRC behavior, that is, that PRC leaders did not have a predetermined future in mind and it made sense to adjust US policy.[18]

It is logically plausible that Clinton's about-face, away from the heat of the campaign and with the spotlight on Tiananmen fading, was spurred by recognition of the new global environment for US-China relations. With the collapse of the Soviet Union in 1991, the signing of defense cooperation and border dispute resolution agreements by Russia and China, and ultimately their formation in 1996 of a "strategic partnership," the Clinton administration faced considerable uncertainty about the prospects for both Chinese and Russian strategic alignments.[19]

But beyond considerations about the global strategic environment, domestic political factors in the United States also appear to have been influential.

After normalization of relations with China in 1979, the executive branch had been able to exercise nearly unilateral control over policy toward China. This changed substantially when congressional members, enraged over the events of 1989, mobilized in new ways to bind the hands of President Bush. Congressional efforts to punish China (notably through Congresswoman Nancy Pelosi's bill to protect the interests of Chinese students and dissidents in the United States and subsequent efforts to condition any renewal of most-favored-nation trading relations) required enormous management efforts from the White House at the same time that the Bush administration was making diplomatic efforts, for strategic reasons, to repair a highly strained relationship.[20] Over the next few years, congressional action became more and more geared toward changing PRC behavior on proliferation and trade but especially on human rights. It was quite clear that, without a different framing of US intentions in China and the benefits of more normal relations, the legislative-executive relationship would remain a hindrance to executive power in handling the China relationship.

Perhaps most important, the advent of the Clinton administration coincided with another trend in US politics: the American business community—those with economic interests in good relations with China—was becoming newly mobilized to influence US policy toward the PRC.[21] While US trade with China and foreign direct investment (FDI) there had grown in the 1980s, it was not until the early 1990s that both began to rise precipitously. Sino-US trade reached US$30 billion in 1994. Even more striking, growth over three years in equity joint ventures (all sources) in particular rose from $2.7 billion in 1990 to $55.1 billion in 1993.[22] Increasingly, US multinationals came to argue that they could no longer afford, competitively, not to be in China, and they proceeded at a greater rate to invest, open representative offices, and commence operations throughout China. In this context, US business advocacy groups such as the US-China Business Council grew in both membership and influence in US politics. Clinton's decision to delink China's trade status from its human rights record is seen as having been heavily influenced by lobbying on behalf of US business interests.[23] American businesses with offensive trade and investment interests in China could watch the domestic Chinese context of the early 1990s, moreover, and conclude that they were making a good bet. Their confidence was heightened, and concerns that China might roll back economic reforms allayed, with Deng Xiaoping's "Southern Tour" in early 1992, in which he declared unambiguously that reform, including China's opening to outside business interests, must continue if China was to modernize and compete in the world.

Also around this time administration officials became more sympathetic to delinking trade and human rights, a key step in the ultimate move—after Clinton's reelection in 1996—toward an unconditional engagement strategy. According to Sutter, in 1994 US officials involved in economy-related agencies—notably the Department of Commerce and the Treasury Department—became increasingly sympathetic to US business interests and, by extension we can presume, an engagement strategy.[24] The visit of Secretary of State Warren Christopher in March 1994, in which human rights issues took center stage, also revealed a tough line by the Chinese government about the linking of its trade status to human rights policy, even to the extent that Chinese security forces detained dissidents prior to the Christopher visit instead of softening their approach, as often had occurred prior to other visits. This hard-line PRC reaction suggested that the linkage strategy was not working, further isolating its advocates in Washington and leading to clear splits on China policy within the administration.[25]

Although by mid-1994 the Clinton administration officials most closely involved in China policy were already disillusioned with efforts to place human rights at the center of policy and to link it to the renewal of most-favored-nation status, other tensions with Beijing—notably over missile sales to Taiwan, the visit to the United States of Taiwanese president Lee Teng-hui, and nonproliferation and intellectual property issues—prevented any major rethinking of the relationship. Clinton's reelection in November 1996, however, precipitated a move to a more pure "engagement" policy centered around the framing idea that positive interactions, including economic interactions, were in the best interest of the United States and were more likely to achieve desired change in China. Clinton himself clearly announced the change of direction in November 1996.

> The emergence of a stable, an open, a prosperous China, a strong China confident of its place and willing to assume its responsibilities as a great nation is in our deepest interest. . . . What the United States wants is to sustain an engagement with China . . . in a way that will increase the chances that there will be more liberty and more prosperity and more genuine cooperation in the future.[26]

Whether it involved "delinking" or full-blown economic engagement, the turn toward a new policy had a threefold rationale. First, as indicated above, too much focus on China's human rights record only served to aggravate Beijing and make its leaders intransigent. Second, as US internationalist business interests stressed (to the increasing chagrin of labor), American economic interests were best served by a more positive bilateral environment. National Security Council deputy Sandy Berger, an advocate of this policy, is reported by Suettinger to have recognized that the president's domestic agenda would be best served by focusing on economic and trade interests with China.[27] Third, the argument made most often in public—such as in Clinton's comment—was that only through cooperative engagement could Washington encourage the kind of change in China that human rights and democracy advocates wanted to see. This line of reasoning was repeated in 2000 as the US Congress considered the administration's arguments to extend PNTR status to China, a key step toward its admission into the WTO: "China's entry into the WTO . . . is about more than our economic interests. It is clearly in our larger national interest. It represents the most significant opportunity that we have had to create positive change in China since the 1980s."[28] The logic underpinning the new engagement policy was somewhat fuzzy—it wasn't entirely clear how engagement would foster changes in Chinese behavior—but to the extent that it was spelled out it appeared to be primarily centered on the first face of security. More specifically, China's increased integration into global markets and institutions would socialize Chinese leaders into global norms and would restructure the incentives facing those leaders by giving China more of a stake in the existing global order.

This exploration of the Clinton administration's move toward engagement suggests the plausibility of our first hypothesis: an engagement strategy ostensibly about influencing China's future helped to frame US interests in a way that would build support for more open trade.

Conversely, Beijing has long been sensitive to perceived outside interference. China's suffering at the hands of imperial powers during the so-called Century of Humiliation has become a standard element of Chinese self-portrayal and is a core element of nationalism under the Chinese Communist Party.[29] Chinese worries about interference are not just memories of imperial times, however. Mao Zedong took umbrage at Secretary of State John Foster Dulles's strategy of "peaceful evolution"—designed to promote the evolution of socialist countries (including China) into systems more acceptable to the United States. Mao is quoted by party elder Bo Yibo as having said, "Dulles wants to change countries like ours. He wants to subvert and change us to follow his ideas. . . . Therefore, the United States is attempting to carry out its aggression and expansion with a much more deceptive tactic."[30] Later, perceived US support of Chinese protesters and dissidents involved in the 1989 Tiananmen movement led to charges in China that the United States was promoting "peaceful evolution."[31] In January 2012, President Hu Jintao once again raised the specter of US interference and called on China to beef up its own efforts to use Chinese culture (including the propaganda system) to fight US cultural hegemony. During many interludes, then, Beijing has pointed to efforts (perceived or real) by the US to meddle and promote regime change as something to be mobilized against.

It is not surprising, therefore, that President Clinton's switch to an economic engagement strategy elicited similar reactions from Beijing. As the administration began to dismantle the linkage policy in late 1993, it suggested that a new bilateral effort should be made to promote more high-level meetings and more intense dialogue, negotiations, and visits compared to those of the previous four years. While one might expect that Beijing welcomed this move away from harsh Tiananmen sanctions, instead it was assumed in some Beijing policy circles that the United States was pursuing a policy of "containment"—the polar opposite of what is intended by engagement.[32] The Xinhua news agency in 1995 proclaimed the US policy to be one of "westernization," an attempt to encourage liberalizing forces within and against the Chinese state.[33] One of China's foremost "America watchers," Chu Shulong, argued in 1996 that the US policy was "a mix of engagement and confrontation. . . . [T]he US says it wants to engage China, but engagement is the form, [and] containment is the real content."[34] To have engagement covering for containment would allow the United States maximum flexibility in its tactical negotiations with China. Of course, in the course of maneuvering to manage pragmatically its most complex bilateral relationship, Beijing's foreign policy leaders offered a mix of positive and negative reactions to initiatives made by the Clinton administration. But throughout it was made clear that China would not accede to US efforts to change Chinese policy, particularly in the area of human rights.[35]

In summary, this short case study confirms the plausibility of both our hypotheses. Using the language of engagement appears to have helped the Clinton administration build broader domestic support for closer commercial ties with the PRC, and domestic political factors appeared to motivate Clinton's interest in expanded commercial ties—at least in part. At the same time, however, explicitly framing trade with China as a force that would help change the PRC appears to have increased suspicion in China about US intentions. That is, by explicitly articulating US motivations—a desire to change China to make it more cooperative—the Clinton administration may have undercut the policy's effectiveness.

China's Economic Engagement Policy toward Taiwan

The relationship across the Taiwan Strait has been characterized for decades by tensions and occasional crises. The dispute centers on Taiwan's sovereign status—whether it is, or should be, a part of China—and dates to the end of the Chinese civil war, when the defeated Kuomintang (KMT or Nationalist Party) retreated to Taiwan. For decades the KMT viewed the PRC regime as illegitimate and claimed that the Republic of China (ROC) remained the legitimate government of all of China. For its part, the PRC viewed Taiwan as unfinished business from the civil war, Chinese territory that must ultimately be liberated and brought under PRC control.

Despite the persistence of the underlying sovereignty dispute, the nature of the conflict has shifted dramatically over time. In Taiwan gradual democratization ensured that Taiwan's status as a part of China became increasingly contested in political discourse. In this environment, President Lee Teng-hui (1988–2000) demanded a greater international profile for Taiwan and increasingly distanced himself from a "one China" principle. His successor, Chen Shui-bian (2000–2008) of the officially pro-independence Democratic Progressive Party (DPP), likewise refused to endorse the principle that Taiwan is a part of China. Chen took steps to weaken symbolic linkages between Taiwan and the mainland, while referring repeatedly it as a sovereign, independent country. The PRC's policy toward Taiwan also changed sharply after the 1970s. After establishing diplomatic ties with the United States on January 1, 1979, China's rhetoric shifted from highlighting the need to liberate the island to an emphasis on peaceful reunification premised on a high degree of Taiwanese autonomy (which later became known as the "one country, two systems" formula). This more conciliatory approach remained in place until the mid-1990s, when PRC leaders became alarmed, believing that Taiwan was moving toward formal independence. Since then the PRC policy has been a combination of tough measures meant to deter Taiwan's independence (such as, e.g., a growing number of missiles deployed within range of Taiwan and instances of bellicose rhetoric) and softer measures meant to entice Taiwan toward ultimate unification (such as increased cross-Strait exchanges). Relations across the Taiwan Strait have stabilized considerably since Ma Ying-jeou was elected Taiwan's president in 2008; compared to his two predecessors, Ma adopted a more conciliatory approach, focusing on the need for détente.

Economic engagement has been a key feature of PRC policy toward Taiwan since the late 1970s. China has consistently welcomed cross-Strait trade and investment flows, a point emphasized repeatedly in major Chinese policy statements related to Taiwan, including the 1981 Nine Points Plan, Jiang Zemin's 1995 Eight Points Proposal, and the 2005 Anti-Secession Law. China has implemented numerous policies designed to encourage increased economic exchange with Taiwan, ranging from the late 1970s decision to locate the original special economic zones (SEZs) near Taiwan (and, of course, Hong Kong) to investment protection provisions aimed at Taiwanese firms and the decision to pursue an Economic Cooperation Framework Agreement (ECFA) with the island. And the Chinese government has been quite frank in suggesting that it encourages cross-Strait economic integration in part because economic integration is conducive to the PRC objectives of blocking Taiwanese independence and fostering eventual unification with the island. For instance, President Jiang Zemin argued explicitly that increased economic ties with Taiwan would promote the goal of national unification.[36] And scholar You Ji writes that by the 1990s even a "portion of the PLA [People's Liberation Army] strongly endorsed the idea of tying Taiwan to the Mainland with 'economic ropes.'"[37] In other words, this is a case in which the deployment of economic statecraft clearly has preceded any effort to find a permanent resolution to the underlying political dispute. China's hope was that increased economic exchange would alter conceptions of national interest in Taiwan—thereby facilitating a political solution that corresponded to PRC preferences.

As relations have improved under the current Ma administration, PRC officials have stepped up efforts to "win Taiwan hearts and minds" (*qude Taiwan renxin*) through a range of commercial deals that benefit Taiwanese businesses and farmers. Since 2009 numerous senior provincial officials have taken high-profile trips to Taiwan—often with large delegations of local businessmen in tow—to sign agreements to purchase various products from Taiwan. In 2010, for instance, the governor of Fujian province led a delegation of over 2,000 to Taiwan; reports indicated that the visit resulted in orders from Taiwan that exceeded US$2 billion.[38] One recent highly publicized effort has focused on milkfish, a freshwater fish farmed in southern Taiwan (a DPP stronghold). The

Taiwanese milkfish industry has faced troubles in recent years, and in 2011 a state-owned PRC firm placed an order for the fish from the town of Syuejia (Xuejia) in Tainan County. Although marketing the fish in the PRC has proven difficult (it is boney, it has an earthy taste, and the first character of its name, *shi*, means "louse"), the PRC has continued to promote its export to the mainland. In early 2012, Zheng Lizhong, the deputy director of China's Association for Relations across the Taiwan Strait (ARATS), visited milkfish farmers in southern Taiwan; reports indicated that he had reached an agreement with local farmers that would facilitate the formation of a joint venture to promote the sale of milkfish in China.[39] The PRC clearly hopes that by pursuing this and similar ventures it will be able to influence the views of farmers in southern Taiwan, who tend to support the DPP, which, in addition to being officially pro-independence, has been much more skeptical of cross-Strait economic integration (including the ECFA) than the current Ma administration. Perhaps, recognizing the benefits that they are reaping from cross-Strait economic exchange, these farmers will be more inclined in future elections to support Taiwanese politicians more sympathetic to cross-Strait exchange and less interested in pushing sovereignty-related issues.[40] Thus, PRC efforts appear to be firmly rooted within a second-face-of-security logic.

At least two interesting questions, related to the hypotheses, emerge from this cursory discussion. First, why do officials and analysts in the PRC persistently frame cross-Strait economic exchange as facilitating political objectives? Second, to what extent do these political frames influence (1) perceptions among Taiwanese officials concerning the desirability of deeper economic exchange and (2) views that those benefiting from cross-Strait exchange hold on sovereignty-related issues? Here we offer just a few thoughts—mostly speculative—related to these questions.

Regarding the first question, clearly the PRC's economic engagement policy toward Taiwan has dovetailed nicely with broader reform and opening policies since the rise of Deng Xiaoping in the late 1970s. Leaders since Deng have persistently painted economic development as China's foremost priority and have pursued a development strategy dependent on integration into global markets. Economic integration with Taiwan, of course, facilitates broader development goals directly: capital from Taiwan has been enormously beneficial to the PRC.[41] But indirectly an engagement strategy offers the promise of a path toward unification that is not premised on the use of military instruments. That is, engagement offers a way to achieve the "core" national objective of unification without putting at risk the arguably more fundamental goal of economic development—as a military conflict in the Taiwan Strait would most certainly do. The promise of engagement-induced unification, then, allows reformist leaders to brush back two types of criticism that might emerge as a consequence of PRC efforts to promote cross-Strait economic exchange and in particular to attract Taiwanese capital to the mainland. First, it provides a potent counter to those opposed to deepening economic ties for straightforward economic (i.e., protectionist) reasons; those who oppose the policy thus potentially run the risk of being cast as unpatriotic.[42] Second, it allows leaders to preempt national-ist critics who might accuse government officials of sacrificing reunification of the motherland for the sake of getting rich. Engagement allows leaders to have their cake and eat it too.

This is not to say that the PRC's engagement policy toward Taiwan is simply a cynical way to frame the leadership's preferred cross-Strait economic poli-cies; we have no reason to believe that these sorts of arguments are not sincere. Indeed, the arguments would stand little chance of persuading nationalists or protectionists unless they were at least plausible. But, by openly framing poli-cies in this way, leaders run the risk of undercutting the efficacy of engage-ment by increasing suspicions in Taiwan. We thus suspect—though again our argument is highly speculative—that a domestic political logic drives the open articulation of an engagement frame by PRC leaders.

And it is quite clear that PRC openness about its political motivations in pursuing cross-Strait exchange raises suspicions in Taiwan. First, officials and societal groups opposed to deepening exchange sometimes point to the PRC's political motivations as a reason to be skeptical. For instance, Tsai Ing-Wen, the 2012 DPP presidential candidate and former party chair, repeatedly suggested in 2010 that the reason the PRC was willing to make concessions to Taiwan in the ECFA negotiations was because China had "ulterior motives" and expected something in return.[43] Lee Teng-hui in 2005 described Hu Jintao's efforts to promote a softer line toward Taiwan as seeking to "buy" the loyalty of Taiwan-ese (*shoumai Taiwan renxin*); DPP politicians and pro-DPP media have por-trayed recent PRC buying sprees in Taiwan using the same term.[44] But, perhaps more fundamentally, PRC efforts have the potential to backfire at the individual level because they can be perceived as insulting. A study by the Taiwan publica-tion *Business Weekly*, for instance, found little evidence that the PRC's milkfish initiative was changing the voting behavior of local fish farmers. While local farmers were strongly supportive of the milkfish deal, they still overwhelmingly indicated that they intended to support Tsai over Ma in the 2012 election; moreover, while Ma supporters credited government policies with facilitating the deal, Tsai supporters credited the hard work of local farmers.[45] One expert following the case suggested a key reason for the limited initial results was that "the big fanfare China made about how much money it was spending to buy milkfish from Taiwan offended Taiwanese people's sense of dignity."[46]

Our analysis in this section is obviously highly speculative. Nevertheless, we believe the cross-Strait case on balance further suggests the plausibility of our hypotheses.

Conclusion

This chapter has aimed to contribute to the growing literature on economic engagement by proposing two straightforward hypotheses. First, the rhetoric of economic engagement serves as a useful frame for political leaders seeking to mobilize public support behind liberal foreign economic policies—especially when those policies are directed at adversarial countries. Second, the public articulation of engagement strategies can undercut their efficacy in target countries because they raise suspicions and can be insulting to target audiences. Two short case studies served to underscore the plausibility of the hypotheses.

More broadly, our argument and case studies offer a cautionary tale concerning the efficacy of economic inducements aimed at an adversary's society. While spelling out the logic of these policies can be useful in building support for them in the sending country, it can also raise suspicions in the target and thereby undercut the utility of the strategy. To answer the fourth question posed by Ripsman and Lobell, there seem to be clear limits to how far these sorts of engagement policies can go in promoting deeper reconciliation. Relations between the United States and China are still tense at times, and trust between Washington and Beijing is—to say the least—often in short supply. While relations across the Taiwan Strait have stabilized greatly in recent years, the PRC's engagement policy has not yielded a fundamentally transformed relationship. Beijing's bottom line—that Taiwan is a part of China and must ultimately be reunified with the rest of the country—remains unchanged; meanwhile, support for unification among Taiwan's citizens has never been lower. Although President Ma briefly floated the idea of a cross-Strait peace agreement in the fall of 2011, he came under withering domestic criticism and quickly dropped the idea. The long-term durability of the present détente, in short, is hardly guaranteed.

In turn we might speculate briefly on the timing of economic statecraft, the third question posed by Ripsman and Lobell. As noted earlier, the cross-Strait case is clearly one in which economic statecraft was deployed prior to a concerted effort to find a lasting settlement of the political dispute. China's hope has been that economic integration would alter preferences in Taiwan—and thereby facilitate a settlement on Beijing's terms. Clearly, China's economic statecraft has not yielded a political resolution. One might thus be tempted to ask the counterfactual question: would inducements have been more effective if Beijing had demanded political progress as a condition for access to China's growing market? That is, would economic statecraft have been more effective had it been timed to coincide with a political process rather than helping to pave the way for a political process? Given the pitfalls of counterfactual reasoning, we demur, except to emphasize two points. First, the PRC clearly derived tremendous economic benefit from cross-Strait trade and investment flows; making those flows conditional on improved relations would have been costly and perhaps not credible. Second, although economic inducements have not led to a resolution of the underlying sovereignty dispute, this does not mean cross-Strait economic integration has not been stabilizing. The costs of a cross-Strait military conflict would be tremendous for both sides—and it is certain that deepening economic ties would raise those costs substantially. Seen in this light, there have been clear advantages to allowing economic integration to precede deeper political reconciliation.

In closing, our preliminary analysis in this chapter suggests that it may be worthwhile for future researchers to evaluate our hypotheses in more systematic fashion. The first hypothesis, in particular, is well suited to testing using simple survey experiments.[47] A simple design, in which some subjects are exposed to an "engagement frame" to a question about trade with an adversary while others are not, may offer some leverage here (especially if other frames—similar to those used by Hiscox—are included in some groups).[48] Designing compelling experimental tests of the second hypothesis may prove more daunting, but nonetheless it strikes us as doable. For instance, a survey of Taiwanese farmers asking about a hypothetical PRC trade agreement might be useful here. In such an experiment, some of the subjects could be primed with a frame that mentions PRC political motivations. Assessing the impact of engagement on identity or voting behavior strikes us as more difficult still. Despite the hurdles involved, further research may be worthwhile simply because our hypotheses, if confirmed, have considerable implications for efforts to gauge the efficacy of economic engagement policies.

NOTES

1. For simplicity, we refer to the country initiating an engagement policy as the "sending country" and the country that is the target of an engagement policy as the "target country."

2. Daniel W. Drezner, "The Hidden Hand of Economic Coercion," *International Organization* 57 (Summer 2003): 643–59.

3. David A. Baldwin, "The Sanctions Debate and the Logic of Choice," *International Security* 24, no. 3 (1999–2000): 80–107, provides a good overview of the problems inherent in assessing the effectiveness of economic sanctions. On the efficacy of sanctions, see also Robert A. Pape, "Why Economic Sanctions Do Not Work," *International Security* 22, no. 2 (1997): 90–136; Gary Clyde Hufbauer, Jeffrey J. Schott, and Kimberly Ann Elliot, *Economic Sanctions Reconsidered* (Washington, DC: Institute for International Economics, 1985); and David M. Rowe, "Economic Sanctions Do Work: Economic Statecraft and the Oil Embargo of Rhodesia," *Security Studies* 9, nos. 1–2 (1999–2000): 254–87. Existing studies have also identified numerous factors that might condition the effectiveness of economic sanctions, including their comprehensiveness and the extent to which they are combined with other coercive instruments, the availability of alternative suppliers of sanctioned goods and the extent to which such suppliers are willing to join the sanctioning regime, expectations of future conflict between the sending and the target state, and the nature of the governing coalition in the target country. See, for instance, Jean-Marc F. Blanchard and Norrin M. Ripsman, "Asking the Right Questions: When Do Economic Sanctions Work Best?," *Security Studies* 9, nos. 1–2 (1999–2000): 219–53; Daniel W. Drezner, "Bad Debts: Assessing China's Financial Influence in Great Power Politics," *International Security* 34, no. 2 (2009): 7–45; Stephan Haggard and Marcus Noland, *Engaging North Korea: The Role of Economic Statecraft*, East West Center Policy Studies, no. 59 (Honolulu: East West Center, 2011); and Risa A. Brooks, "Sanctions and Regime Type: What Works and When?" *Security Studies* 11, no. 4 (2002): 1–50.

4. For studies of engagement, see Miles Kahler and Scott L. Kastner, "Strategic Uses of Economic Interdependence: Engagement Policies on the Korean Peninsula and across the Taiwan Strait," *Journal of Peace Research* 43, no. 5 (2006): 523–41; Daniel W. Drezner, "The Trouble with Carrots: Transaction Costs, Conflict Expec-

tations, and Economic Inducements," *Security Studies* 9, nos. 1–2 (1999–2000): 188–218; Michael Mastanduno, *Economic Containment: COCOM and the Politics of East-West Trade* (Ithaca: Cornell University Press, 1992); David A. Baldwin, *Economic Statecraft* (Princeton: Princeton University Press, 1985); Rawi Abdelal and Jonathan Kirshner, "Strategy, Economic Relations, and the Definition of National Interests," *Security Studies* 9, nos. 1–2 (1999–2000): 119–56; Albert O. Hirschman, *National Power and the Structure of Foreign Trade* (Berkeley: University of California Press, 1945); Christina L. Davis, "Linkage Diplomacy: Economic and Security Bargaining in the Anglo-Japanese Alliance, 1902–23," *International Security* 33, no. 3 (2008–9): 143–79; Paul A. Papayoanou and Scott L. Kastner, "Sleeping with the (Potential) Enemy: Assessing the U.S. Policy of Engagement with China," *Security Studies* 9, nos. 1–2 (1999–2000): 157–87; and Steven E. Lobell, "Second Face of Security Strategies: Anglo-German and Anglo-Japanese Trade Concessions during the 1930s," *Security Studies* 17, no. 3 (2008): 438–67.

5. Mastanduno, *Economic Containment*; Drezner, "Trouble with Carrots"; Kahler and Kastner, "Strategic Uses of Economic Interdependence."

6. For an elaboration of these points, see Kahler and Kastner, "Strategic Uses of Economic Interdependence." Studies that focus on these sorts of second-face, transformational effects include Hirschman, *National Power and the Structure of Foreign Trade*; Abdelal and Kirshner, "Strategy, Economic Relations, and the Definition of National Interests"; and Lobell, "Second Face of Security Strategies."

7. Mastanduno, "The Strategy of Economic Engagement."

8. Michael J. Hiscox, in "Through a Glass and Darkly: Attitudes toward International Trade and the Curious Effects of Issue Framing," *International Organization* 60, no. 3 (2006): 755–80, conducts a survey experiment and finds that negative frames (which emphasize potential job losses) significantly reduce support for trade, while positive frames (which emphasize lower prices) have little effect.

9. Edward D. Mansfield and Diana C. Mutz, "Support for Free Trade: Self-Interest, Sociotropic Politics, and Out-Group Anxiety," *International Organization* 63, no. 3 (2009): 425–57.

Though for an alternative interpretation of these findings, see Benjamin O. Fordham and Katja B. Kleinberg, "How Can Economic Interests Influence Support for Free Trade," *International Organization* 66, no. 2 (2012): 311–28.

10. Patrick Buchanan, "Free Trade vs. National Security," *Buchanan.org* (blog), May 26, 1998, http://buchanan.org/blog/pjb-free-trade-vs-national-security-305.

11. "Trade Deficit with China Rises in May: Alliance for American Manufacturing (AAM) Statement," July 3, 2013, Alliance for American Manufacturing: http://www.americanmanufacturing.org/press-releases/entry/trade-deficit-with-china-rises-in-may-alliance-for-american-manufacturing-a (accessed Aug. 11, 2015).

12. See, for instance, James Heyman and Dan Ariely, "Effort for Payment: A Tale of Two Markets," *Psychological Science* 15, no. 11 (2004): 787–93. In one experiment, for example, the authors found that students were significantly less willing to help move a sofa for low payment than they were for no payment. A large literature considers the impact of incentives on effort and how incentives can undermine motivation to participate in socially desirable activities (such as donating blood). For a review of some of this literature, see Uri Gneezy and Aldo Rustichini, "Pay Enough or Don't Pay at All," *Quarterly Journal of Economics* 115, no. 3 (2000): 791–810, which concludes through a series of experiments that small monetary incentives can backfire (being perceived as insulting perhaps), but large incentives tend to improve performance.

13. For an extended discussion, see Dan Ariely, *Predictably Irrational: The Hidden Forces that Shape Our Decisions* (New York: Harper, 2008).

14. Robert Sutter, *Chinese Foreign Relations: Power and Policy since the Cold War*, 3rd ed. (Lanham, MD: Rowman and Littlefield, 2012).

15. Peter Baker, "Bush, Clinton, and China," *Washington Post*, April 8, 2008, http://voices.washingtonpost.com/44/2008/04/bush-clinton-and-china.html.

16. Congress did not grant PNTR status to China until near the end of the Clinton administration, in 2000.

17. Sutter, *Chinese Foreign Relations,* 8.

18. A categorization of foreign views according to, among other things, the ability of Beijing to be influenced can be found in Aaron L. Freidberg, "The Future of U.S.-China Relations: Is Conflict Inevitable?," *International Security* 30, no. 2 (2005): 7–45. On the mid-1990s, see David Shambaugh, "Containment or Engagement of China: Calculating Beijing's Responses," *International Security* 21, no. 2 (1996): 180–209.

19. Sutter, *Chinese Foreign Relations.*

20. Robert Suettinger, *Beyond Tiananmen* (Washington, DC: Brookings Institution Press, 2003).

21. American defensive trade interests did not turn their sights on China until the early 2000s, after China joined the WTO in 2001. Suettinger, in *Beyond Tiananmen,* notes that in the late years of the Bush administration, lobbying by outside groups—on human rights and business—was not yet crucial in determining congressional votes on most-favored-nation status.

22. Harry Broadman and X. Sun, "The Distribution of Foreign Direct Investment in China," *World Economy* 20, no. 3 (1997): 339–61.

23. Robert Sutter and Kerry Dumbaugh, *China-U.S. Relations,* Issue Briefs, no. 94002 (Washington, DC: Congressional Research Service, 1996); David M. Lampton, "America's China Policy in the Age of the Finance Minister: Clinton Ends Linkage," *China Quarterly* 139 (September 1994): 597–621.

24. As criticism of the Christopher trip escalated, economic agencies within the Cabinet also became more active in trying to protect US economic interests in the relationship. See Suettinger, *Beyond Tiananmen*.

25. Sutter, *Chinese Foreign Relations*; Suettinger, *Beyond Tiananmen*.

26. Suettinger, *Beyond Tiananmen*, 283.

27. Ibid.

28. Ibid., 393.

29. He Yinan, "History, Chinese Nationalism, and the Emerging Sino-Japanese Conflict," *Journal of Contemporary China* 16, no. 50 (2007): 1–24.

30. Geremie Barmé, "The Harmonious Evolution of Information in China," *China Beat* January 29, 2010, http://www.thechinabeat.org/?p=1422.

31. Beijing also launched a campaign against what it termed US "peaceful evolution" strategies following the Tiananmen crackdown.

32. Suettinger, *Beyond Tiananmen*.

33. Xinbo Wu, "China: Security Practice of a Modernizing and Ascending Power," in Muthiah Alagappa, ed., *Asian Security Practice: Material and Ideational Influences* (Stanford, CA: Stanford University Press, 1998), 115–56.

34. Phillip C. Saunders, "China's America Watchers: Changing Attitudes Towards the United States," *China Quarterly* 161 (March 2000): 47.

35. Interestingly, Saunders argues that during the 1990s, Chinese scholars and government analysts who were critical of the nationalist turn against the United States following Tiananmen often self-censored or even wrote under pseudonyms, as it was too risky to challenge views alleging containment and "peaceful evolution" (ibid.).

36. Suisheng Zhao, "Economic Interdependence and Political Divergence: A Background Analysis of the Taiwan Strait Crisis," in Suisheng Zhao, ed., *Across the Taiwan Strait: Mainland China, Taiwan, and the 1995–1996 Crisis* (New York: Routledge, 1999), 21–40.

37. You Ji, "Taiwan in the Political Calculations of the Chinese Leadership," *China Journal* 36 (July 1996): 122.

38. "China Flaunts Buying Power," *Taipei Times*, May 15, 2010, http://www.taipeitimes.com/News/taiwan/archives/2010/05/15/2003473036.

39. See Annie Huang, "China Uses Trade to Influence Taiwan Election," Associated Press, January 9, 2012, available at http://news.yahoo.com/china-uses-trade-influence-taiwan-election-081715266.html; Sophia Wu, "Talk of the Day: Beijing's New Strategies toward Taiwan," *Focus Taiwan* (Taiwan Central News Agency), February 24, 2012; Jens Kastner, "Mainland Slips on Fishy Plan to Boost Cross-Strait Business," *Taiwan Reports*, March 23, 2012, http://taiwanreports.wordpress.com/2012/03/23/mainland-slips-on-fishy-plan-to-boost-cross-strait-business/. The ARATS is China's quasi-official organization tasked with negotiating with Taiwan.

40. Analysts in the PRC sometimes framed ECFA as undercutting the support in Taiwan for independence. See, for instance, Yin Maoxiang, "Jiedu ECFA Zhengzhi Xiaoying," *Zhongguo Wang*, July 20, 2010, http://www.china.com.cn/news/tw/2010-07/20/content_20538624_2.htm.

41. For example, see Douglas B. Fuller, "The Cross-Strait Economic Relationship's Impact on Development in Taiwan and China: Adversaries and Partners," *Asian Survey* 48, no. 2 (2008): 239–64; You-tien Hsing, *Making Capitalism in China: The Taiwan Connection* (New York: Oxford University Press, 1998); and John Q. Tian, *Government, Business, and the Politics of Interdependence and Conflict across the Taiwan Strait* (New York: Palgrave, 2006).

42. For an example of a protectionist critique of ECFA, see Zhang Luqiang, "ECFA Dui Dalu Bi Dayu Li, Yingdang Huanxing," *Lianhe Zaobao Wang*, December 24, 2009, http://www.zaobao.com/special/china/taiwan/pages12/taiwan091224a.shtml.

43. See, for instance, "Talks End with No Early Harvest List," *Taipei Times*, June 15, 2010, http://www.taipeitimes.com/News/front/archives/2010/06/15/2003475536.

44. See "Taiwan Qianzongtong Li Denghui Di Huashengdun Fangwen," *Da Ji Yuan*, October 18, 2005; Xie Weicheng, "Beijing Zhaofu Nan Taiwan," *Ziyou Shibao*, February 16, 2012; and Li Wenzhong, "Tanpan Shishang Zuiguaide ECFA," *Ziyou Shibao*, April 12, 2010.

45. "2012 Elections: Milkfish Order Would Not Sway Voters, Poll Finds," *Taipei Times*, October 29, 2011, 3.

46. Du Yu, "Chinese Delegation Comes Fishing," *Taipei Times*, February 25, 2012, 8.

47. Survey experiments are proving increasingly possible in the PRC. See particularly Peter Hays Gries, Jennifer L. Prewitt-Freilino, Luz-Eugenia Cox-Fuenzalida, and Qingmin Zhang, "Contentious Histories and the Perception of Threat: China, the U.S., and the Korean War, an Experimental Analysis," *Journal of East Asian Studies* 3, no. 3 (2009): 433–65; and Peter Hays Gries, "Experimental Methods and Psychological Measures in the Study of Chinese Foreign Policy," in Allen Carlson, Mary E. Gallagher, Kenneth Lieberthal, and Melanie Manion, eds., *Contemporary Chinese Politics: New Sources, Methods, and Field Strategies* (Cambridge: Cambridge University Press, 2010).

48. Hiscox, "Through a Glass and Darkly."

CHAPTER 8

Economic Statecraft as a Tool of Peacemaking?

China's Relationships with India and Russia

William Norris

This chapter examines the use of economic statecraft as a tool of peacemaking in China's relations with two of its most important great power neighbors: Russia and India.[1] As is well known in the realist tradition of international relations, power—especially on one's border—constitutes a potential threat. Such fears are well grounded in China's historical experience. In fact, throughout its long history, the periphery of China has frequently been the source of external invasions and conquest. China's contested peripheral boundaries provide fertile hunting ground for exploring peacemaking efforts.

The overarching inquiry motivating this book is how economic statecraft can be used to encourage peacemaking between regional rivals. In particular, can economic statecraft be used effectively to drive the peace process forward? The "Introduction," by Norrin M Ripsman and Steven E. Lobell, provided a number of questions related to the timing, sequencing, and targeting of economic statecraft as a peacemaking tool of national power. The cases examined in this chapter will explore whether economic statecraft, including incentives and sanctions, has been an effective method of forging regional peace.

The other questions I examine more briefly involve the targets and timing of economic statecraft. Broadly speaking, economic statecraft has not been the leading edge driving regional peace in either of these cases. To the extent that economics has played a role in facilitating peacemaking, it has been as a consolidating engine. Only after both sides have mustered the political and diplomatic will to forge a peace can economics backfill to help stabilize the relationships. When economics helps to reassure the parties and build longer-term cooperative dynamics, such patterns of trade and investment can solidify and reinforce a regional peace. I find support for Ripsman's proposition that most successful peacemaking endeavors start as "top-down" settlements reached by the political elites of states.[2] Economic ties tend to come afterward as part of a general effort to solidify a negotiated peace.

Perhaps, somewhat unexpectedly, one limitation of economic statecraft is that it can serve as a driver feeding regional suspicions and insecurities. When economic activity is perceived to be advancing the goals of one side at the expense of the other or when economic interests are viewed as agents of an expansionist state or even when economic growth is seen as fueling a generally rising power, the economic activity can produce security consequences that actually work against peacemaking efforts. Similar to the findings of Jean-Marc F. Blanchard in chapter 6, I think of these as the security externalities that result from economic interaction. These externalities can be positive or negative for the states involved. They need not necessarily be zero-sum, although they sometimes are. When states deliberately seek to shape the behavior of commercial actors so as to generate such security externalities, states are engaging in economic statecraft. It is important to recognize that sometimes states may not be deliberately seeking to use economic statecraft, but the commercial actors' pursuit of "normal" economic activity might, nonetheless, produce security externalities for the states involved. As we see in contemporary Chinese-Russian relations in the Russian Far East (RFE), "normal" economic activity in an insecure and highly sensitive regional rivalry context can carry important strategic ramifications for the states concerned. But, before we examine the contemporary role of economics and its relationship to regional peace, we will explore the historical role that economics has played in Sino-Soviet relations.

Economic Statecraft and Peacemaking in the Broader Historical Context

Although this chapter will focus on the modern Sino-Russian relationship, it is important to note that the strategic distrust between these two great powers has a much longer historical antecedent. Contemporary relations are inescapably anchored in this larger historical context. Since the Ming dynasty, the Russian Empire has historically been fairly aggressive as it sought to consolidate its sprawling domain and test the limits of its ability to project power into Asia. Russian expansionism would eventually come to test the strength of both the late Ming and Qing Chinese dynastic boundaries. Although the early Qing enjoyed a respectable military advantage over the expanding czarist presence, Russia was able to take advantage of both the fading Ming and late-nineteenth-century Qing weakness. Czarist Russia would participate in China's colonial experience right up to the end of czarist rule itself. Although the new Soviet Union would eventually find fertile ground for exporting its Communist revolution to China, even this ideological compatibility provided only a short-lived respite to the uneasy great power neighbors. Indeed, even as the People's Republic of China (PRC) was being established, the honeymoon period of Mao Zedong's "leaning to one side" policy seemed all too short. Disagreements over the very ideology that bound these Cold War allies together and a host of other factors would eventually result in the Sino-Soviet split a decade later. China's subsequent international realignment and the economic reform path it embarked on would come to redefine the contemporary PRC. Throughout this history, these two polities have interacted with each other on both strategic and economic terms. This portion of the chapter unpacks the causal connections between economic statecraft and the process of peacemaking in the Sino-Russian relationship.

I have chosen to focus on three specific periods of conflict and/or peace-making in the Sino-Russian relationship with a view toward examining the strategic role that economics may have played during them.[3] The cases I examine are early Cold War cooperation, the border skirmish on Zhenbao Island in 1969 during the height of the Sino-Soviet split, and finally the repairing of Sino-Russian relations at end of the Cold War. In each of these cases, I focus on how (if at all) the economic dynamics played into peacemaking.

"Leaning to One Side"

The relative weakness of the Chinese polity characterized the regional security dynamics until 1949 when the PRC was established. Up to that time, other regional powers, such as Russia and Japan, would continue to take advantage of internal instability and general weakness in China dating back to the Opium Wars of the mid-nineteenth century. In 1949, however, several factors converged to bring about the beginning of what constitutes the first case in this analysis of economic statecraft and regional peacemaking in Sino-Russian relations. With the decisive defeat of Japan at the end of World War II, the great power regional dynamics reverted to revolving around the Sino-Russian relationship. With the overthrow of the czar in 1917, a new regime was created: the Union of Soviet Socialist Republics (Soviet Union or USSR). The institutional and ideological ties between the Communist Party of China and the Soviet Communist Party would lay the foundation for this phase of the Sino-Russian relationship.

Although strikingly brief, this period represents what is perhaps the highwater mark of economic and strategic cooperation between Russia and China. During this early Cold War period, both the USSR and the PRC shared a common enemy in a hostile US-led capitalist order. When Mao established the PRC in October 1949, China had very few strategic options. The country had endured decades of civil war and was economically decimated. By June 1950 it would find itself enmeshed in a regional conflict of epic proportions: the Korean War. Under these circumstances it is not difficult to understand Mao's strategic decision to "lean to one side" and align China with the USSR. On February 14, 1950, the Soviet Union and the PRCsigned the Sino-Soviet Treaty of Friendship, Alliance, and Mutual Assistance. As the Cold War began to unfurl in Asia, the USSR and the PRC were initially able to enjoy some of the closest strategic cooperation to characterize the Sino-Russian relationship since the earliest encounters of the seventeenth century. It seems natural, then, for this study to inquire about the role that economic statecraft may have played in bringing about this period of relative tranquility.

As a part of the alliance, the Soviet Union would provide a good deal of foreign aid in the form of direct economic and development assistance to China. In addition to the provision of an important $300 million loan, Soviet advisers were instrumental in sharing scientific and industrial technologies to help with China's modernization efforts. Although these advisers would be withdrawn by the late 1950s, their initial presence and contributions to China's scientific, military, and industrial development were important.[4] Between 1950 and 1956, trade between the Soviet Union and the PRC increased six and a half times. By 1955, more than 60 percent of China's trade in goods was with the Soviet Union.[5] This economic statecraft was a state-based expression of transparty cooperation between Cold War communist allies.

It would, however, be incomplete to consider this economic statecraft in the absence of the important ideological common ground between the USSR and the PRC. Mao held a view that the US-led imperialist camp was intent on subverting the Communist cause. The Soviet Union and the PRC were to be united in their anti-imperialist vision, and the economic relationship was simply a natural extension of that ideologically based strategic cooperation. Thus, the Sino-Soviet peacemaking that we observe during this period is only partially attributable to economic statecraft. Clearly, the much larger driver of this treaty alliance was the common ideological ground and shared geostrategic interests of the USSR and the PRC in the early 1950s. A more accurate accounting of the causality in this case would note that both the economic aid and the regional peace were caused by ideological compatibility, which generated shared strategic interests during this period. This causal logic is clearly borne out by the next case, in which we observe the breakdown of this ideological bond and the subsequent souring of the Sino-Soviet relationship, which ultimately would manifest itself once more (as it had during the colonial period) in blood along their eastern boundary.

Peacemaking in the Wake of the 1969 Border Conflict

The second historical case of regional peacemaking starts with the Sino-Soviet split of the late 1950s. Although this case of regional conflict is complex and a thorough treatment of the Sino-Soviet split would fill volumes, for our purposes, I focus only on how the breakdown of the amity that characterized the previous case bears on the regional border conflict that erupted in March 1969. Whereas the previous case involved the role of economic statecraft as it related to the Sino-Soviet alliance, this case explores the breakdown in that relationship and the eventual Cold War border conflict between two nuclear superpowers.

Once again economics plays only an indirect role in explaining the breakdown of the relationship. The more significant factor is the ideological divergence that emerged between Mao and the Soviet Union following the death of Stalin.[6] As Mao began to adopt the rural and peasant-oriented economic development policies that he felt were better suited to Chinese conditions, it became increasingly clear that his interpretation of Marxist-Leninist thinking as he was adapting it to China's situation did not conform to the version espoused by Moscow. When Nikita Khrushchev gave his "Secret Speech" in 1956, in which he criticized Stalin, Mao became convinced that the USSR had lost the vision and resolve required to lead the world communist revolution.[7]

By promoting an alternative interpretation of communism based on China's own peasant-oriented experience, Mao was laying claim to the ideological leadership of the movement. Given the importance for legitimacy of these communist regimes, such an ideological challenge was inherently threatening to the other side. Although relations would sour and progressively worsen though the rest of the 1950s and into the 1960s, the division did not generate outright conflict until 1969 when China ambushed a Russian patrol on Zhenbao Island, located in the Ussuri River.[8] As relations worsened, the two sides mobilized additional military forces on their borders. By 1968, the Soviet Union had 16 divisions stationed on the Sino-Soviet border. These were arrayed against 47 Chinese divisions.[9]

So what drove the particular clash on Zhenbao Island? Was there a significant breakdown of some sort of economic ties that previously bound both sides and held the growing tensions in check? As it turns out, economic statecraft (or the absence of it) did not feature prominently in explaining the outbreak of this regional conflict. To the extent that economics did factor in, it was via the ideological implications of Mao's direction of communist economic development in China in the late 1950s that initially fueled the Sino-Soviet split. The conflict on Zhenbao Island was largely precipitated by Chinese military provocations in the context of the split. Despite effective Soviet control over most of the area's islands, Mao had been providing indications, both directly to the USSR and indirectly to visiting delegations, that previous treaties that had established the boundary were a legacy of China's "unequal treaties" and thus unjust and in need of reconsideration. On February 19, 1969, the green light was given to the Heilongjiang provincial military command to conduct an ambush on Zhenbao Island.[10] On March 2, 1969, Chinese forces ambushed Soviet border guards on the island, killing more than 30. On March 15, the Soviets struck back with artillery fire and four T-62 tanks but were unable to retake the island. Tensions ratcheted up quickly, with both sides making nuclear allusions. In August the second secretary of the Soviet embassy in Washington even broached the possibility of a strike on China's nuclear facilities over a lunch with an American diplomat to gauge possible US responses should the conflict escalate.[11] China was seriously preparing for a Soviet nuclear strike during the late summer and early fall of 1969. Although the strike never materialized, both sides would maintain a highly militarized border for the duration of the Cold War.

A modus vivendi would gradually emerge, but peace would not really return to the Sino-Russian relationship until the end of the Cold War. Mikhail

Gorbachev was instrumental in deescalating what had become a long-standing source of tension in Sino-Russian relations. His visit on the eve of the Tiananmen Square incident in 1989 was the culmination of increasingly high-level diplomatic efforts to make peace in the region. These efforts would eventually result in the May 1991 Sino-Soviet Border Demarcation Agreement. When the Soviet Union dissolved, the Russian Federation continued with the peacemaking effort. The agreement that was ratified in February 1992 left a few of the more difficult islands for later negotiations. The status of these was eventually resolved by the 2004 Complementary Agreement between the PRCand the Russian Federation on the Eastern Section of the China–Russia Boundary, which was ratified by both sides in the spring of 2005. This resolution of the border dispute was really the first time that the two sides were able to relax their forward-deployed positions.[12] So what was the role played by economic statecraft in the context of driving this peacemaking effort?

Once again economic relations accelerated only in the wake of the larger diplomatic/political peacemaking efforts. Throughout the 1990s and into the 2000s, Sino-Russian economic relations improved dramatically. Deng Xiaoping's southern tour in 1992 relaunched China's economic liberalization efforts. This timing coincided with the shock therapy efforts in the Russian Federation. As Russia encountered difficult economic headwinds in the aftermath of the 1998 ruble crisis, China provided a ready market for one of the former Soviet Union's most competitive products: military equipment. Sales of military equipment from the former Soviet Union to China during this period accelerated rapidly and was an instrumental part of Sino-Russian cooperation.[13] The arms sales and other Sino-Russian trade helped to reinforce the peacemaking efforts, but their primary motivation seems to have been driven by a Russia in search of markets and supplies of consumer goods on the one hand and a modernizing China in need of advanced military hardware and raw material resources to feed its rapidly growing economy on the other. To the extent that these economic relationships in the 1990s and 2000s helped to reinforce and solidify the peacemaking effort, they offer some additional empirical evidence in support of Ripsman's hypothesized sequencing of economic statecraft—that economics can be used to reinforce top-down, state-led peacemaking efforts.

Tellingly, these economic relations eventually seem to have grown into a source of strategic concern in the Sino-Russian relationship. As we will see in the final Sino-Russian case study, the underlying insecurity that is still present in the relationship continues to contextualize the economic interaction between the two states. In such an environment, we might not be surprised to learn that trade flows primarily rooted in advanced military platforms and strategic raw materials have a tendency to generate long-term security concerns about the consequences of such technology transfer and market dependence.

Economic Statecraft and Peacemaking in the Contemporary Sino-Russian Relationship

As should be evident by this point, the Sino-Russian relationship has been fraught with strategic regional competition from the very earliest encounters between the two polities. However, this relationship has also witnessed a series of regional peacemaking efforts. The historical case studies above explore the role that economics has played in these peacemaking efforts. In this section, I examine the economic dimensions of the contemporary Sino Russian strategic relationship. In particular, I have chosen to focus on two specific contemporary regional empirical contexts: the two sides' differing visions for the Shanghai Cooperation Organization (SCO) and the strategic concerns stemming from China's economic engagement with the RFE.

With the open break of the Sino-Soviet split, a regional rivalry emerged, and both sides engaged in a competition for influence. Even with the end of the Cold War, the region still seems decidedly unsettled due to latent competition for regional influence between a declining Russia and a rising China. The creation of the SCO in 2001 provided a multilateral institution that could facilitate cooperation in Central Asia. The institutional development of the SCO, however, suggests that the formalization of the regional economic grouping has not done much to ameliorate the underlying great power competition. If anything, the SCO and the need to agree on its mission and agenda merely institutionalized the realm of regional contestation. This multinational forum provides an interesting institutionalized setting for examining the underlying struggle for regional influence between Russia and China. Russia prefers to see the SCO function primarily as a security-oriented regional cooperation organization (thus playing into Russia's relative strength).[14] This stands in contrast to China's preferred version of the SCO, which would look more like a cooperative, regional economic organization (thus complementing China's strengths).[15] The SCO case suggests that if a great power rivalry exists in a region, simply institutionalizing it will only serve to channel the regional great power competition and the alignment of smaller regional players.

Beyond the SCO, China's economically motivated strategy also colors its relations with the RFE. The RFE is an important source of timber and energy for China.[16] Given its sparse population and relative developmental neglect under the Soviet Union, some in Moscow are particularly sensitive to growing Chinese economic influence there.[17] The region is woefully underdeveloped and suffering from depopulation. China's economic engagement has injected much-needed commercial activity and provided a migrant, entrepreneurial labor force. Over time these dynamics will likely bind the region even more closely to China. These kinds of strategic dynamics are a source of security concern for Russia. On the one hand, Russia looks forward to and embraces the Chinese economic regional growth engine. On the other hand, the historical memory of Russia's own economic penetration into this region at a time when China was unable to solidify its grasp on these peripheral areas now hauntingly echoes on the streets of Vladivostok.[18]

The contemporary Sino-Russian relationship suggests that the role of economic statecraft as it relates to peacemaking is perhaps more complicated than might be first assumed. As mentioned at the outset, economic interaction can often carry security externalities. In some cases, economic interaction produces positive security externalities that can reinforce peacemaking efforts. But in other instances economic interaction might simply serve to exacerbate preexisting strategic security concerns about projecting regional influence and growing regional power: "[T]he limitations of the [Sino-Russian] relationship are more bound up with economic asymmetries and uncertainties regarding the future scope of China's power at the global and regional level than an inherent antipathy based on cultural factors. Nonetheless, at the rhetorical level, old enmities and suspicions can be played on."[19] Contemporary suspicions are fed by an often violent and brutish regional history. For example, today's growing Chinese economic ties to the RFE are often seen as fifth-column, colonizing efforts that will eventually be used to wrest control of these territories from Russia.[20]

Given the historical pattern of economic penetration followed by expansionist imperial tendencies, the regional context for relying on economic statecraft to drive peacemaking along the Sino-Russian eastern border does not hold out much cause for optimism. The memory of the 1969 border war, with its rapid escalation to the nuclear threshold, and the militarized confrontation that followed in its wake still hangs heavy over prospects for long-term Sino-Russian strategic relations.[21] Moreover, the nature of Sino-Russian economic interaction predisposes it toward strategic sensitivity. Such dynamics tend to suggest that Sino-Russian economic interaction in the future will be at least as likely to exacerbate strategic concerns as it will be to ameliorate them.

But, perhaps this pessimism concerning the use of economic statecraft to forge contemporary peacemaking is merely an artifact of the peculiarities of the Sino-Russian relationship. Perhaps China's other great power regional rivalry with India holds out more reason to hope that economic statecraft will be able to drive the peacemaking effort.

Economic Statecraft and Peacemaking in the Sino-Indian Relationship

The Sino-Indian case is divided into four periods.[22] The first centers around Chinese regime consolidation in Tibet (1950–53). This Chinese presence generated friction along the contested border, which ultimately provided the precipitating cause for open conflict in 1962. As was the case with the effect of the 1969 border clash on Sino-Soviet relations, this conflict represented a watershed in contemporary Sino-Indian relations. China's 1962 clashes sowed the seeds of the distrust and animosity that spawned a closer Chinese-Pakistan alignment, as well as ongoing strategic distrust between the two rising powers of Asia that continues to this day.

Early Modern Sino-Indian Encounters

The preface to the 1962 Border War begins with China's consolidation of the PRC. At that time, the strategic disparity between the newly formed PRC and the recently independent India was stark. At the end of the Chinese Civil War, even after the PLA demobilized, the country was left with 3 million soldiers. India, on the other hand, possessed only 350,000 in the aftermath of its World War II demobilization.[23] The second important factor during this period was China's military momentum. At the end of World War II, the Chinese Communists' deepest base of support was centered in the central and northern parts of China. As it gained momentum over the KMT forces in the Civil War, the PLA was able to "conquer" China beginning from this geographic base and sweeping in a southwesterly direction. By 1950, this increasingly successful consolidation effort had reached Tibet. When India gained its independence from Great Britain in 1947, its northern boundaries were not fully delineated. After China conquered Tibet and folded it into the PRC, this imperfectly specified border would become a source of friction between India and China.[24] Many of these border issues remain unresolved today and continue to present serious challenges to peacemaking in this relationship.

In addition to these structural features, each side took destabilizing actions that the other side perceived as threatening during the lead-up to the 1962 conflict. Although India had enjoyed a vigorous trading relationship with Tibet prior to the Chinese invasion, it began to reduce this trade after the PLA moved into the region.[25] This reduced economic activity made it difficult for China to sustain its PLA operations in the region. In 1958, India discovered that China had built a road in Aksai Chin that would enable more effective deployment and mobilization in some of the disputed territory.[26] The Indian side was alarmed by what it saw as a Chinese attempt to extend regime consolidation to include Chinese territorial claims.[27] To make matters worse, in 1959 there was a large-scale Tibetan revolt in Lhasa, which the PLA successfully put down. However, to respond to this revolt, the Chinese side had to deploy a significantly higher number of troops in the region. Not surprisingly, the Indian side responded by increasing its military presence near the border. In another act that China viewed as provocative, India granted the Dalai Lama asylum. This pattern of early Sino-Indian interaction did not produce much strategic trust between the newly independent India and the emergent PRC.[28]

The two sides encountered each other in a series of relatively small-scale conflicts in the late summer and early fall of 1959. In late August, Chinese border troops shot at an Indian patrol at Longju in the eastern sector.[29] The Soviet Union (China's erstwhile ally) took a neutral position on the border conflict issue—much to Beijing's consternation.[30] On October 20, 1959, Chinese forces attacked an Indian patrol in Aksai Chin and killed nine Indians at the Kongka Pass.[31] There does not seem to have been any effort to use economic statecraft to reestablish peace in the aftermath of any of these clashes. Rather, on November 7, 1959, Zhou Enlai proposed that both China and India withdraw troops from within 20 kilometers of the McMahon Line (India's primary basis for its territorial boundary in the area) and the Line of Actual Control (the de facto border). However, a subsequent diplomatic negotiation and official committee investigation both were unable to resolve the issue. In April 1960, Zhou Enlai floated the idea that China and India could essentially "swap" their opposing claims in the western and eastern sectors, but this proposal was rejected by India.[32]

During 1960 and 1961, China began establishing outposts in the disputed territory. When Indian intelligence sources reported this activity, Jawaharlal Nehru responded with the decision to move Indian troops forward in what was called the "Forward Policy" to check Chinese consolidation.[33] Although it may not have been intended as such, China viewed the Forward Policy as intolerably threatening.[34] Specifically, the outposts were seen as incremental efforts to seize Chinese territory.[35] By the end of that summer, China's senior leadership had decided that a military response would be necessary to check India's growing presence in the region.

The 1962 Border War

The eventual clash would come in early October 1962 in the eastern portion of the border region. As part of the high-altitude chess game, Chinese forces crossed Thag La Ridge on September 8, 1962, and took up a blocking position, which threatened an outpost India had recently established below the ridge.[36] Andrew Kennedy makes the case that India believed it would enjoy a locally superior position in the region.[37] There was an Indian outpost in that location, and India began to reinforce the neighboring sectors. On October 8, China's senior military command authorized the start of operations. On October 10, Chinese troops overwhelmed a smaller Indian force in the area. By October 11, India realized that it was facing an entire Chinese division and suspended its operations.[38] On October 20, China launched a coordinated assault along the border in both the eastern and western sectors.[39] China had a militarily superior fighting force and handed the Indians a decisive defeat. In late October and early November, India refused to enter into negotiations on China's terms. On November 14, it attempted to launch what would prove to be an unsuccessful local offensive at Walong. The Chinese successfully counterattacked the following day at Walong, as well as along the rest of the eastern border region to Tawang. On November 18, China conducted another successful offensive foray and decimated India's remaining forces in the eastern sector, capturing Bomdila about 50 kilometers southeast of Tawang.[40] The war was a clear victory for the PLA. Following this victory, on November 21, 1962, China unilaterally withdrew its forces to a position 20 kilometers behind the original line of control. But trust between India and China would continue to suffer for another half century.

The Aftermath

The ghosts of the 1962 Border War would continue to haunt Sino-Indian relations for years to come. In response to the decisive Chinese victory and the clear vulnerabilities that it exposed, India nearly doubled its military capacity.[41] As part of the overall mistrust between China and India, China began improving its strategic relations with Pakistan. In addition to China's alignment with Pakistan, the 1962 Border War would be followed by a couple of periods of continued (albeit on a smaller scale) territorial clashes between India and China. The first of these occurred in 1967. Following the conclusion of the Border War, both sides generally withdrew from their forward positions along the contested boundary. An exception to this was the region around a strategic mountain pass called Natu La in the central sector of the disputed territories. In this area, both sides maintained a forward presence after 1962. As part of the effort to consolidate their defenses, Indian troops constructed fences and built additional defensive structures in late August and early September 1967.[42] In mid-September, Chinese troops in the region launched an attack that lasted several days, with numerous soldiers killed on both sides. Another skirmish occurred nearly 20 years later in a valley called Sumdurong Chu.[43] It is located south of the Thag La Ridge, the initial site of the 1962 conflict. Sumdurong Chu is located north of the McMahon Line (as depicted in the Simla Treaty map) but south of the highest ridgeline that runs along Thag La.[44] Both sides had left this region unoccupied following the Border War, but India constructed a seasonal observation post in Sumdurong Chu in 1984. Talks to resolve the boundary stalled in November 1985. Indian troops occupied this observation post during the summer of 1986 and vacated it that winter. The PLA sent troops into the valley before the spring thaw to preempt the return of the Indian patrols in 1987. There they built a helipad. Both sides began the escalation by deploying several divisions to the region. By the beginning of summer 1987, the two sides seemed to be once again locked on the path toward a high-stakes collision. This time, however, a series of high-level diplomatic talks were able to bring both sides back from the brink of war.

Post-1962 Border Conflict Peacemaking

The Indian episodes are unlike many of my Russian observations in that the Indian case does not really fulfill the primary screening criterion: peace was never really fully made. To the extent that one can pinpoint the moment of "peacemaking" for the 1962 Border War, it would be the proposals brokered by six nonaligned nations in Colombo, Sri Lanka, in December 1962.[45]

Two features of this "peacemaking" are important to note. First, there does not seem to be any indication that economic statecraft played a role. Second, the "peace" that was made simply confirmed the results on the battlefield and the subsequent unilateral Chinese withdrawal. The territorial disputes remain unresolved. Although relations have improved since 1962, the underlying issues of strategic mistrust, outstanding territorial disputes, and the competitive dynamics of two rising powers in the region continue to color Sino-Indian relations.[46] These fundamental issues are compounded by China's support for Pakistan and its sensitivity about Indian interference in Tibetan affairs. The Sino-Indian animosity that spawned a closer Chinese-Pakistani alignment also engendered a deep sense of betrayal and an ongoing strategic distrust between the two rising powers of Asia, which continues to this day. "Moreover, as both countries have developed economically, modernized their militaries, and expanded their regional and global interests, new sources of mistrust and potential competition have emerged."[47] These factors may partly account for the relatively low levels of trade and investment in the relationship today.

Early on, the potential for economic statecraft to contribute to a peaceful Sino-Indian relationship seemed promising. Relations got off to a good start on December 30, 1949, when an optimistic Nehru's India became the second noncommunist country (after Burma) to recognize the PRC. An "Agreement on Trade and Intercourse" was signed between the two sides in the spring of 1954. This was followed two weeks later by the well-known "Five Principles of Peaceful Co-Existence," which India and China signed on May 15, 1954, and a trade agreement five months later. At the Bandung Conference in April 1955, China and India jointly sought to cooperate with other third-world nations in forging a nonaligned movement. However, none of these diplomatic and economic niceties would prove sufficient to overcome the security threats presented by the Chinese consolidation of Tibet and the subsequent territorial conflicts. Economic relations by and large reflected the relatively poor state of Sino-Indian border relations and would remain frigid for most of the Cold War, with cross-border trade nonexistent from 1962 to 1992.

By the mid-1980s, however, there were some signs of an economic thaw. On August 15, 1984, India and China agreed to reciprocal most favored nation status. This seems to have been enabled by a series of Sino-Indian diplomatic initiatives following China's relative restraint in 1971 (compared to its military deployments in support of Pakistan in its 1965 war with India). In the aftermath of the 1987 border tension at Sumdurong Chu, these diplomatic talks proved resilient. In December 1988, both sides agreed to create a working group to address the boundary issues and another joint group to explore opportunities in economics, trade, science, and technology cooperation. The peacemaking effort that kept Sumdurong Chu from boiling over into another round of deadly clashes seems to have been directly driven not by any economic statecraft but rather by determined diplomatic efforts and a willingness on both sides to deescalate the tensions. However, economics was seen as a potential solidifying measure to help reinforce peace. This evidence also seems to support the notion that political decisions (rather than a strictly economic logic) on the part of contending parties are the critical driver of peacemaking.

In the early 1990s, a series of confidence-building measures and joint communiqués were signed by the two sides, and by July 1992 border trade (which had ended in 1962) began to resume. In June 1993, another border trading post was opened. The deescalation via diplomatic channels continued, with further troop reductions in 1993 and 1994, although my read of this history suggests that improved economic ties came in response to the reduced security concerns rather than driving the peacemaking per se. The peacemaking was done by political elites who negotiated with their counterparts for the political terms of the peacemaking. In the summer of 1995, border talks were broadened to include discussions of cooperation in cross-border crime. Further troop withdrawals were agreed to that summer in New Delhi as well. The agreements in 1993 and 1996 to observe the Line of Actual Control and limit the number of troops deployed in sensitive areas have reduced the propensity for localized conflict in the region. In 1998, both sides began talks to reopen a trade route in the west-central sector.

Economic Statecraft and Peacemaking in the Contemporary Sino-Indian Relationship

The contemporary Sino-Indian relationship might provide a good test case for whether economic statecraft can lead to a permanent resolution of outstanding territorial disputes. The current economic relationship between India and China reflects the diplomatic warming of the past 30 years. So far economic statecraft has not resulted in a permanent peace that resolves the countries' territorial disputes. The economic dimension of the relationship remains stunted by continued strategic concerns. Although trade has grown considerably since the diplomatic efforts following the end of the Cold War in 1992, it has grown from a base of effectively zero since 1962. Not surprisingly, the trade relationship received a considerable boost with China's accession to the WTO in 2001.

However, despite these positive trends, trade between China and India continues to fall short of its potential.[48] By 2011, Indian imports had grown to $55 billion while India's exports to China were only $19 billion (needless to say, this growing trade deficit is another point of Indian discontent in the relationship).[49] India-China cross-border investment has also been paltry, with less than $500 million in Indian direct investment flowing into China in 2011 and less than half of that coming into India from China. This growing economic relationship does provide some support for the notion that political will and diplomacy can provide an important foundation to support economic activity (even in the absence of a complete resolution of the underlying sources of conflict). Perhaps the most powerful evidence in favor of the hypothesis that economic statecraft can be used to achieve peacemaking goals is the 2006 reopening of Natu La Pass. The strategic significance of this sector derives from its geographic role as a chokepoint. Discussions about reopening the pass began in 2004. Reopening it to international trade and commerce can be considered a form of economic statecraft in which the negotiating parties agreed to set aside military differences in the interest of economic cooperation.

Productive and wide-ranging diplomatic talks continued throughout the 2000s, but just below the surface there continues to be strategic mistrust and sensitivity over the unresolved issues. For instance, in 2009 China apparently sought to block a $2.9 billion loan to India from the Asian Development Bank for a watershed development project in Arunachal Pradesh on the grounds that the territory was not recognized by China as a state belonging to India.[50] Indeed, even as this chapter was being written, tensions erupted once again in the western region.[51] Chinese troops moved into this area and set up tents on the Indian side of the Line of Actual Control.[52] For our purposes, it is telling that this escalation took place in spite of a rapidly growing economic relationship in recent years, the foundations of which we have discussed.[53]

Beyond the narrow territorial issues, the power transition dynamics that both China and India are currently navigating will pose difficult international structural challenges for building greater strategic trust in the Sino-Indian relationship. In this dyad, economic growth on each side is fueling a rising power dynamic that feeds into preexisting strategic security concerns posed by the other. Although economic ties might help reinforce the peacemaking effort that has been in place since 1987, these larger competitive power dynamics are likely to weigh against any attempt to make the peace permanent. Although it still may be too early to draw a definitive conclusion regarding whether or not economic statecraft can be used to drive regional peacemaking in this case, the history of animosity in the long-standing territorial disputes suggests that economic dynamics can be just as likely to feed mutual suspicions as they can be to advance peacemaking between these two rising powers of twenty-first-century Asia.

Conclusion: Economic Statecraft, Peacemaking, and the Broader Regional Context

This chapter has examined economic statecraft's relation to peacemaking in the Sino-Russian and Sino-Indian relationships, but how do these bilateral dynamics scale up to the regional level, the final question raised in the introduction to this volume? What is the nature of the ties between these regional great-powers and the Central and South Asian regions as a whole? Although this discussion has focused on the role of economic statecraft in peacemaking efforts in the context of China's bilateral relationships, I would suggest that the Sino-Russian and the Sino-Indian relationships serve as the primary axis for regional dynamics in both Central Asia and the Himalayan region. The overwhelming power disparity between these large regional powers and their much smaller neighbors means that the tenor of these key relations drives most of the other regional alignment dynamics. Peacemaking between these regional great powers is an important part of the greater regional peace. In the same way, friction in these great power rivalries generates regional insecurity and destabilization and increases the potential for regional conflict escalation, as evidenced by China's role in the Pakistan-India rivalry, Sino-Russian competition for influence and its impact on the SCO, and the Sino-Soviet split (along with the USSR-PRC-US triangle diplomacy of the 1970s and 1980s). Many of these regional alignment dynamics are the result of classic power balancing and bandwagoning behaviors that are derivative of the state of China's relations with Russia and India.[54]

This chapter's analysis of the cases of Sino-Russian and Sino-Indian relations concludes that for effective peacemaking to occur the conflicting parties must first expend the diplomatic capital needed to establish the initial conditions for peace. This often entails demilitarization of the conflict. Another interesting dimension of peacemaking among regional great powers suggested by these two cases is the important role played by territorial disputes. While economic statecraft may play a significant role in reinforcing and solidifying peacemaking efforts, the evidence presented by these cases does not seem to suggest that economic statecraft, itself, brings conflict-ridden states to the peacemaking table. This chapter's analysis suggests that economic statecraft can be used to reinforce a peacemaking effort, but it has a fairly limited independent ability to drastically alter the status quo.[55]

That is not to say that economic statecraft is only a tool of peace reinforcement. These cases suggest that economic interaction may be just as likely a cause for strategic concern as it can be a cause for strategic stability; as Blanchard notes, the strategic effect depends on the security externalities that are produced. Economic interaction (particularly in the context of a long-standing rivalry or preexisting insecurity) can just as easily generate security externalities that are disruptive to regional peace and stability. For example, in the case of the Sino-Indian relationship, continued economic growth is underwriting both powers' military modernization and their growing power-projection capabilities. These kinds of security externalities reinforce strategic mistrust in the region rather than promote peacemaking. The Sino-Russian relationship is also bedeviled by historical fears of military encroachment and great power threats at the periphery of empire. In that context, China's growing economic presence in the RFE contributes to Russian regional insecurities—another example of negative security externalities that exacerbate strategic mistrust rather than fuel peacemaking.

So, does this mean that economic statecraft must be relegated to a secondary, reinforcing role in peacemaking among regional rivals? Not necessarily. Economic statecraft played a critical driving role in the case of Taiwan. Future work ought to explore how those cross-strait circumstances differ from the regional dynamics discussed in this chapter. One key feature is that Taiwan no longer poses much of a security threat to China.[56] In contrast, Russia, and perhaps to lesser extent India, still features prominently on Beijing's radar screen as a potential long-term regional security rival. Under these circumstances, using economic statecraft as a tool to drive peacemaking is a more difficult proposition since the requisite political and diplomatic will is not really present. As Lobell and Ripsman state in their introduction, economic statecraft cannot succeed "when noneconomic interests dominate calculations in the rival states."

NOTES

1. These two states, Russia and India, constitute China's two most powerful continental neighbors. One of the immutable geographic challenges for the Peo-

ple's Republic of China (PRC) is that it possesses the longest land border in the world (22,147 km). A quick decomposition of this land border suggests the relative importance of these two relationships for China's security. China's second-longest border is shared with Russia (3,645 km), while its third-longest border is with India (3,380 km). Incidentally, China's longest land border is with Mongolia (4,677 km). For most of its modern history, Mongolia has served as a buffer state between its more powerful neighbors, Russia and China.

2. See Norrin M. Ripsman, "Top-Down Peacemaking: Why Peacemaking Begins with States and Not Societies," in T. V. Paul, ed., *International Relations Theory and Regional Transformation* (Cambridge: Cambridge University Press, 2012).

3. This sort of historical analysis can shed light on the role of economic statecraft as it relates to regional peacemaking.

4. Stalin personally promised 50 industrial development projects to aid in China's initial industrialization effort. In 1951, the promised Soviet economic aid was being built into China's First Five Year Plan. By the time it was adopted in the spring of 1953, it included 141 Soviet-sponsored industrialization projects. This economic aid and development assistance flowed to China as an expression of political solidarity and support. It was also strategically useful for the USSR to help shore up China as a Cold War ally. Harry Schwartz, *Tsars, Mandarins, and Commisars: A History of Chinese-Russian Relations* (Garden City, NY: Anchor Books, 1973), 149–51.

5. Lorenz M. Luthi, *The Sino-Soviet Split: Cold War in the Communist World* (Princeton: Princeton University Press, 2008), 37.

6. Economics does play a supporting role in this story, but it is tangential to the larger ideological causality. For more on this perspective, see ibid.

7. Schwartz, *Tsars, Mandarins, and Commisars*, 156–58.

8. See Yang Kuisong, "The Sino-Soviet Border Clash of 1969: From Zhenbao Island to Sino-American Rapprochement," *Cold War History* 1, no. 1 (2000): 21–52; Odd A. Westad, ed., *Brothers in Arms: The Rise and Fall of the Sino-Soviet Alliance, 1945–1963* (Palo Alto, CA: Stanford University Press, 1998).

9. Luthi, *Sino-Soviet Split*, 340. Although there were some border skirmishes in late 1967 in this region, the first Chinese fatalities do not seem to have occurred until early 1968.

10. China seems to have selected Zhenbao Island for its proximity to the Chinese shore. It is located on the Chinese side of the main navigation channel of the Ussuri River, and thus China claimed, by international convention, that it should have been considered Chinese territory.

11. For the declassified document, see US State Department Memorandum of Conversation, "US Reaction to Soviet Destruction of CPR [Chinese Peoples Republic] Nuclear Capability; Significance of Latest Sino-Soviet Border Clash,"

August 18, 1969, US National Archives, SN 67–69, Def 12 Chicom, http://www. gwu.edu/~nsarchiv/NSAEBB/NSAEBB49/sino.sov.10.pdf.

12. The agreements meet the requirement for a peacemaking treaty that Ripsman and Lobell laid out in the introduction to this volume: "When peace is achieved, both sides have an expectation that the treaty will be respected, and they no longer invest as much time, energy, or resources in defending the border against the former enemy." On the Chinese side, this process enabled the People's Liberation Army (PLA) to demobilize, reassign, and redeploy many border troops as part of its military modernization effort in the 1990s and 2000s.

13. This trade was beneficial to both parties. It provided China with the relatively advanced military equipment it was not able to produce domestically. This equipment constituted an important part of the PLA's military modernization efforts. At the same time, the sales helped prop up flagging domestic demand for the products of the Russian military-industrial complex and were an important source of hard currency.

14. Russia has tended to emphasize traditional military and security elements in its vision for the SCO.

15. China tends to stress a more economically oriented mandate centered around regional integration and development. China's economics-based vision for the SCO aims to enhance Chinese influence in Central Asia over the long term. Each power's view of the organization's future is emblematic of its relative strengths: China as the dynamic up-and-coming economic powerhouse and Russia as the legacy Cold War military force in the region. China has more easily found partners willing to sign on to its economically oriented vision. China's economic approach comes across as less threatening and more beneficial than Russia's military-oriented emphasis. The direction the institution ultimately takes may make it relatively easier for Russia or China to dominate it.

16. "In 2000, raw materials made up 5% of Russian exports to China, and by 2008, this figured had reached to 40%." Natasha Kuhrt, "The Russian Far East in Russia's Asia Policy: Dual Integration or Double Periphery?," *Europe-Asia Studies* 64, no. 3 (April 2012): 471–93, at 481.

17. Christina Yeung and Nebojsa Bjelakovic, "The Sino-Russian Strategic Partnership: Views from Beijing and Moscow," *Journal of Slavic Military Studies* 23, no. 2 (May 2010): 243–81.

18. Although economic statecraft might prove to be a positive force for reinforcing the peacemaking efforts that continue to be consolidated in the aftermath of the Cold War, the region's history does not provide much to suggest optimism.

19. Kuhrt, "Russian Far East in Russia's Asia Policy," 476.

20. Such fears of a Chinese fifth-column effect seem to have been behind the

Russian effort in 1900 to "deport" ethnic Chinese from the Russian side of the Amur River in the city of Blagoveshchensk during the Boxer Rebellion. At the height of this antiforeign sentiment, the governor of Blagoveshchensk issued an order to send all ethnic Chinese back across the river to Manchuria. The city's cossack garrison (assisted by local "volunteers") forced the Chinese into the river at bayonet point. Those who refused to enter the water (and thus did not drown in the current) were slaughtered on the bank. Accounts of the massacre are gruesome. See, for instance, "Horrors in Manchuria: River Amur Choked Full of Corpses after the Massacres," *New York Times*, November 14, 1900, http://query.nytimes.com/mem/archive-free/pdf?res=F60A14FF3F5B11738DDDAD0994D9415B808CF1D3.

21. China also continues to harbor a sense that even during the high point in Sino-Soviet relations, the Soviet Union treated Mao and the PRC as a junior partner, one that was ultimately abandoned during several difficult Cold War confrontations such as the 1958 Taiwan Strait crisis and the friction with India in the early 1960s. Luthi, *Sino-Soviet Split*, 101–2, 141–46, 148.

22. India represents a suitable comparative case for this chapter's analysis. Like the conflict with the USSR in 1969, China also fought a border war with India in 1962. As is the case with China's Russian relations, the tone of the Sino-Indian relationship exerts a fundamental shaping influence on regional dynamics. Both Russia and India are regional great powers on China's immediate border, and Both have had (or still have) territorial disputes with China.

23. Andrew Kennedy, *The International Ambitions of Mao and Nehru: National Efficacy Beliefs and the Making of Foreign Policy* (Cambridge: Cambridge University Press, 2012), 217.

24. John W. Garver, *Protracted Contest: Sino-Indian Rivalry in the Twentieth Century* (Seattle: University of Washington Press, 2001), 41.

25. Ibid., 60–61, 84–86.

26. Ibid., 58, 79–86; Kennedy, *International Ambitions of Mao and Nehru*, 227.

27. For an excellent source on the details of these territorial disputes, see M. Taylor Fravel, *Strong Borders, Secure Nation* (Princeton: Princeton University Press, 2008), especially 326–28; and M. Taylor Fravel, "Power Shifts and Escalation: Explaining China's Use of Force in Territorial Disputes," *International Security* 32, no. 3 (2008): 44–83.

28. Srinath Raghavan, "Sino-Indian Boundary Dispute, 1948–60: A Reappraisal," *Economic and Political Weekly* 41, no. 36 (2006): 3890.

29. Kennedy, *International Ambitions of Mao and Nehru*, 227.

30. Luthi, *Sino-Soviet Split*, 141–42, 145.

31. Kennedy, *International Ambitions of Mao and Nehru*, 228.

32. Ibid.

33. Over the summer of 1962, India established 36 outposts in the disputed western sector and another 34 in the eastern sector. Several of these appear to have been located north of the McMahon Line. The move was apparently prompted by the desire to claim higher terrain (a more advantageous military position). It was justified by an Indian claim that the McMahon Line was originally supposed to run along the highest ridge.

34. Steven A. Hoffman, *India and the China Crisis* (Berkeley: University of California Press 1990), 92.

35. See John Garver, "China's Decision for War with India in 1962," in Alastair Iain Johnston and Robert Ross, eds., *New Directions in the Study of China's Foreign Policy* (Stanford, CA: Stanford University Press, 2005).

36. Kennedy, *International Ambitions of Mao and Nehru*, 230.

37. Ibid., 230–31.

38. Ibid., 230.

39. Ibid., 233.

40. This was significant because once Bomdila fell there was little to prevent an extensive conquest of Indian territory beyond the disputed border region. Ibid., 234–35.

41. Garver, *Protracted Contest*, 63. In particular, India created ten new high-altitude divisions to deploy in its disputed territories.

42. G. S. Bajpai, *China's Shadow over Sikkim: The Politics of Intimidation* (New Delhi: Lancer Publishers, 1999).

43. Garver, *Protracted Contest*, 97.

44. Because India claims that the McMahon Line was defined as running along the highest ridge of the Himalayas, it believes Sumdurong Chu ought to be in Indian territory.

45. These accords provided for the withdrawal of Chinese forces 20 kilometers behind the traditional lines as these are understood by China.

46. Jing-dong Yuan, "The Dragon and the Elephant: Chinese-Indian Relations in the 21st Century," *Washington Quarterly* 30 (Summer 2007): 131–44.

47. "The Indians are threatened by China's moves to improve relations with and provide limited assistance to Myanmar, Pakistan, Bangladesh, and Sri Lanka, and worry that these ties are forming a ring of encirclement around India to restrain its influence. The early manifestations of India's 'Look East' policy have also threatened China's interests, as it perceives India as intruding upon its sphere of influence in Myanmar and Indochina. Mutual suspicions have also been stirred by each nation's military build-up and by evidence of the early stages of competition over control of the Indian Ocean and a potential arms race." Michael A. Glosny, "China and the BRICs: A Real (but Limited) Partnership in a Unipolar World," *Polity* 42, no. 1 (January 2010): 100–129, at 127.

48. Although it is growing, the Sino-Indian economic relationship has fallen short of what might be "normally" expected given the countries' relative sizes and geographic proximity. Economists typically use gravity models to estimate expected levels of trade between two nations. The simplest techniques estimate expected trade as a function of their distance (usually approximated by the distance between their capitals) and the size of their economies. Closer, larger economies are more likely to experience higher trade volumes. Of course these models can be significantly more complex and might account for factors such as openness, geography, conflict, levels of development, and transportation technology.

49. Figures are from the Direction of Trade Statistics (DOTS), and the Coordinated Direct Investment Survey (CDIS), both of the International Monetary Fund (IMF). Data were extracted from the IMF Data Warehouse on April 2, 2013.

50. In the end, the loan was approved. Pranab Dhal Samanta, "India-China Face-Off Worsens over ADB Loan for Arunachal, Bank Doesn't Help," *Indian Express*, May 15, 2009, http://www.indianexpress.com/news/indiachina-faceoff-worsens-over-adb-loan-for-arunachal/459910/.

51. In April 2013, India accused China of violating the border, conducting provocative patrol operations, and constructing encampments in Indian territory "19km past a line of actual control (LAC), in the Despang area of Ladakh, a part of Jammu & Kashmir state that is wedged between Tibet proper and the vale of Kashmir." "India and China Square Off: High Stakes," *Economist,* April 30, 2013, http://www.economist.com/blogs/banyan/2013/04/india-and-china-square.

52. Jake Maxwell Watts, "Are China and India about to Fight over Their Border?," *Atlantic,* May 2, 2013, http://www.theatlantic.com/china/archive/2013/05/are-china-and-india-about-to-fight-over-their-border/275518/.

53. "The value of bilateral trade, skewed heavily in China's favour, has grown from just $2.9 billion a year at the start of the millennium to some $66 billion annually." "India and China Square Off."

54. The power disparity between these regional great powers and the smaller states in the region often means that the presence or absence of great power peace frequently shapes what the alignment options look like for these smaller states. Because it is often a bit harder to detect "dogs that did not bark" in international relations, it may be easier to observe how the absence of cordial regional great power relations can lead to regional instability rather than observing how the presence of peaceful great power relations bolsters regional tranquility.

55. Once conflicting parties have agreed diplomatically and politically to move toward peace and shift from a status quo of conflict toward a status quo that is peaceful, economic ties may prove useful to cement this more peaceful state of affairs.

56. This has probably been true at least since economic statecraft has been in a position to be used as a tool for peacemaking.

CHAPTER 9

The Institutional Design of Preferential Trade Agreements and the Maintenance of Peace

Edward D. Mansfield and Jon C. W. Pevehouse

In the introduction to this volume, Norrin M. Ripsman and Steven E. Lobell raise the question of whether economic tools can be used to promote peace throughout a geographic region. In this chapter, we address one particular type of conflict-reducing instrument, a preferential trade agreement (PTA), and consider its potential for reducing regional conflict and stabilizing troubled regions.

Social scientists and policy makers have expressed a long-standing interest in the effects of international trade on political conflict. For centuries commercial liberals have argued that open trade dampens hostilities. Mercantilists, however, have challenged this view, claiming instead that unfettered commerce often contributes to belligerence. Realists and others charge that, in contrast to both views, trade is unrelated to interstate disputes. Over the past 20 years, a burgeoning empirical literature has addressed these competing claims. The vast bulk of that literature has analyzed the effects of bilateral trade flows on military disputes between states. But most of this research has paid little attention to the institutional context in which trade is conducted.

Central to that context are PTAs, a broad class of institutions that include free trade areas, common markets, and customs unions.[1] In earlier research, we have found that parties to the same PTA are less prone to disputes than other states and that hostilities between PTA members are less likely to occur as trade flows rise between them.[2] Moreover, heightened commerce is more likely to inhibit conflict between states that belong to the same preferential grouping than between states that do not.

In that earlier research, we treated all PTAs as homogeneous. In this chapter, we relax the assumption that all preferential groupings are alike, allowing us to address whether variations in the institutional design of PTAs and in their members' characteristics influence the outbreak of hostilities. More specifically, we analyze whether the size of the agreement (bilateral or multilateral), the extent of integration that a PTA aims to achieve, and the presence or absence of a dispute settlement mechanism (DSM) affect the use of force. We find that multilateral PTAs tend to dampen conflict to a greater extent than bilateral arrangements but that these other institutional features have little effect on the outbreak of hostilities. We conclude that multilateral PTAs in which regional members trade extensively can significantly reduce conflict, rendering them useful tools with which to cement and reinforce bilateral peace treaties between regional rivals. In this regard, PTAs can help embed bilateral peace settlements in broader regional economic arrangements, thereby enhancing the durability of peace. Consequently, this chapter can shed light on the fifth question posed by Ripsman and Lobell's introduction, which focuses on moving from a bilateral peace agreement to a multilateral regional arrangement.

PTAs and International Conflict

Largely neglected in the burgeoning empirical literature on the relationship between trade flows and political conflict are the international institutions designed to guide overseas commerce.[3] Particularly important in this regard are PTAs, commercial institutions that have become increasingly pervasive over the past 60 years.[4] We argue that military disputes are less likely to occur between PTA members than between other states and that parties to the same preferential arrangement are less prone to conflict as the flow of trade expands between them. We also argue that heightened commerce is more likely to dampen hostilities between parties to the same PTA than between other states. In this regard, we embrace the commercial liberal argument to a greater degree than Jean-Marc F. Blanchard does in chapter 6 in this volume.

The claim that PTAs reduce the prospect of military conflict has been advanced for centuries, and since World War II various governments have established preferential groupings in an effort to stimulate peace as well as prosperity.[5] Nonetheless, systematic analyses of the links between PTA membership and conflict have been lacking. In some preliminary research on this topic, we have argued that the effects of PTAs on conflict stem partly from the economic benefits that states expect to derive from membership.[6] As these expected gains increase, so do the economic costs of military disputes, which threaten to degrade economic relations between states and to damage PTAs. Preferential agreements reduce trade barriers among members and limit the ability of participants to subsequently raise these barriers. Hence, a state entering into a PTA helps to insure itself against the possibility of future surges in protectionism on the part of other members.[7] From that state's standpoint, the benefits of obtaining such insurance grow if the other members include its key trade partners, since increases in protection by these partners are likely to yield considerable harm. The benefits of PTA membership also grow if states fear that they will be left without adequate access to crucial international markets unless they belong to a preferential grouping, a concern that has contributed greatly to the rush of states entering PTAs over the past few decades.[8]

Parties to a preferential agreement have reason to anticipate a rise in investment as well.[9] Firms can generate substantial benefits from locating assets in a PTA member because doing so vests them with preferential access to each participant's market.[10] Equally, since PTAs diminish the capacity of governments to engage in opportunistic behavior, firms investing in a preferential grouping limit the prospect that the profitability of their assets will be jeopardized due to state actions.[11] Even if states' economies are not highly complementary, thereby restricting the gains from commercial liberalization, they may form a preferential grouping in the hopes of luring foreign investment, as often occurs in the case of PTAs established between developed and developing countries.[12] Furthermore, countries joining a PTA frequently expect to enhance their position in international economic negotiations, since they may exert greater leverage via-à-vis third parties as a group than individually. For example, entrants into the European Economic Community (EEC) expected this organization to bolster their bargaining position with respect to the United States, and various developing countries have formed PTAs in an effort to improve their leverage in negotiations with advanced industrial counterparts.[13]

Interstate conflict can hamper the ability of states to realize these expected gains from PTA membership by undermining commitments to sustain commercial liberalization, inhibiting investment on the part of firms that are reluctant to operate in unstable regions and damaging the bargaining power of members in negotiations with third parties. Even if trade flows are relatively small and states actually derive few economic gains from membership—conditions that have characterized various efforts at regional integration since World War II—preferential groupings can reduce the prospect of hostilities if participants anticipate that sizable economic benefits will be forthcoming. The repeated efforts that countries have made to invigorate dormant PTAs and the rarity with which these arrangements have been cast aside without a replacement quickly being established suggest that members of unsuccessful PTAs have harbored such hopes.[14]

For states that trade heavily, however, the future stream of gains from participating in a preferential arrangement is likely to appear especially large. The institutional mechanisms that PTAs provide to deepen integration and avert the future breakdown of economic relations help to ensure that ties between key trade partners will be sustained, if not expanded. As Miles Kahler argues, extensive economic interaction within a regional institution contributes to "perceptions that enhance the prospects for cooperation and reinforce institutions: an expectation that interactions will continue and a declining discount rate in evaluating future pay-offs from those interactions."[15] By jeopardizing existing trade relations and the realization of potentially significant future economic benefits, military conflict threatens to exact a particularly heavy toll on states that have dense commercial ties and belong to the same PTA.[16] As such, PTA members that trade extensively have a strong incentive to avoid military confrontations.[17]

In addition, PTAs can inhibit antagonism by establishing a forum for bargaining and negotiation among members, thereby facilitating the resolution of interstate tensions prior to the outbreak of open hostilities.[18] Various preferential groupings have crafted dispute settlement mechanisms to mediate economic conflict, institutional devices that may prove especially useful for states that trade heavily.[19] Heightened commerce raises the costs of military conflict, but it also can generate economic conflict that, unless contained, has the potential to sow the seeds of political discord.[20] Preferential agreements aid in containing and resolving economic disputes before they damage political relations. Moreover, many PTAs have become venues for addressing political disputes between participants and fostering cooperation. It is widely acknowledged, for example, that the Association of Southeast Asian Nations (ASEAN) has helped to manage tensions in Southeast Asia.[21] Mercosur has done likewise, improving political-military relations throughout the Southern Cone.[22]

Furthermore, PTAs can help to address concerns about the distribution of gains stemming from economic exchange that, in the view of many observers, impede international cooperation.[23] One way they can do so is by promoting reciprocity among members, helping to guarantee that economic concessions made by one party will be repaid, rather than exploited, by its counterparts.[24] Preferential trade agreements can also address such concerns by providing information about the gains and losses that members have accrued, thereby reducing uncertainty about the distribution of benefits from economic exchange. More generally, PTAs facilitate the construction of focal points that forestall breakdowns in cooperation by shaping states' expectations about what constitutes acceptable behavior and facilitating the identification of deviations from such behavior.[25]

The Effects of Institutional Variations across PTAs on Interstate Conflict

Thus far we have treated PTAs as a homogeneous class of institutions, since all such arrangements vest participants with preferential access to other members' markets. At the same time, however, the goals, rules, procedures, and institutional designs of PTAs often vary. Whether these differences influence the ability of PTAs to contain political conflict has rarely been explored to date.[26] We probe this issue by addressing three types of institutional variation across PTAs: the extent of the integration they aim to achieve, the mechanisms they put in place to resolve disputes among member states, and the number of member states.

One key source of institutional variation among PTAs is the degree of economic integration they propose to achieve. Common markets, for example, aim to generate substantial integration by fostering the free movement of factors of production, as well as finished goods, across national borders. Customs unions aim to achieve somewhat less integration than common markets but nonetheless involve open trade among members and the establishment of a common external tariff. Free trade areas (FTAs) are less ambitious initiatives than customs unions, focusing primarily on efforts to eliminate trade barriers among member states. Other preferential arrangements attempt to reduce trade barriers among participants without eliminating them.

As preferential groupings try to achieve greater trade liberalization and economic integration, there is a greater need for them to become more formal, extensive, and comprehensive institutions.[27] For example, customs unions require additional infrastructure to monitor compliance with their common external tariffs, while common markets require the creation of supranational institutions to control monetary and/or labor market integration. Furthermore, the anticipated gains from PTA membership are likely to rise if the arrangement holds out the promise of greater integration and liberalization among members. As these expected gains increase, so do the economic costs of military disputes, which threaten to degrade economic relations between combatants and to damage the PTA itself.

Another key source of institutional variation across PTAs stems from whether members establish a formal dispute resolution and settlement mechanism.[28] Although most mechanisms of this sort are designed to resolve economic disputes, they may dampen political tensions in the process. For example, the creation of mechanisms to facilitate the peaceful settlement of disputes has played an important role in inhibiting conflict within ASEAN, many members of which have a border dispute or an overlapping "exclusive economic zone" claim with another participant.[29] Evaluating the arrangement's history of dispute resolution, Hans H. Indorf argues that ASEAN "has increased the likelihood that conflicts of peripheral national value would not explode into open confrontation, and those of a more serious nature would not tear the organization asunder. Personal consultations and periodic meetings have had a mitigating effect on potential bilateral hostilities."[30] The considerable amount of institutional variation among existing dispute settlement mechanisms may have an important bearing on the links between PTA membership and military disputes.

Finally, the likelihood of conflict may depend on whether a PTA is bilateral (comprised of two members) or multilateral (comprised of more than two members). It is well known, for example, that collective action problems become more severe as the number of members in an organization rises.[31] Perhaps states are more likely to free ride and avoid intervening in conflicts between fellow members as a PTA becomes larger. In addition, negotiating and enforcement become increasingly difficult as a PTA's membership expands.[32] If the provisions of preferential agreements are not enforced, member states are likely to heavily discount future gains provided by the organization. In these cases, larger PTAs may be less effective in diminishing conflict between members than their smaller counterparts.

Alternatively, a rising number of PTA members also increases the number of countries that could help broker a resolution to a dispute and that have an incentive to avoid the economic damage to the grouping as a whole that conflict could precipitate. More generally, a PTA tends to provide members with greater benefits as its internal market size increases, and, all other things being equal, the size of its internal market is directly related to the number of member states.[33] Thus, in larger PTAs, military disputes will generate more market disruptions, raising the cost of disputes and providing a strong incentive for participants to resolve differences short of military conflict.

The Statistical Model

We begin by estimating the following model.

$$
\begin{aligned}
ONSET_{ij} = \ & \beta_0 + \beta_1 PTA_{ij} + \beta_2 TRADE_{ij} + \beta_3 (TRADE_{ij} \times PTA_{ij}) + \beta_4 GDP_i \\
& + \beta_5 GDP_j + \beta_6 \Delta GDP_i + \beta_7 \Delta GDP_j + \beta_8 DISTANCE_{ij} \\
& + \beta_9 CONTIGUOUS_{ij} + \beta_{10} ONGOING\ MID_{ij} + \beta_{11} ALLIES_{ij} \\
& + \beta_{12} CAPRATIO_{ij} + \beta_{13} MAJOR\ POWER_{ij} + \beta_{14} REGIME_i \\
& + \beta_{15} REGIME_j + \beta_{16} GATT_{ij} + \beta_{17-20} SPLINES_{ij} + e_{ij}
\end{aligned}
$$

where $ONSET_{ij}$ is the probability of the onset of a militarized interstate dispute (MID) between two states, i and j, in a given year, t.[34] The observed value of the variable is 1 if a dispute begins between countries i and j in year t and 0 otherwise. After generating some initial estimates, we also analyze only those MIDs that yielded battlefield fatalities.

The first three independent variables are included to test the hypothesis that PTAs tend to inhibit conflict and that the effects of trade flows on hostilities depend on whether trade partners also participate in the same PTA. PTA_{ij} equals 1 if states i and j are parties to the same PTA in year $t - 1$, and 0 otherwise. $TRADE_{ij}$ is the natural logarithm of the total trade flow (expressed in constant U.S. dollars) between states i and j in year $t - 1$. Because we argue that the impact of trade flows on military hostilities is influenced by PTA membership, we also include $TRADE_{ij} \times PTA_{ij}$.[35]

GDP_i and GDP_j are the natural logarithm of the gross domestic products (GDPs) in year $t - 1$ (expressed in constant US dollars) of each state in the dyad, and ΔGDP_i and ΔGDP_j tap the extent of economic growth in these countries.[36] We include these variables because the size of a state's economy and fluctuations in its business cycle might affect its trade flows, whether it participates in PTAs, and the likelihood of military conflict. Next, $DISTANCE_{ij}$ is the natural logarithm of the capital-to-capital distance between countries i and j, and $CONTIGUOUS_{ij}$ indicates whether these countries are geographically contiguous. Geographically proximate states have much greater opportunity to enter into a dispute and more issues to fight over than distant states.[37] Equally, states in close proximity tend to conduct more trade and have a greater likelihood of entering the same PTA than other countries.[38] As such, we need to ensure that any observed relationship between disputes and either trade or PTAs is not due to the effects of proximity.

In addition, it is widely understood that political-military relations between states influence their proneness to hostilities.[39] We therefore address the effects of four crucial political-military factors. First, we include $ONGO$-$ING \ MID_{ij}$, which equals 1 if states i and j are already in a MID in year $t -$ 1 and 0 otherwise. States that are enmeshed in one MID may be less likely to start another one; alternatively, conflict over one unresolved issue may lead the belligerents to lock horns over other issues too. Second, we include $ALLIES_{ij}$ to account for the influence of political-military alliances on conflict. This variable is coded 1 if states i and j are allied in year $t - 1$ and 0 otherwise.[40] Third, to control for the dyadic balance of power, we introduce $CAPRATIO_{ij}$. This variable is the natural logarithm of the ratio of the stronger state's military capabilities to the weaker state's capabilities in year $t - 1$. To calculate annual values of $CAPRATIO_{ij}$, we rely on the Correlates of War (COW) project's national military capabilities index, which is based on each state's total population, urban population, energy consumption, iron and steel production, military manpower, and military expenditures.[41] Fourth, it is widely recognized that major powers are more likely to become embroiled in military conflict than other states. They also play an important role in shaping the international trading system. To account for their influence, we include $MAJOR \ POWER_{ij}$, which equals 1 if either state i or state j is a major power in year $t - 1$ and 0 otherwise.

In light of the voluminous literature on the democratic peace, it is important to control for the influence of regime type. Keith Jaggers and Ted Robert Gurr have developed a widely used index of regime type that ranges from 0 (least democratic) to 20 (most democratic).[42] $REGIME_i$ and $REGIME_j$ are the values of this index for states i and j in year $t - 1$. The bulk of the literature on the democratic peace concludes that democratic country pairs are more peaceful than other dyads, suggesting that an inverse relationship should exist between each of these variables and the probability of a militarized dispute.[43]

Although our argument is that PTAs inhibit conflict, they might not be the only international commercial institutions that have such an effect. The General Agreement on Tariffs and Trade (GATT) and the World Trade Organization (WTO) undergirded the global trading system during the period examined here, and, like PTAs, they may have created a setting that reduced the likelihood of military conflict between members. Moreover, since many PTAs were formed under the GATT's and WTO's authority, we need to make sure that any observed relationship between PTAs and conflict is not simply an outgrowth of GATT or WTO membership. To this end, we include $GATT_{ij}$, which equals 1 if states i and j are GATT or WTO members in year $t - 1$ and 0 otherwise.[44] Finally, e_{it} is a stochastic error term.

The following analysis covers the period from 1950 to 2000. Since our dependent variable is dichotomous, logistic regression is used to estimate the model. To account for any temporal dependence in the data, we introduce a cubic spline function with three knots of the number of years that have elapsed since a MID last began between states i and j.[45] In order to conserve space, however, we do not present the coefficient estimates of these variables in the following tables. We also rely on clustered standard errors to take account of any heteroskedasticity, as well as the grouped nature of the data.

Initial Findings

Initial estimates of the model are presented in the first column of table 9.1. In our model, the coefficient of $TRADE_{ij}$ measures the influence of trade flows on disputes for states that do not belong to the same PTA. Clearly, this influence is weak: the estimated coefficient of $TRADE_{ij}$ is positive, but it is not large and only marginally statistically significant. Hence, outside of a preferential trade agreement, the flow of commerce has little influence on the prospect of military hostilities. Heightened trade does serve to dampen conflict between PTA members, however, as indicated by the negative and statistically significant coefficient estimate of $TRADE_{ij} \times PTA_{ij}$. We attach little importance to the coefficient of PTA_{ij}, which reflects the influence of a preferential arrangement on conflict when members engage in no trade. Nonetheless, among states that conduct no trade, PTA members are more likely to experience armed hostilities than non-PTA members.[46]

To more fully analyze the links between commerce and conflict, it is useful to assess the magnitude of the estimated effects of both trade flows and PTAs on military disputes. We therefore generate the predicted probability of a dispute's outbreak for PTA members and non-PTA members while varying the amount of commerce being conducted. To compute these probabilities, all continuous variables except $TRADE_{ij}$ (and $TRADE_{ij} \times PTA_{ij}$) are set to their means; $ALLIES_{ij}$, $GATT_{ij}$, $CONTIGUOUS_{ij}$, $ONGOING\ MID_{ij}$, and $MAJOR\ POWER_{ij}$ are set to 0, which is the modal value of each variable. As shown in figure 9.1, PTA membership tends to inhibit conflict, and this effect grows quite large as the flow of trade increases. Moreover, the effect of trade flows on belligerence is much larger for participants in a preferential grouping than for other states.

TABLE 9.1. Estimates of the Influence of PTAs and Trade on the Onset of Militarized Disputes

Variable	(1) MID Onset	(2) Fatal MIDs	(3) Prior MIDs
Trade	0.031*	−0.042*	−0.020
	(0.017)	(0.024)	(0.012)
PTA	0.485***	0.491***	−0.084
	(0.113)	(0.163)	(0.093)
Trade × PTA	−0.128***	−0.083***	−0.034**
	(0.018)	(0.023)	(0.017)
Δ GDP$_i$	−0.193	0.434	−0.115
	(0.376)	(0.797)	(0.296)
Δ GDP$_j$	0.176	0.232	0.198
	(0.393)	(0.600)	(0.343)
Distance	−0.270***	−0.311***	−0.067***
	(0.034)	(0.056)	(0.025)
Contiguity	2.145***	2.337***	0.968***
	(0.114)	(0.175)	(0.091)
GDP$_i$	0.247***	0.214***	0.070***
	(0.027)	(0.045)	(0.025)
GDP$_j$	0.176***	0.142***	0.009
	(0.028)	(0.043)	(0.025)
Regime$_i$	−0.020***	−0.020***	0.004
	(0.005)	(0.007)	(0.004)
Regime$_j$	−0.012**	−0.021***	0.011**
	(0.005)	(0.008)	(0.005)
Capability Ratio	0.638***	0.748***	0.227
	(0.159)	(0.235)	(0.160)
Ongoing MID	1.682***	1.888***	0.744***
	(0.162)	(0.216)	(0.101)
Allies	−0.242**	−0.378***	−0.064
	(0.094)	(0.138)	(0.075)
GATT	−0.463***	−0.433**	−0.329***
	(0.113)	(0.206)	(0.092)
Major Power	0.649***	0.909***	0.236**
	(0.131)	(0.235)	(0.119)
Constant	−10.683***	−10.724***	−3.420***
	(0.846)	(1.355)	(0.751)
N	404,133	404,133	17,952

Note: Robust standard errors clustered on the dyad are in parentheses; *** $p < 0.01$, ** $p < 0.05$, * $p < 0.10$.

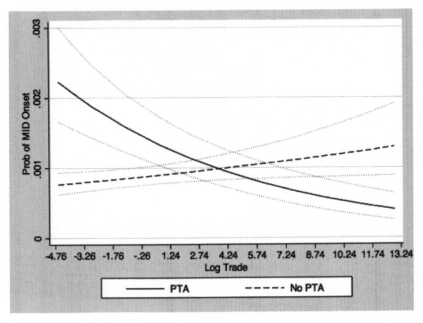

Fig. 9.1. The influence of trade on the predicted probability of MID onset for PTA members and states that are not PTA members. (Predicted effects are calculated based on the results in the first column of table 9.1. Lighter lines represent 95 percent confidence intervals.)

Interestingly, though, such groupings do little to inhibit conflict at the very lowest levels of trade. In fact, as we noted earlier, for states that conduct no trade, PTA membership actually gives rise to a slight increase in the predicted probability of a military dispute. This finding is not entirely surprising. We have argued that the effects of PTAs on conflict stem partly from the future stream of economic benefits that these arrangements promise to participants—including providing institutional mechanisms that help to ensure that ties between key trade partners will be sustained, if not expanded. That future stream of benefits is likely to appear very meager if no trade is being conducted by PTA partners. Moreover, if expectations regarding the gains from regional integration are unmet—which is quite likely to be the case if little or no trade is conducted within a PTA—it is not hard to understand why political tensions might flare between member states.

As trade grows, however, the pacifying influence of preferential arrangements becomes quite evident. Indeed, given even a relatively modest rise in the amount of trade in a dyad, PTA membership yields a dramatic reduction in the prospect of hostilities. An increase from the median to the 75th percentile of dyadic trade yields a 30 percent decrease in the predicted probability of a militarized dispute between PTA members. That same increase in dyadic trade yields nearly a 15 percent rise in the predicted probability of a MID between states that do not belong to the same PTA.

However, PTAs are not the only trade agreements that affect conflict. The estimated coefficient of $GATT_{ij}$ is negative and statistically significant, indicating that members of the multilateral regime are less likely to become embroiled in conflict than other states. Furthermore, economically large states are more likely to engage in military disputes than their smaller counterparts, since the estimated coefficients of GDP_i and GDP_j are positive and statistically significant. In contrast, the business cycle has little bearing on hostilities. Neither the coefficient of ΔGDP_i nor that of ΔGDP_j is significant.

As expected, distance also affects the outbreak of hostilities. States are especially likely to fight with their neighbors, and they are especially unlikely to fight with distant counterparts. The coefficient estimate of $DISTANCE_{ij}$ is negative, that of $CAPRATIO_{ij}$ is positive, and both are statistically significant. That the estimated coefficients of $REGIME_i$ and $REGIME_j$ are negative and statistically significant indicates that states are less likely to become enmeshed in hostilities as they become more democratic. Finally, political-military relations also play an important role in shaping the outbreak of conflict. Disputes become more likely as the disparity in capabilities widens, and conflicts are particularly likely to break out between states that are not allies and those that include a major power. Equally, the existence of an ongoing MID between a given pair of states increases the odds that this dyad will experience the onset of a second conflict, suggesting that MIDs tend to cluster among country pairs.

Fatal Disputes and Prior Antagonism

Many of the conflicts included in the MIDs data set are low-intensity events in which force is threatened or displayed, but no shots are fired. The factors stimulating such events may differ in important ways from the causes of episodes marked by battlefield fatalities. To ensure that our results reflect the effects of trade relations on the use of force, we estimate our model after redefining $ONSET_{ij}$ as the probability of the onset of a MID marked by battlefield deaths in a given year, *t*. Again, the observed value of the variable equals 1 if a dispute begins between countries *i* and *j* that yields at least one such fatality and 0 otherwise.

The results, shown in the second column of table 9.1, are remarkably similar to those based on all MIDs, indicating that our results are not being driven by low-intensity conflict. Especially important for our purposes is that the estimated coefficient of $PTA_{ij} \times TRADE_{ij}$ remains negative and significant when we shift our attention to fatal MIDs. Interestingly, however, the estimated coefficient of $TRADE_{ij}$ becomes negative and is marginally significant. The effect of an increase in trade between PTA members from the median to the 75th percentile continues to be sizable, yielding a 35 percent decline in the predicted probability of a fatal MID. Outside a PTA, this same increase in trade yields a predicted decline of only about 15 percent.

In addition, it is important to address whether trade and PTA membership reduce the likelihood of conflict between states with a history of antagonism. One concern in an analysis of this sort is that PTAs—and trade relations more generally—might be an outgrowth of political cooperation. If PTAs form and trade flows are extensive among states that have similar political interests and few reasons to fight, then our earlier results might be a product of endogeneity.

To address this concern, we conduct three additional analyses. First, we restrict our sample to countries that have already experienced a MID, thereby addressing whether PTAs and trade flows affect conflict among countries that have a history of discord.[47] The results, shown in the third column of table 9.1, indicate that the effects of trade agreements and trade flows are even more striking among this group of countries than among all states. The coefficient estimates of PTA_{ij}, $TRADE_{ij}$, and $TRADE_{ij} \times PTA_{ij}$ are negative, and the latter estimate continues to be statistically significant. Moreover, the effects of trade flows between PTA members are quite sizable. Heightened trade flows between PTA members that have experienced a military conflict play a substantial role in reducing the odds of future discord.

Second, we include a measure of the similarity of states' preferences that is based on voting records in the United Nations (UN) General Assembly and that has been widely analyzed in models like ours.[48] While there are some limitations associated with using the votes of UN members to measure their underlying foreign policy preferences, accounting for these preferences is important. States with similar preferences are unlikely to become embroiled in military conflicts and are quite likely to have close economic ties. To ensure that any observed effect of PTAs or trade flows does not stem from the influence of states' preferences, we include the measure of the similarity of state i's and state j's UN voting profiles in year $t - 1$, labeled $TAU\text{-}B_{ij}$.

Third, we include a measure of enduring rivalries developed by William R. Thompson.[49] Such states might be less likely to form PTAs or trade extensively, and there is ample evidence that they are more likely to experience the onset of hostilities. Although we do not show these results to conserve space, $TAU\text{-}B_{ij}$ does not have a significant effect on the outbreak of MIDs, but enduring rivalries significantly increase the likelihood of a new conflict. Of particular importance for our purposes, though, is that the estimated coefficient of $TRADE_{ij} \times PTA_{ij}$ remains negative, statistically significant, and sizable when these variables are included in the model. Taken together the results in this section strongly suggest that our results are not a product of endogeneity.

The Effects of Institutional Design

A central purpose of this chapter is to address whether design features of PTAs influence their ability to dampen conflict and how these agreements can be used to move from a bilateral peace agreement to regional peace. In particular, we focus on whether membership is limited to two states (a bilateral agreement) or more (a multilateral agreement), the extent of integration that the PTA aims to achieve, and whether the PTA has a dispute settlement mechanism. We examine each of these factors in turn.

Multilateral versus Bilateral PTAs

First, as previously discussed, there are competing logics about whether larger or smaller trade agreements are better suited to dampening military disputes. To test these arguments, we classify each PTA in our sample as bilateral or multilateral.[50] We define a new variable, $BILATERAL_{ij}$, which equals 1 if a given dyad has a bilateral PTA and 0 otherwise. Likewise, we set $MULTILATERAL_{ij}$ equal to 1 if both states in the dyad participate in the same multilateral PTA. We include these variables and the interaction between each of them and $TRADE_{ij}$ to determine whether the effect of trade on conflict among PTA members depends on the size of the trade agreement.

The first column of table 9.2 presents the estimates of this model. Although

TABLE 9.2. Estimates of the Effects of PTA Characteristics on the Onset of Militarized Disputes

Variable	(1)	(2)	(3)
Trade	0.031*	0.031*	0.027
	(0.017)	(0.017)	(0.017)
Multilateral PTA	0.483***		
	(0.113)		
Multilateral PTA × Trade	−0.133***		
	(0.018)		
Bilateral PTA	0.147		
	(0.360)		
Bilateral PTA × Trade	−0.015		
	(0.064)		
FTA		0.440***	
		(0.115)	
FTA × Trade		−0.132***	
		(0.017)	
CET		0.804***	
		(0.268)	
CET × Trade		−0.105**	
		(0.054)	
DSM			1.211***
			(0.276)
DSM × Trade			−0.270***
			(0.036)
No DSM			0.429***
			(0.114)
No DSM × Trade			−0.086***
			(0.017)
ΔGDP_i	−0.189	−0.206	−0.165
	(0.377)	(0.371)	(0.378)
ΔGDP_j	0.183	0.162	0.226
	(0.395)	(0.390)	(0.408)
Distance	−0.270***	−0.271***	−0.275***
	(0.034)	(0.034)	(0.034)
Contiguity	2.144***	2.143***	2.144***
	(0.114)	(0.113)	(0.113)
GDP_i	0.247***	0.248***	0.246***
	(0.027)	(0.027)	(0.027)
GDP_j	0.176***	0.177***	0.176***
	(0.028)	(0.028)	(0.028)
$Regime_i$	−0.020***	−0.020***	−0.019***
	(0.005)	(0.005)	(0.005)
$Regime_j$	−0.012**	−0.011**	−0.011**
	(0.005)	(0.005)	(0.005)
Capability Ratio	0.646***	0.636***	0.678***
	(0.158)	(0.159)	(0.157)
Ongoing MID	1.682***	1.676***	1.675***
	(0.162)	(0.162)	(0.161)

TABLE 9.2.—*Continued*

Variable	(1)	(2)	(3)
Allies	−0.240**	−0.227**	−0.239**
	(0.094)	(0.094)	(0.094)
GATT	−0.461***	−0.463***	−0.424***
	(0.113)	(0.114)	(0.112)
Major Power	0.653***	0.649***	0.686***
	(0.129)	(0.130)	(0.129)
Constant	−10.678***	−10.735***	−10.701***
	(0.842)	(0.849)	(0.837)
N	404,133	404,133	404,133

Note: Robust standard errors clustered on the dyad are in parentheses; *** $p < 0.01$, ** $p < 0.05$, * $p < 0.10$.

the coefficient estimates of $BILATERAL_{ij}$ and $MULTILATERAL_{ij}$ are positive and the estimate of each variable's interaction with trade is negative, only the two variables associated with multilateral agreements achieve statistical significance. Thus, it appears that multilateral groupings largely drive the relationship between PTAs and conflict that we uncovered earlier. This finding may reflect a tendency for larger PTAs to have members that can help broker a resolution if conflict breaks out between a given pair of participants. Furthermore, greater institutionalization may help dampen conflicts between participants.[51] Multilateral agreements are usually more highly institutionalized than bilateral trade agreements, which almost always have the sparest institutional infrastructures.

Finally, we use this model to analyze our two other dependent variables: the onset of a MID that yields battlefield fatalities and the onset of a MID between countries that previously experienced a military dispute. These results are reported in the first columns of tables 9.3 and 9.4, respectively. The results for fatal MIDs are strikingly similar to the earlier findings: heightened trade depresses conflict between participants in multilateral arrangements, whereas bilateral arrangements appear to have no appreciable influence on the onset of deadly MIDs. Furthermore, as shown in the first column of table 9.4, the estimated coefficient of $MULTILATERAL_{ij} \times TRADE_{ij}$ for dyads that previously experienced a MID is negative and statistically significant. However, further analysis indicates that there is no statistically significant difference between this estimate and the estimate of $BILATERAL_{ij} \times TRADE_{ij}$.

TABLE 9.3. Estimates of the Effects of PTA Characteristics on the Onset of Fatal Militarized Disputes

Variable	(1)	(2)	(3)
Trade	−0.040*	−0.042*	−0.043*
	(0.024)	(0.024)	(0.024)
Multilateral PTA	0.413**		
	(0.162)		
Multilateral PTA × Trade	−0.100***		
	(0.023)		
Bilateral PTA	0.400		
	(0.588)		
Bilateral PTA × Trade	−0.000		
	(0.082)		
FTA		0.434***	
		(0.166)	
FTA × Trade		−0.092***	
		(0.023)	
CET		0.759**	
		(0.340)	
CET × Trade		−0.037	
		(0.077)	
DSM			1.498***
			(0.433)
DSM × Trade			−0.276***
			(0.045)
No DSM			0.445***
			(0.164)
No DSM × Trade			−0.057***
			(0.022)
ΔGDP_i	0.430	0.412	0.433
	(0.792)	(0.788)	(0.791)
ΔGDP_j	0.234	0.219	0.268
	(0.599)	(0.593)	(0.614)
Distance	−0.313***	−0.313***	−0.315***
	(0.056)	(0.056)	(0.056)
Contiguity	2.344***	2.336***	2.338***
	(0.175)	(0.174)	(0.174)
GDP_i	0.212***	0.215***	0.213***
	(0.045)	(0.045)	(0.045)
GDP_j	0.140***	0.143***	0.141***
	(0.043)	(0.043)	(0.043)
$Regime_i$	−0.020***	−0.019***	−0.019***
	(0.007)	(0.007)	(0.007)
$Regime_j$	−0.022***	−0.021***	−0.020**
	(0.008)	(0.008)	(0.008)
Capability Ratio	0.771***	0.748***	0.796***
	(0.232)	(0.236)	(0.232)
Ongoing MID	1.885***	1.883***	1.883***
	(0.216)	(0.215)	(0.215)

TABLE 9.3.—*Continued*

Variable	(1)	(2)	(3)
Allies	−0.356***	−0.359***	−0.372***
	(0.137)	(0.139)	(0.137)
GATT	−0.418**	−0.435**	−0.388*
	(0.205)	(0.209)	(0.202)
Major Power	0.912***	0.909***	0.951***
	(0.232)	(0.235)	(0.231)
Constant	−10.641***	−10.754***	−10.707***
	(1.353)	(1.359)	(1.349)
N	404,133	404,133	404,133

Note: Robust standard errors clustered on the dyad are in parentheses; *** $p < 0.01$, ** $p < 0.05$, * $p < 0.10$.

From Regional Trade Relations to Regional Peacemaking

In the introduction to this volume, Ripsman and Lobell ask what types of economic statecraft can be used to promote regional peace. We examine whether bilateral economic agreements can be used to promote peace within regions or whether multilateral agreements are better able to promote regional peacemaking. To generate some evidence bearing on this issue, we restrict our sample to dyads located in the same geographic region, based on the COW project's coding of each country's regional location. We then reestimate the model discussed in the previous section, in which we distinguish the effects of bilateral and multilateral PTAs.

We do not present these results in tables 9.2–9.4 to conserve space and because the results are nearly identical to the previous estimates. But figure 9.2 shows the predicted probability of the onset of a MID for regional neighbors that do not belong to the same PTA and for such neighbors in a multilateral PTA, respectively. We do not include bilateral PTAs in this figure since $BILAT$-$ERAL_{ij}$ and its interaction with trade are not jointly statistically significant. As before, there is a strong inverse relationship between trade and the onset of a dispute between regional neighbors that participate in the same multilateral PTA. Outside a PTA, by contrast, trade between states in the same region has no bearing on the outbreak of conflict. Estimating this model using our two additional dependent variables, however, yields less robust results. For MIDs marked by battlefield fatalities and MIDs between states that have a history of conflict, the effects of trade within multilateral PTAs are much weaker.

TABLE 9.4. Estimates of the Effects of PTA Characteristics on the Onset of Militarized Disputes between States with a History of Antagonism

Variable	(1)	(2)	(3)
Trade	−0.020	−0.019	−0.021*
	(0.012)	(0.012)	(0.012)
Multilateral PTA	−0.106		
	(0.093)		
Multilateral PTA × Trade	−0.036**		
	(0.017)		
Bilateral PTA	0.629		
	(0.506)		
Bilateral PTA × Trade	−0.107		
	(0.101)		
FTA		−0.085	
		(0.098)	
FTA × Trade		−0.039**	
		(0.017)	
CET		−0.099	
		(0.220)	
CET × Trade		−0.012	
		(0.051)	
DSM			0.706*
			(0.404)
DSM × Trade			−0.166**
			(0.067)
No DSM			−0.116
			(0.094)
No DSM × Trade			−0.019
			(0.015)
ΔGDP_i	−0.114	−0.122	−0.103
	(0.296)	(0.294)	(0.296)
ΔGDP_j	0.192	0.186	0.215
	(0.342)	(0.340)	(0.349)
Distance	−0.067***	−0.067***	−0.070***
	(0.025)	(0.025)	(0.025)
Contiguity	0.968***	0.972***	0.969***
	(0.091)	(0.091)	(0.091)
GDP_i	0.069***	0.070***	0.070***
	(0.024)	(0.024)	(0.025)
GDP_j	0.008	0.009	0.009
	(0.025)	(0.025)	(0.025)
$Regime_i$	0.004	0.004	0.004
	(0.004)	(0.004)	(0.004)
$Regime_j$	0.010**	0.011**	0.011**
	(0.005)	(0.005)	(0.005)
Capability Ratio	0.242	0.229	0.245
	(0.160)	(0.159)	(0.159)
Ongoing MID	0.741***	0.745***	0.740***
	(0.102)	(0.102)	(0.101)

TABLE 9.4.—*Continued*

Variable	(1)	(2)	(3)
Allies	−0.059	−0.059	−0.063
	(0.075)	(0.075)	(0.075)
GATT	−0.325***	−0.323***	−0.310***
	(0.092)	(0.092)	(0.092)
Major Power	0.246**	0.238**	0.254**
	(0.119)	(0.119)	(0.119)
Constant	−3.394***	−3.424***	−3.451***
	(0.744)	(0.749)	(0.757)
N	17,952	17,952	17,952

Note: Robust standard errors clustered on the dyad are in parentheses; *** $p < 0.01$, ** $p < 0.05$, * $p < 0.10$.

Proposed Integration

Next we analyze whether a PTA's proposed level of integration affects the likelihood of hostilities between its member states. Preferential agreements include FTAs, customs unions, common markets, and economic unions. The latter three types of PTAs are all marked by a common external tariff (CET) on the products of third parties, where FTAs do not have this design feature. As such, we consider customs unions, common markets, and economic unions as a group.

More specifically we define FTA_{ij} and CET_{ij}, as well as the interaction between each of these variables and $TRADE_{ij}$, to address whether the combination of heightened trade between members of arrangements that have particularly ambitious economic objectives is an especially potent deterrent to conflict. The estimates of this model are shown in the second column of table 9.2. Both trade agreements with and trade agreements without a common external tariff depress the level of military conflict as trade rises. Furthermore, there is no statistically significant difference between the two effects: the simulated predicted probabilities from this model indicate that there is no variation between FTAs and arrangements with a CET in reducing the onset of militarized conflict.

When examining only MIDs marked by fatalities (the second column of table 9.3) or disputes involving states that have fought in the past (the second column of table 9.4), trade in agreements without a CET is inversely related to the onset of conflict. The coefficient estimates of $FTA_{ij} \times TRADE_{ij}$ are negative and statistically significant, whereas the estimated coefficients of $CET_{ij} \times TRADE_{ij}$ are not statistically significant. However, it is important to recognize that,

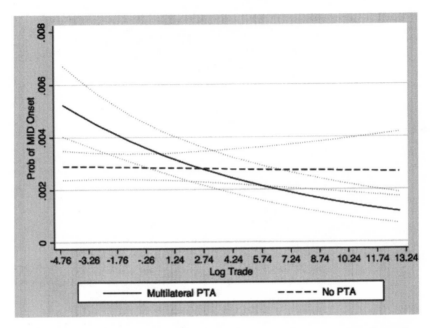

Fig. 9.2. The effects of trade on conflict between states in the same region, depending on whether they participate in the same multilateral PTA. (Lighter lines represent 95 percent confidence intervals.)

in all of these tests, there is no statistically significant difference between the effects of FTAs and agreements characterized by a CET.[52]

Dispute Settlement Mechanisms

Finally, we examine the effects of a DSM. James McCall Smith has measured the extent of formal legalization of DSMs within a set of PTAs.[53] His measure includes information on (1) whether disputes are delegated to third-party review, (2) whether these reviews are binding, (3) the nature of the agents (judges) conducting the review, (4) who has standing before the review agents, and (5) the nature of remedies provided by the review system. Based on these five characteristics, Smith created an ordinal indicator of the level of "legalism" in the organization. We utilize Smith's coding scheme to code DSMs across PTAs. We also use Smith's data, after supplementing them in several ways. First, Smith excluded a number of agreements. Many of these omitted PTAs are bilateral agreements, which are often less institutionalized than the groupings included in Smith's sample. Excluding these less institutionalized PTAs could bias an investigation of DSMs and conflict. Second, Smith's coding was largely static, but DSMs can change over time.[54] We revisit Smith's coding to capture these institutional changes and fill in missing data.

All other things being equal, we expect more formalized DSMs to depress political-military conflict, since this institutional feature should assist states in ameliorating tensions before open hostilities break out. To test this hypothesis, we create two variables: (1) DSM_{ij} equals 1 if the dyad is a member of a PTA with a DSM and 0 otherwise, and (2) $NO\ DSM_{ij}$ equals 1 if states i and j are members of a PTA without a dispute settlement mechanism and 0 otherwise. The absence of a PTA is the baseline category. In addition, we include the interaction between each of these variables and $TRADE_{ij}$.

The initial estimates of this model are reported in the third column of table 9.1. Both PTAs with and PTAs without DSMs condition the impact of trade on militarized disputes. However, neither the difference between these two coefficient estimates nor the difference between the coefficients of the two associated interaction terms is statistically significant. Thus, whether or not a PTA is marked by a formal DSM has little bearing on the prospects for military conflict between member states.[55]

This conclusion also holds when examining the influence of DSMs on the onset of fatal MIDs (the third column of table 9.3) and the onset of MIDs between dyads that have experienced prior conflict (the third column of table 9.4). In the former case, the estimated coefficients of DSM_{ij} and $NO\ DSM_{ij}$ are statistically significant but not significantly different from each other. The same is true for the interactions between these variables and $TRADE_{ij}$. In the latter case, only the estimated coefficients of DSM_{ij} and $DSM_{ij} \times TRADE_{ij}$ are statistically significant, yet again these estimates are not distinguishable from the estimates of $NO\ DSM_{ij}$ and its interaction with $TRADE_{ij}$. Dispute settlement mechanisms seem to have little bearing on the onset of fatal MIDs or MIDs between dyads that have experienced conflict.

Conclusion

The past 20 years have witnessed a substantial increase in the number of preferential trade agreements throughout the world. While most research on these arrangements has focused on their economic causes and effects, we have argued that they also influence political-military relations between states. Our past work has confirmed this claim, showing that PTA members that trade extensively tend to have more pacific relations than other states.

In this chapter, we have arrived at the same conclusion, based on an extended and updated data set. Heightened trade has little effect on the prospects for military disputes outside a PTA. Extensive trade between members of a PTA, however, significantly reduces the prospects for military violence. This result holds when focusing on all MIDs, those that result in battlefield fatalities, and MIDs between states with a history of military antagonism.

We also extended our previous work by differentiating PTAs across three institutional characteristics: whether they are bilateral or multilateral, their proposed level of integration, and whether they contain a dispute settlement mechanism. We found that multilateral agreements are the institutions driving the relationship between PTAs and conflict. This finding is especially strong when limiting the sample to dyads that inhabit the same geographic region, providing some evidence for Ripsman and Lobell's conjecture in the introduction to this volume about whether bilateral or multilateral institutions are better at fostering regional peace. Furthermore, bilateral PTAs have little effect on disputes, and because they virtually never expand, take on additional members, and become multilateral, there is little reason to believe that they can evolve in a way that would be useful from the standpoint of regional peacekeeping.[56] Alternatively, there is no evidence that the level of proposed integration or the presence of a DSM affects interstate hostilities.

In sum, it appears that institutional design plays only a marginal role in the way PTAs influence political-military relations between states. Rather, the key factor influencing the pacific effect of PTAs is the level of bilateral trade between their members. If PTAs can serve to reinforce high levels of trade between member states, they are likely to augur well for promoting peaceful relations between states within a region. They are, consequently, also useful for maintaining and reinforcing bilateral peace agreements within a broader regional institutional context, provided that member states in such institutions trade extensively. Nonetheless, while economic tools do promote peace between regional participants, there is no preferred path to regional arrangements, nor are regional efforts necessarily better than bilateral ones.

NOTES

1. For discussions of the types of PTAs, see Kym Anderson and Richard Blackhurst, "Introduction and Summary," in Kym Anderson and Richard Blackhurst, eds., *Regional Integration and the Global Trading System* (London: Harvester Wheatsheaf, 1993); and Jaime de Melo and Arvind Panagariya, "Introduction," in Jaime de Melo and Arvind Panagariya, eds., *New Dimensions in Regional Integration* (New York: Cambridge University Press, 1993).

2. Edward D. Mansfield and Jon C. Pevehouse, "Trade Blocs, Trade Flows, and International Conflict," *International Organization* 54, no. 4 (2000): 775–808; and Edward D. Mansfield and Jon C. Pevehouse, "Institutions, Interdependence, and International Conflict," in Gerald Schneider, Katherine Barbieri, and Nils Petter Gleditsch, eds., *Globalization and Armed Conflict* (Lanham, MD: Rowman and Littlefield, 2003).

3. This section draws on Mansfield and Pevehouse, "Trade Blocs, Trade Flows, and International Conflict." For discussions of the relationship between trade and military conflict, see Michael W. Doyle, *Ways of War and Peace: Realism, Liberalism, and Socialism* (New York: W. W. Norton, 1997); Robert O. Keohane, "Economic Liberalism Reconsidered," in John Dunn, ed., *The Economic Limits to Politics* (Cambridge: Cambridge University Press, 1990); Arthur A. Stein, "Governments, Economic Interdependence, and International Cooperation," in *Behavior, Society, and Nuclear War*, Philip E. Tetlock, Jo L. Husbands, Robert Jervis, Paul C. Stern, and Charles Tilly, eds., vol. 3 (New York: Oxford University Press, 1993); and Edward D. Mansfield and Brian Pollins, eds., *Economic Interdependence and International Conflict: New Perspectives on an Enduring Debate* (Ann Arbor: University of Michigan Press, 2003). For competing perspectives on this "opportunity cost" argument, see Solomon W. Polachek, "Conflict and Trade," *Journal of Conflict Resolution* 24, no. 1 (1980): 55–78; Norrin M. Ripsman and Jean-Marc F. Blanchard, "Commercial Liberalism under Fire: Evidence from 1914 and 1936," *Security Studies* 6, no. 2 (1996–97): 4–50; James D. Morrow, How Could Trade Affect Conflict?," *Journal of Peace Research* 36, no. 4 (1999): 481–89; Erik Gartzke, Quan Li, and Charles Boehmer, "Investing in the Peace: Economic Interdependence and International Conflict," *International Organization* 55, no. 2 (2001): 391–438; and Solomon W. Polachek and Jun Xiang, "How Opportunity Costs Decrease the Probability of War in an Incomplete Information Game," *International Organization* 64, no. 1 (2010): 133–44.

4. WTO [World Trade Organization], *World Trade Report 2011: The WTO and Preferential Trade Agreements* (Geneva: WTO, 2011).

5. Raquel Fernández, and Jonathan Portes, "Returns to Regionalism: An Evaluation of Nontraditional Gains from Regional Trade Agreements," *World Bank*

Economic Review 12, no. 2 (1998): 197–220; and Joseph S. Nye, *Peace in Parts: Integration and Conflict in Regional Organization* (Boston: Little, Brown, 1971).

6. Mansfield and Pevehouse, "Trade Blocs, Trade Flows, and International Conflict"; Mansfield and Pevehouse, "Institutions, Interdependence, and International Conflict"; and Edward D. Mansfield, Jon C. Pevehouse, and David H. Bearce, "Preferential Trading Arrangements and Military Disputes," *Security Studies* 9, nos. 1–2 (1999–2000): 96–118.

7. Fernández and Portes, "Returns to Regionalism"; Edward D. Mansfield, "The Proliferation of Preferential Trading Arrangements," *Journal of Conflict Resolution* 42, no. 5 (1998): 523–43; and John Whalley, "Why Do Countries Seek Regional Trade Arrangements?," in Jeffrey A. Frankel, ed., *The Regionalization of the World Economy* (Chicago: University of Chicago Press, 1998).

8. De Melo and Panagariya, "Introduction," 5–6; Carlo Perroni and John Whalley, "How Severe Is Global Retaliation Risk under Increasing Regionalism?," *American Economic Review* 86, no. 2 (1996): 57; and Beth V. Yarbrough and Robert M. Yarbrough, *Cooperation and Governance in International Trade: The Strategic Organizational Approach* (Princeton: Princeton University Press, 1992), 105–6.

9. Tim Büthe and Helen Milner, "The Politics of Foreign Direct Investment into Developing Countries: Increasing FDI through International Trade Agreements?," *American Journal of Political Science* 52, no. 4 (2008): 741–62.

10. WTO, *World Trade Report 2011*.

11. Fernández and Portes, "Returns to Regionalism"; and Yarbrough and Yarbrough, *Cooperation and Governance in International Trade*.

12. Mark S. Manger, *Investing in Protection: The Politics of Preferential Trade Agreements between North and South* (New York: Cambridge University Press, 2009); and Denis Medvedev, "Beyond Trade: The Impact of Preferential Trade Agreements on FDI Inflows," *World Development* 40, no. 1 (2012): 49–61.

13. Richard Pomfret, *The Economics of Regional Trading Arrangements* (New York: Oxford University Press, 1997); and Whalley, "Why Do Countries Seek Regional Trade Arrangements?"

14. There are numerous instances in which a struggling PTA has been replaced. For example, the Latin American Integration Association replaced the Latin American Free Trade Association, the Central African Customs and Economics Union succeeded the Equatorial Customs Union, and the Caribbean Community and Common Market replaced the Caribbean Free Trade Association.

15. Miles Kahler, "Institution-Building in the Pacific," in Andrew Mack and John Ravenhill, ed., *Pacific Cooperation: Building Economic and Political Regimes in the Asia-Pacific Region* (Boulder: Westview, 1995), 29.

16. For an analysis of how the anticipation of future gains from trade can

reduce the prospect that commercial partners will become embroiled in political disputes, see Dale Copeland, "Economic Interdependence and War: A Theory of Trade Expectations," *International Security* 20, no. 4 (1996): 5–41.

17. Keohane, "Economic Liberalism Reconsidered." Clearly, this argument is subject to qualification. If states anticipate that they could easily replace the economic benefits from PTA membership or if they heavily discount these benefits, then PTAs may do little to inhibit hostilities regardless of the volume of trade that countries conduct. However, so long as key trade partners expect that the benefits from PTA membership will outweigh the costs of participation and the potential benefits of a military dispute, the prospect of antagonism is likely to be small. See Mansfield, Pevehouse, and Bearce, "Preferential Trading Arrangements and Military Disputes."

18. Nye, *Peace in Parts*, 109.

19. Beth V. Yarbrough and Robert M. Yarbrough, "Dispute Settlement in International Trade: Regionalism and Procedural Coordination," in Edward D. Mansfield and Helen V. Milner, eds., *The Political Economy of Regionalism* (New York: Columbia University Press, 1997).

20. Stein, "Governments, Economic Interdependence, and International Cooperation."

21. Kusuma Snitwongse, "Thirty Years of ASEAN: Achievements through Political Cooperation," *Pacific Review* 11, no. 2 (1998): 183–94; and Timo Kivimäki, "Southeast Asia and Conflict Prevention: Is ASEAN Running Out of Steam?" *Pacific Review* 25, no. 4 (2012): 403–27.

22. Luigi Manzetti, "The Political Economy of MERCOSUR," *Journal of Interamerican Studies and World Affairs* 35, no. 4 (1993–94): 101–41; and Peter H. Smith, "The Politics of Integration: Concepts and Themes," in *The Challenges of Integration*, ed. Peter H. Smith (New Brunswick, NJ: Transaction Publishers, 1993).

23. Joseph M. Grieco, "Anarchy and the Limits of Cooperation: A Realist Critique of the Newest Liberal Institutionalism," *International Organization* 42, no. 3 (1990): 485–507; and Michael Mastanduno, "Do Relative Gains Matter? America's Response to Japanese Industrial Policy," *International Security* 16, no. 1 (1991): 73–113.

24. Fernández and Portes, "Returns to Regionalism," 213.

25. Geoffrey Garrett and Barry R. Weingast, "Ideas, Interests, and Institutions: Constructing the European Union's Internal Market," in Judith Goldstein and Robert O. Keohane, eds., *Ideas and Foreign Policy* (Ithaca: Cornell University Press, 1993).

26. For important exceptions, see David H. Bearce and Sawa Omori, "How Do Commercial Institutions Promote Peace?," *Journal of Peace Research* 42, no. 6

(2005): 659–78; and Yoram Z. Haftel, *Regional Economic Institutions and Conflict Mitigation: Design, Implementation, and the Promise of Peace* (Ann Arbor: University of Michigan Press, 2012).

27. Roberto Bouzas, "Regional Trade Arrangements: Lessons from Past Experiences," in M. Mendoza, P. Low, and B. Kotschwar, eds., *Trade Rules in the Making* (Washington, DC: Brookings Institution Press, 1999).

28. Haftel, *Regional Economic Institutions and Conflict Mitigation*; Cherie O'Neal Taylor, "Dispute Resolution as a Catalyst for Economic Integration and an Agent for Deepening Integration: NAFTA and MERCOSUR?," *Northwestern Journal of International Law and Business* 17, no. 1 (1997): 850–99; and Yarbrough and Yarbrough, "Dispute Settlement in International Trade."

29. It should be noted that while intra-ASEAN border disputes—such as the Singapore-Malaysia dispute over Pedra Branca Island and the Indonesia-Malaysia dispute over the Sipadan and Litigan islands—have often been resolved by the World Court and not the ASEAN High Council, some analysts maintain that ASEAN-reinforced norms led the states to seek dispute mediation. See Sheldon W. Simon, *Economic Crisis and ASEAN States' Security* (Carlisle Barracks, PA: Strategic Studies Institute, 1998), 198–200.

30. Hans H. Indorf, *Impediments to Regionalism in Southeast Asia* (Singapore: Institute of Southeast Asian Studies, 1984), 85.

31. Mancur Olson, *The Logic of Collective Action: Public Goods and the Theory of Groups* (Cambridge, MA: Harvard University Press, 1965).

32. Yarbrough and Yarbrough, *Cooperation and Governance in International Trade*, 17–19.

33. On the relationship between market size and the growth of PTA membership, see Edward D. Mansfield and Jon C. W. Pevehouse, "The Expansion of Preferential Trading Arrangements," *International Studies Quarterly* 57, no. 3 (2013): 592–604.

34. For a summary of the MIDs data, see Daniel M. Jones, Stuart A. Bremer, and J. David Singer, "Militarized Interstate Disputes, 1816–1992: Rationale, Coding Rules, and Empirical Patterns," *Conflict Management and Peace Science* 15, no. 2 (1996): 163–213.

35. Data on PTA membership and trade flows are taken from Edward D. Mansfield and Helen V. Milner, *Votes, Vetoes, and the Political Economy of International Trade Agreements* (Princeton: Princeton University Press, 2012). In our analysis, we exclude PTAs that are nonreciprocal since these arrangements do not provide market access to all parties. Rather, they are usually agreements whereby advanced industrial countries grant preferential market access to developing countries.

36. These data are taken from Alan Heston, Robert Summers, and Bettina

Aten, Penn World Table Version 7.0., Center for International Comparisons of Production, Income, and Prices at the University of Pennsylvania, May 2011, http://pwt.econ.upenn.edu/php_site/pwt_index.php. Both variables are randomized with respect to which state is designated as *i* and *j*.

37. Randolph Siverson and Harvey Starr, *Diffusion of War: A Study of Opportunity and Willingness* (Ann Arbor: University of Michigan Press, 1991).

38. Alan V. Deardorff, "Determinants of Bilateral Trade: Does Gravity Work in a Neoclassical World?," in Jeffrey A. Frankel, ed., *The Regionalization of the World Economy* (Chicago: University of Chicago Press, 1998); and Mansfield and Milner, *Votes, Vetoes, and the Political Economy of International Trade Agreements.*

39. See, for example, Robert Gilpin, *War and Change in World Politics* (New York: Cambridge University Press, 1981).

40. These data are taken from the Alliance Treaty Obligations and Provisions project and are available at atop.rice.edu.

41. J. David Singer and Melvin Small, *National Material Capabilities Dataset*, Study no. 9903 (Ann Arbor: Inter-university Consortium for Political and Social Research, 1993).

42. Keith Jaggers and Ted Robert Gurr, "Tracking Democracy's Third Wave with the Polity III Data," *Journal of Peace Research* 32, no. 4 (1995): 469–82. Their original index ranges from −10 to 10. To aid in interpreting the results, we add 10 to every state's annual score.

43. See, for example, Doyle, *Ways of War and Peace;* and Bruce Russett and John R. Oneal, *Triangulating Peace: Democracy, Interdependence, and International Organizations* (New York: W. W. Norton, 2001).

44. Data on GATT membership are taken from Mansfield and Milner, *Votes, Vetoes, and the Political Economy of International Trade Agreements.*

45. Nathaniel Beck, Jonathan N. Katz, and Richard Tucker, "Beyond Ordinary Logit: Taking Time Seriously in Binary Time-Series Cross-Section Models," *American Journal of Political Science* 42, no. 4 (1998): 1260–88.

46. On the interpretation of interaction terms, see Bear F. Braumoeller, "Hypothesis Testing and Multiplicative Interaction Terms," *International Organization* 58, no. 4 (2004): 807–20.

47. On the related issue of how trade relations affect the cessation of conflict and peacemaking, see Galia Press-Barnathan, *The Political Economy of Transitions to Peace* (Pittsburgh: University of Pittsburgh Press, 2009).

48. Erik Gartzke, "Kant We All Just Get Along? Opportunity, Willingness, and the Origins of the Democratic Peace," *American Journal of Political Science* 42, no. 1 (1998): 1–27; Mansfield and Pevehouse, "Trade Blocs, Trade Flows, and International Conflict," 796–97; and Russett and Oneal, *Triangulating Peace*, 228–37.

49. William R. Thompson, "Identifying Rivals and Rivalries in World Politics," *International Studies Quarterly* 45, no. 4 (2001): 557–86.

50. Although we measure this variable each year and allow it to vary, nearly all PTAs that begin as bilateral remain as such throughout their existence, whereas various multilateral PTAs do take on new members. See Mansfield and Pevehouse, "The Expansion of Preferential Trading Arrangements."

51. Haftel, *Regional Economic Institutions and Conflict Mitigation.*

52. This is counter to the finding of Vicard, who finds that deeper integration schemes lead to fewer conflicts. However, he does not examine the interaction between PTAs and bilateral trade. See Vincent Vicard, "Trade, Conflict, and Political Integration: Explaining the Heterogeneity of Regional Trade Agreements," *European Economic Review* 56, no. 1 (2012): 54–71.

53. James McCall Smith, "The Politics of Dispute Settlement: Explaining Legalism in Regional Trade Pacts," *International Organization* 54, no. 1 (2000): 137–80.

54. Yarbrough and Yarbrough, "Dispute Settlement in International Trade."

55. For studies that arrive at a similar conclusion, see Bearce and Omori, "How Do Commercial Institutions Promote Peace?"; and Haftel, *Regional Economic Institutions and Conflict Mitigation.*

56. Mansfield and Pevehouse, "The Expansion of Preferential Trading Arrangements."

Conclusion

Economic Statecraft and Regional Peacemaking

Peter Dombrowski

In focusing on the use of economic instruments to terminate regional rivalries, the editors and contributors to this volume address what has been one of the most pernicious security challenges. Most regions of the world have been plagued with long-standing conflicts, periodic wars, and general instability. Often the source of these conflicts is enduring rivalries between specific country dyads that both contribute to and are exacerbated by wider regional problems. As Karen Rasler, William R. Thompson, and Sumit Ganguly note, citing earlier research, about 1 percent of possible state dyads account for nearly 80 percent of the interstate warfare that has taken place over the past 200 years.[1] Moreover, at several points in world history long-standing rivalries between individual states have embroiled entire regions in open warfare, and on three or four occasions flared into global wars that transformed the world's distribution of power and wealth. Israel's conflicts with Egypt, for example, have spilled over to multinational conflicts that threatened to draw extraregional powers into conflict in ways that, given bad luck or a little worse judgment, could have escalated to global nuclear war. Several hundred years of enmity between France and Germany (or various configurations of Germanic states) plunged Europe into world wars during the Napoleonic period, World War I, and World War II.

Few regions have managed to escape this dynamic, even temporarily, and, if we are to believe the most pessimistic international relations scholars, even those that have managed to establish peace temporarily may someday return to the normal state of affairs: conflict and warfare. Today Europe, the most prominent exception to the general norm of regional conflict, is enjoying its seventh decade largely free of war. Several historical European rivalries, most prominently that between France and Germany, have diminished to the point of vanishing. Perhaps more accurately, the historical intra-European conflicts have been channeled into commercial competition, cultural rivalry, and even political maneuvering within the comfortable institutional confines of the North Atlantic Treaty Organization (NATO) and the European Union (EU). As several chapters in this volume recount, the peace settlements between Germany and France in the decade following World War II laid the foundation for this enduring regional peace.

The costs of regional conflicts are incalculable in material terms, and their impact on social relations in other spheres is beyond mere speculation. Philosophers, political leaders, and, more recently, social scientists have thus sought an explanation for why such conflicts have endured both between individual states and within entire geographic spaces almost as long has human society has been chronicled. The reason is simple and ultimately practical. They search for solutions, means of promoting peace in these trouble regions applicable to the real world, not simply theoretical constructs divorced from the necessity of providing advice to "princes."

The contributors to this volume on the political economy of regional peacemaking have undertaken a difficult but valuable task: to examine the dynamics underlying the emergence of peace between regional rivals in a wide range of cases separated by time and space. Even more significantly, they have eschewed the research strategies common to many similar efforts. Rather than focusing on politics, diplomacy, strategy, or military operations, they explore in detail the relationship between the political process of regional peacemaking and economic statecraft.

Questions Asked and Answered

In the introduction to the volume, the editors, Norrin M. Ripsman and Steven E. Lobell, provide a valuable summary of the scholarly literatures relevant to the challenging problem of using economic instruments to resolve dyadic conflicts and contribute to regional peace. More important, they pose five questions to guide the contributors.

Ripsman and Lobell asked the contributors to frame their empirical analyses around these five interrelated questions about the political economy of regional transitions. In short, how have the instruments of economic statecraft been used by states to build peace between rival dyads, and how does peacemaking engage the entire geographic region? Each chapter then explores the history of important dyadic conflicts or engages in large-*N* analyses to determine what types of economic statecraft played a role in the process, what segment of society was targeted in the recipient state, and how the timing influenced outcomes. Stepping back from the events leading to peace (or in some cases not) Ripsman and Lobell also asked the contributors to evaluate the downsides to economic statecraft and what risks, if any, might accrue for state strategies relying on economic instruments. In most cases, though by no means all, the dyadic process contributes to the reduction of regional conflict. With exceptions discussed below, the contributors thus found cautious support for the importance of economic statecraft. After comparing and contrasting the cases both within and between chapters, however, it is clear that the relative contribution of the critical factors (as theorized by Ripsman and Lobell) varied greatly over time and space.

Types of Economic Statecraft

David Allen Baldwin's classic study of economic statecraft identified numerous types of negative and positive economic instruments ranging from embargoes to investment promotion to tariffs.[2] Subsequently, a cottage industry of scholarship developed to test the efficacy of Baldwin's instruments and to identify other possible instruments in both theory and practice.[3] Of the volume's chapters, those of Ripsman, Lobell, and Jean-Marc F. Blanchard pay the closest attention to the specific instruments of economic statecraft identified by Baldwin. According to the qualitative and quantitative evidence presented in this volume, the utility of economic instruments employed to support peacemaking has been somewhat limited.

In chapters 1 and 2, Ripsman and Lobell examine the roles of economic statecraft in crafting peace agreements in two cases: Egypt-Israel and Jordan-Israel. Ripsman covers the Franco-German and Egypt-Israel cases, while both recount the Jordan-Israel peace process from top-down and bottom-up perspectives. Ripsman concludes that in all three cases "peace settlements were facilitated through the promise of large economic assistance programs or grants" by the United States Lobell concludes that third parties, such as the

United States, the International Monetary Fund (IMF), and the World Bank, helped create a larger win-set for both societies by signing preferential trade agreements (PTAs) and agreeing to structural adjustment programs with both Israel and Jordan. Third-party interventions were intended to not only achieve the standard goals of the so-called Washington Consensus and economic liberalization but also, more important to the cause of peace, create internationally oriented domestic coalitions with an overarching interest in peace because of second order economic benefits. Taken together, the Middle Eastern peace process benefited from economic statecraft exercised by a range of external actors. A similar claim could be made for the Franco-German settlement.[4] The Marshall Plan promised direct aid from the United States, while the institutional dimensions of European integration and the wider Bretton Woods arrangements established a fertile institutional context for the long-term growth of economic interdependence, leading in time to the economic integration represented by the Single Market and the EU.

In chapter 6, Blanchard looks carefully at four positive sanctions—trade, foreign aid, low-interest loans, and foreign direct investment (FDI)—with regard to bringing about long-term peace between China and Japan. However, as he acknowledges, these economic interactions are part of a wider pattern of growing economic interdependence if not economic integration. Within a geopolitical rivalry characterized by mistrust and growing militarization, neither government has used economic instruments to support the peaceful resolution of long-standing diplomatic, political, and territorial disputes. In fact it appears that Chinese and Japanese firms do business with each other despite rather than because of the enduring rivalry. Moreover, as China has become a leading economic power in its own right, Japan's willingness to provide foreign assistance and low-interest loans has diminished.

Several chapters consider means of economic statecraft neither identified by Baldwin nor explicitly considered in the wide-ranging literature following in his footsteps. In chapter 4, Marie-Joëlle Zahar combines two understudied strands of thought in the overarching literatures—(1) the role played by nonstate actors and (2) the material motivations of the targets of inducements—with her own empirical work to offer important hypotheses about which types of statecraft are most likely to be successful.

Chapter, 9, by Edward D. Mansfield and Jon C. Pevehouse, contributes important findings about one specific type of economic statecraft, PTAs. They find that PTAs do have a positive effect, particularly on sustaining peace once bilateral peace agreements have been signed. More significantly for exploring the specific types of economic statecraft that are effective in promoting regional peace, they look closely at the institutional design of PTAs. Their analysis finds support for the contribution of multilateral PTAs (vs. bilateral arrangements), but, perhaps surprisingly, it also finds that the level of integration associated with the PTA and the presence of dispute resolution mechanisms (DSMs) do not affect interstate hostilities. This is the type of finding that could influence negotiators seeking to design PTAs to support regional stability. Rather than devoting time and energy to working out the details of future integration or dispute resolution, ensuring that the agreement is concluded and includes as many parties as possible might be more effective.[5]

Targets in Rival States

In general there are three target audiences for economic incentives and sanctions: (1) leaders, (2) elites, and (3) society. For the most part, the chapters in this volume focus most closely on leaders or elites. One major exception is the China-Japan dyadic relationship explored by Scott L. Kastner and Margaret Pearson in chapter 7. In this relationship, especially once Japan stopped providing direct aid and investment incentives, FDI and trade largely influenced society as whole and to some extent economic or business elites who profit from bilateral commercial relations. Yet *targeting* seems too strong a term in this context because for the most part economic interactions between the two societies are less a result of strategic decisions to promote peaceful relations than a by-product of commercial behavior. Moreover, contrary to the expectations of some of the commercial peace literature broadly understood, growing economic interdependence between Japan and China has not reduced tension let alone led to the equivalent of a peace agreement.

Zahar steps outside the conceptual framework developed by Ripsman and Lobell by identifying targets outside their tripartite division. In part this is because she frames the issue in terms of the hypothesis that "material sanctions are likely to be more effective when yielded against organizationally complex nonstate armed actors." Thus, her analysis prioritizes nonstate, societal actors (and in her cases nonstate actors with elements that reside outside the state—the Palestine Liberation Organization [PLO]). Organizationally complex actors are led and managed by individuals and groups with stakes in the long-term future. They present opponents or third parties with a variety of levers (see below on smart or targeted sanctions) to influence belligerents using negative sanctions or positive inducements. Thus, the first Intifada allowed Israel to destroy the PLO's infrastructure and assets while the PLO's refusal to condemn Iraq's invasion of Kuwait forced the Arab Gulf states to suspend their aid. In short the time became "ripe" for the Oslo Accords because Yasser Arafat and the PLO were materially weakened by negative inducements.

Timing of Economic Statecraft

As a process with many stops and starts, as well as uncertain phases, peace negotiations allow us to explore the timing of economic statecraft. Ripsman and Lobell's introduction posits three straightforward phases: prenegotiation, negotiation, and postagreement. What instruments work best during what phase of the process?

Zahar demonstrates how economic statecraft can be used to affect the fundamental balance of power between two parties in conflict. In effect, in a civil war or other conflict, one side can use negative or positive inducements to weaken or strengthen the other. Peacemaking is thus contingent on creating a window of opportunity ("a ripe moment") when negotiations have a chance to succeed. Time is ripe for agreement when one side is on the "precipice" of losing or perhaps both sides recognize the futility of continuing the conflict absent hope of victory or a workable military resolution.

If coaxing rivals to the negotiating table is a difficult task that economic statecraft can facilitate, the same is true for ensuring that peace agreements hold. Thus, at the opposite end of the spectrum from Zahar's research, and in line with William R. Thompson's focus on forward-looking agreements in chapter 5, is the central conclusion of Mansfield and Pevehouse that PTAs make "useful tools to cement and reinforce bilateral peace treaties between regional rivals." Building on their long-standing research program, Mansfield and Pevehouse make a strong case that embedding bilateral peace within a strong regional institutional context makes it more likely that peace will last. Their empirical findings are consistent with the general logics expressed in several of the other chapters. Peace arrangements between France and Germany have lasted more than 50 years at least in part because of the interlocking web of regional organizations that exist in Europe, the strongest of which is that internal market associated with the EU. By contrast, peace between Israel and its various adversaries remains tenuous for many reasons, including the lack of strong free trade institutions in the Middle East as a whole. Commerce between Israel and its neighbors is relatively modest and threatened almost continuously by political and military crises. There are no multilateral commercial forums available in which to mediate disputes and channel conflicts in less escalatory directions.

Limits and Risks

Not all contributors to this volume identified specific risks associated with using economic instruments in the pursuit of peace. Those that did, however, are quite clear about the potential costs of peacemaking strategies that rely on economic inducements or sanctions.

Perhaps the most important limitation is the general and even obvious caveat identified by Thompson, who writes, "[E]conomic incentives are but one factor among many." In two of the cases he examines—the Franco-German and Brazilian-Argentine rivalries—other factors included the defeat of one party in each dyad in a war. Even Thompson's presentation of the Israeli case stressed the importance of Israel's "near defeat" at the hands of Egypt because it shook Israel's political leadership. If Thompson is the author who stresses most closely the importance of overall context and multicausal explanations, a close reading of the other chapters highlights similar points. All of this is not to deny the various roles played by economic statecraft but rather to make certain that in our interpretations of individual cases and further theorizing we take care not to overlook the contributing factors or underemphasize the wider political, economic, and military context in which economic statecraft is employed to pursue peace agreements.

Another key finding from the Blanchard chapter makes this point with regard to a specific subset of dyadic rivalries. Namely, "[T]he problem is that economic interactions take place within a relationship characterized by power relations and a security dilemma, which constrains their positive externalities." Put differently, economic statecraft has less impact when the relationship between the rivals is already highly securitized. Although Blanchard does not make too much of the significance of this finding, taken to its logical conclusion it calls into question the applicability of economic sanctions to many long-standing dyadic rivalries. After all, these rivalries endure and have importance more generally for regional stability and international relations precisely because the parties interact through "power relations," leading to long-standing security dilemmas. Nonetheless, Blanchard's conclusions are not completely at odds with Ripsman and Lobell's theoretical perspective in the introduction because, as Blanchard acknowledges, the current and historical Sino-Japanese rivalry involves "massive bilateral economic ties rather than targeted economic sanctions or incentives," that is, what we traditionally understand as economic statecraft.

Kastner and Pearson draw insight from social psychology, observing that "the introduction of monetary incentives into social market interactions can backfire." Economic statecraft, represented in their chapter by policies of "engagement," may encourage increased gains (or presumably losses) from economic incentives rather than the potential overarching benefits of the peaceful resolution of long-term conflicts. Further, the targets of negative or positive sanctions may question the motives of their benefactor(s). Are the incentives some form of Trojan horse or "bait and switch" that promises to contribute to peace building while actually opening the door for the resolution of long-standing disputes on less than favorable terms? In chapter 8, William Norris extends these insights with an observation: "When economic activity is perceived as advancing the goals of one side at the expense of the other or when economic interests are viewed as agents of an expansionist state, or even when economic growth is seen as fueling a generally rising power, the economic activity can produce security consequences that work against peacemaking efforts."

Norris implies that perceptions on the part of various domestic constituencies within both parties to a dispute matter a great deal. Yet neither the Norris chapter nor the others in the volume address what strategic studies scholars sometimes call strategic communications.[6] Diplomats call this public diplomacy,[7] business scholars call it public relations, and political operatives call it messaging. In using economic statecraft (regardless of the specific instruments or even sequencing), both parties, and likely third-party participants as well, need to communicate their intentions and purposes. Or perhaps in some circumstances the parties might decide to divert the attention of particular factions during some steps in the three-phase negotiation process in order to give peace a chance. Of course the credibility of such communications is quite likely to be called into question, especially when those communicating are working their way out of long-term, often hostile rivalries.

From Bilateral to Regional Peace

Of the three wider regions encompassing the dyadic cases examined in this volume—Europe, the Middle East, and the Asia-Pacific—only Europe can be said to be peaceful as a result of resolving long-standing bilateral conflicts.

Clearly, the ability of France and Germany to overcome historic enmities and the legacies of multiple, deeply violent, region- and globe-reshaping wars to make bilateral peace and lead an entire continent into economic, security, and political integration that to date has proved remarkably resilient is a remarkable achievement. The start provided by Germany and France allowed for the gradual but virtually inexorable "widening and deepening" of Europe up to and including the peaceful management of the collapse of the Soviet bloc.

The other two regions—the Middle East and Asia—are more problematic. In each region, modest progress in resolving (or in the case of Taiwan and China, perhaps, managing) specific bilateral conflicts has not extended to the wider region. As I will discuss, despite the successes of Israel and Egypt and Israel and Jordan in developing peaceful relationships, Israel remains mired in multiple bilateral conflicts with both state and nonstate actors. Moreover, although the Arab-Israeli conflict remains a primary driver of adversarial regional trends, there are many other sources of conflict disrupting the region. In Asia, although the main protagonists have not directly fought wars or even proxy wars, there have been, and continue to be, sporadic tensions. From Quemoy and Matsu in the 1950s to recent tensions between China and Japan in the East China Sea, local tensions remain high. Certainly China and Japan, like many countries in East Asia, are currently engaging in a quiet, if expensive and dangerous, arms buildup.[8]

The possibility of moving from bilateral peacemaking to wider regional settlements is yet another area in which, given the findings of this volume's chapters, additional research is required. Regional organizations, regional powers, and great powers with global interests, such as the United States, have many interests in wider settlements. Resolving specific dyadic conflicts obviously helps enormously, but, as the impact of Israel's numerous conflicts on the greater Middle East demonstrates, resolving one conflict completes only part of the job. In policy and analytic terms, there are many interaction effects between and among dyadic conflicts and regional peace. Both positive and negative inducements can and should be crafted by regional players to take this into account.

Questions Raised

In a volume that presents as many rich case studies as this one, it is not surprising that the analyses raise nearly as many questions as they fully answer. The next section considers several avenues for future research that lead to important questions scholars can pursue in both the cases presented here and others that develop over time.

Policy Implications

No brief chapter can be expected to answer all questions or present a full account of any particular case. One lacuna in virtually all the chapters is a discussion, however brief, of how the public policy apparatus of each country involved is equipped to formulate and implement decisions regarding the peace process across the necessary sequence of events.[9] This, of course, is by design, as the editors wanted to address the theoretical foundations of using economic statecraft in the service of peacemaking to enable a meaningful policy discussion to take place.

Yet, from my perspective, a better understanding of how economic statecraft can support a peace process is essential to understanding whether the policy institutions and policy makers in adversary countries and interested third parties have the wherewithal to pursue prescribed approaches. In chapter 2, Lobell briefly alludes to the importance of "foreign policy executives" but largely as those acted upon (by the instruments of statecraft pursued by other states and nonstate actors) rather than as actors making choices about alternative courses of action. Which inducements (positive or negative) are employed, when, and in what sequences depends on a complex set of decisions made by politicians and policy professionals operating within a domestic institutional structure that often places severe limits on what is possible. Understanding the impact of this reality will provide greater depth to understanding the successes and failures of peacemakers under particular circumstances.[10] Focusing on foreign policy executives, both as those "acted upon" by other states seeking to influence policy choices or as decision makers choosing from alternative policies, comes with a cost however. Such granularity complicates the ability of scholars to model and conduct empirical research; the already daunting task of understanding and documenting the important of economic statecraft on peacemaking becomes still more challenging.

Thus, one next step in pursuing the analytic threads opened up by this volume would be to take seriously the argument of Valerie M. Hudson that we should pursue an understanding of foreign policy that is "characterized by an actor-specific focus, based upon the argument that all that occurs between nations and across nations is grounded in human decision makers acting singly or in groups."[11] Insights on specific economic instruments, timing in the peace process, limits to statecraft, and so forth thus can contribute both to theory building and to understanding how policy makers operate.

Economic Statecraft

Ripsman and Lobell are two of the major contributors to the large and successful literature on economic statecraft. As such, it is a bit surprising that, with the exception of their own chapters, the role of economic statecraft is relatively undertheorized and empirically deemphasized in some of the volume's other contributions.

One important exception is the chapter by Kastner and Pearson. The authors introduce the concept of engagement, long essential to thinking about the strategic choices available to states, particularly the United States and other great powers making choices about how to interact with peers, rivals, so-called rogue states, and especially non-status-quo powers.[12] Although engagement has long been associated with economic statecraft, this chapter opens the door to thinking more systematically about economic policy instruments in the context of establishing peace. Specifically, a strategy of engagement connotes two dynamics often underemphasized in the literatures on peacemaking and economic statecraft. First, it encourages scholars (and perhaps politicians and policy makers) to stop thinking about economic sanctions, be they positive or negative, in a tit-for-tat fashion. Rather economic instruments are not simply responses to stimuli by the other actor but part of a multiphase, multi-instrument, integrated plan. Second, it hints that the best approaches to bilateral relationships—especially those marked by armed conflict, mutual suspicion, and distrust—are, in the jargon of the day, characterized as encompassing a "whole of government" approach.[13] In short, rather than thinking about policies in binary terms—military or economic or in institutional terms the military or the Treasury Department—policies in pursuit of dyadic peace can and should be comprehensive and all encompassing. Engagement, broadly understood, is not simply about economic relations but rather the entire range of interactions, public and private, between two armed rivals.

Another interesting strand, emerging most notably in Zahar's chapter, concerns nonstate actors and some states involved in conflicts that threaten their survival. As Peter Andreas and others have analyzed in the path first blazed by Mary Kaldor in *New Wars and Old Wars*, clandestine economies represented by smugglers and pirates contribute to the outbreak, the sustainment, and, crucially, the termination of conflicts.[14] Inducements likely should take into account the impact of illicit economic activities on war (and in enduring rivalries) because the individuals and organizations involved may hold the keys to altering the incentives of both the governments in question and third parties (state and nonstate) playing roles in the dyadic and regional conflicts. Moreover, in follow-on research, Andreas demonstrated that economic sanctions may play an even more pernicious role by "unintentionally contribut[ing] to the criminalization of the state, economy, and civil society of both the targeted country and its immediate neighbors, fostering a symbiosis between political leaders, organized crime, and transnational smuggling networks."[15]

Third Parties

Ripsman and Lobell are correct to emphasize in their introduction that third parties can have an important impact on peacemaking and, especially, the provision of either negative or positive inducements. Nonetheless, contrasting accounts of the Franco-German rapprochement by Press-Barnathan and Thompson suggest, at least in the European case, that deeper theorizing and more research are necessary. In Press-Barnathan's chapter, the story of how France's relations with Germany were transformed and vice versa is largely bilateral. Both France and Germany responded and reacted to initiatives and development without a great deal of reference to the United States, Russia, or the nascent institutions that would eventually, many decades later, form the EU. By contrast, for Thompson the shift of France and Germany from enmity to "competition and cooperation within regional institutions took place within a specific context of US preponderance, US involvement in European affairs, and US support for regional integration." In sum, the bilateral peace alone does not explain the shift, and third-party involvement (on the part of the United States) was important.

Some international relations scholarship assigns greater importance to the United States, as the world's lone superpower, in politics of all regions of the world than is suggested by several authors in this volume. Peter J. Katzenstein, for example, views the world as a set of porous regions loosely under an overarching American "imperium" with differing territorial and nonterritorial dimensions that shape economic and security arrangements.[16] In his understanding, this imperium is both an "actor and a system" such that American policies help shape regions.[17] If the world can be understood as an imperium, then it makes sense that the United States has a central role in peace building involving dyadic conflicts that threaten both regional and global stability. Powerful global and regional states, including the United States, Japan, some members of the EU, and, increasingly, China, are better able to be coercive. A great power like the United States might not shy away from using force, but it might also work to create and maintain peace using economic instruments among conflict dyads in key regions.

Dyads to Regions

As complicated as the peace processes are in virtually all the dyadic cases analyzed in this volume, the regional level is even more so. Even if two countries manage to navigate the give-and-take associated with hashing out agreements that satisfy both parties and manage to implement the agreement, the region itself might not become peaceful. In many regions there are multiple and overlapping causes of conflict and war. Even with one dyadic issue resolved, others might remain. Indeed, in some regions other actors not part of an enduring dyadic rivalry might actively seek to undermine even the beginnings of peace. Andrew Kydd and Barbara F. Walter find, for example, that "Hamas acted quite strategically from 1993 to 2001 timing its violence to coincide either with the signing of a peace treaty [between the Palestinian Authority and Israel] or with elections in which soft-line administrations could be unseated.[18] It is not a stretch to suggest that other third parties might have similar motivations to undermine peace processes in progress or to reverse the effects of those already concluded, what Stephen John Stedman terms "spoilers.[19] Of course this opens up the possibility that economic incentives, especially in forward-looking agreements (see Thompson's chapter), could be used to help both parties to an agreement weather efforts by other governments or nonstate actors to disrupt dyadic peace within a region; "outside" spoilers, especially if they are "greedy," in Stedman's terms, may be susceptible to inducements.

Without undertaking a follow-on analysis of several of the cases discussed here, it is somewhat futile to speculate on the next stages of crafting and enduring peace—moving beyond the dyad to a region. The chapters addressing the Franco-German example provide some insight into how such an analysis might unfold. After World War II, the gradual rapprochement and then developing partnership between the two nations were embedded within several region-wide and even global processes. First and foremost, the two-country dynamic was part and parcel of the regional integration process associated with the construction of the European Coal and Steel Community and beyond (eventually leading to the formation of the EU). Second, relations between the two states were complicated by the fact that France was one of the four powers charged with administering a divided Germany in the postwar period. Dyadic peace-making was at least partially determined by the complicated quadripartite negotiations among France, Great Britain, the Soviet Union, and the United States. Third, and intimately related to the latter point, is the need to understand how the construction of the regional security structures eventually associated with NATO and the Warsaw Pact allowed, and was allowed by, the bilateral arrangements between France and Germany. Fourth, and especially relevant to questions of economic statecraft, is the simultaneous construction of the liberal economic order in the West associated in the immediate postwar period with the Bretton Woods institutions.

The point is not to turn honest scholarship intended to investigate the role of positive and negative sanctions on dyadic peacemaking into a quest for a universal theory of everything that must include such disparate macroprocesses as represented by the reestablishment of German sovereignty, the security community of Europe, and the building of the liberal international order but to acknowledge that these macroprocesses both enable and constrain dyadic peacemaking. Conversely, the ability to construct wider economic and security settlements in Europe and the world (given Europe's central historical role) also depended on German and French progress toward a bilateral peace settlement.

Cases from other regions such as the Middle East reveal that even this level of complexity might not be sufficient. If we step back from the particularities of the Israel-Egypt relationship and peace building, we can see that the settlement, or rather nonsettlement, between those counties held only one key to regional stability. Israel has many other enemies equally enduring—including Syria, Iran, Iraq, and beyond. Moreover, the regional fault lines are seemingly endless. Intra-Arab national rivalries add yet another layer of complexity, as do confessional challenges related to Sunni and Shia disputes, not the least because they force an endlessly complicated political and strategic calculus on prospective peacemakers. Finally, centuries-old conflicts remain between Persians and Arabs, meaning, for the Israelis at least, that even if Camp David and Oslo could be built upon, the dangerous ethnic and national tensions within the region that affect Israeli security but have little to do with Israel itself very well might continue.

Concluding Thoughts

The research into the political economy of regional transitions analyzed and extended by Ripsman and Lobell, not to mention the contributors to this volume, is a vibrant one. It intersects with a variety of literatures and issue areas within the overlapping subdisciplines of political science, most notably international relations and comparative politics. This volume makes a major contribution by focusing closely on the role of economic statecraft and peacemaking. Because enduring rivalries are such an important source of regional conflict and regional conflicts involving great powers often lead to global conflicts, resolving them peacefully matters. As has been increasingly clear in both theory and practice, military, diplomatic, and political instruments alone are likely to be insufficient tools with which to craft sustainable peace. Economic instruments targeted on various actors at the appropriate time can supplement diplomacy by building support to both the negotiations and any ensuring agreements. Although it is not a point under consideration in the volume, I suspect that whatever the costs of economic statecraft (and in cases like the Marshall Plan the cost can be considerable), they are likely to be lower than those of outright military conflicts, the development of garrison states, or the long-term resources required to sustain arms races. This topic is therefore of considerable importance.

Conceptual Innovations

Since the publication of Baldwin's *Economic Statecraft* and the extensive literature exploring his ideas, new theories and concepts regarding economic instruments have been introduced. Both practitioners seeking pragmatic, policy-friendly approaches and theorists identifying and studying real world phenomena have made progress. For example, to a much greater extent than is evident in older historical cases and scholarship, sanctions are now "smart" and/or "targeted."[20] Targeted sanctions "include[e] arms embargoes, financial sanctions on the assets of individuals and companies, travel restrictions on the leaders of a sanctioned state, and trade sanctions on particular goods."[21] What makes them distinct is that the very terms *targeted* and *smart* implicitly answer Ripsman and Lobell's question in the introduction about which part of the target state's population the state employing economic statecraft should seek to influence; targeted sanctions are smart because they focus on actors capable of directly affecting state decisions and policies. In the case of peacemaking leading potentially to peace agreements that can help resolve dyadic conflicts and lead to regional peace, the targets would presumably be political leaders and negotiators. In ethical terms, this approach reduces the pain, at least in theory, of those who may not have the ability to influence state choices—except very indirectly, perhaps, through social movements or popular protests of some form. Several chapters in this volume, however, recognize that targeting leaders and social groups may also produce negative security externalities that impede progress toward peace. Thus, seeking more definitive answers to Ripsman and Lobell's targeting question remains on the future research agenda.

Moreover, targeted sanctions reach into areas of finance, for example, in more sophisticated and subtle ways, even against specific individuals and families. Juan Zarate observes that targeted financial sanctions require "a deeper involvement of the private sector in arenas previously confined to the halls of governments, with a commensurate and widening appreciation within governments of the power of markets and the private sector to influence international security."[22] A number of scholars have worked to provide advice that bridges the academic divide with manuals and training on how to apply new instruments of economic statecraft.[23] Time and further scholarship will determine how well such efforts succeed by promoting, among other things, dyadic peace processes and conflict resolution. In all likelihood, such analyses will involve new cases of conflict too recent to have generated the scholarship necessary for theory development.

New Cases

Most obviously, many of the cases examined in this volume's chapters remain not fully resolved both at the dyadic (e.g., Israel and Egypt and China and Taiwan) and at the regional (e.g., the Middle East and East Asia) levels. Policy makers continue to look for practical policies that will promote the peaceful resolution of conflicts even in the face of long-standing historical enmity and contemporary actors uninterested in peace. Even with the well-studied conflicts, such as between France and Germany, much remains to be done. The cases in this volume point to conceptual puzzles and controversies worthy of further empirical analyses.

In terms of other dyads, a number of cases could potentially make for excellent future research. Four examples with consequences for the future are Iraq-Iran, China-Vietnam, South Korea–North Korea, and India-Pakistan. To a greater or lesser extent, economic statecraft has played a role in tentative efforts to negotiate the peaceful resolution of these conflicts. In contrast, India and Pakistan have consistently traded and invested less with each other on a bilateral basis than the structure of their respective economies would suggest is possible and likely should the conflict wane or the countries reach a long-term and sustainable settlement.[24] For two nuclear powers that have fought three times since independence, have unresolved territorial disputes, and harbor terror groups on both sides, it would seem worthwhile to use economic statecraft during the "prenegotiation phase" at the very least to create a moment "ripe" for negotiations. Zahar's chapter, of course, argues that ripeness—for successful negotiations—is easier to produce using negative sanctions rather than positive inducements. This would suggest that actions threatening even the relatively limited bilateral economic interactions between India and Pakistan might push the conflict toward resolution. Policy makers in both countries must weigh the welfare implications (in terms of human costs and the effects on individual businesses, commercial sectors, and geographic regions) of negative sanctions against the possibility that they might support peacemaking.

Finally, to pursue threads introduced by Zahar and others, exploring additional cases involving long-term conflict and enmity between states and non-state actors such as terrorists would have several scholarly advantages. First, while terrorist activities are rarely as deadly as interstate conflicts or civil wars, terrorism as an instrument of state and nonstate groups greatly complicates interstate relations, contributes to regional instability, and intensifies threat perception in many societies in ways that may obscure real international security concerns.[25] Second, from a theoretical perspective, looking intensively at the state-nonstate dynamic would allow scholars to pursue a number of important themes explored in this volume. Timing and sequencing (as we have seen, terrorist acts and state responses committed during delicate phases of peace negotiations can serve as a spoiler), the nature of inducements (could positive vs. negative sanctions actually support bad behavior by those one are trying to make peace with), and the role of third parties (again, the United States is an example) might have different impacts when the relevant actors are not states

238 THE POLITICAL ECONOMY OF REGIONAL PEACEMAKING

and/or have motivations different from those of sovereign actors. Third, as a practical matter, a number of countries, including the United States, have prioritized counterterrorism measures, particularly against groups like al-Qaeda, with "global reach," or al-Shabaab, with regional reach. Already some scholars have investigated the intersection of terrorism and multilateral institutions.[26] More research along these lines would have conceptual and public policy benefits, a mix I believe the editors of this volume would support and do justice to the research program they have worked hard to encourage.

NOTES

1. Karen Rasler, William R. Thompson, and Sumit Ganguly, *How Rivalries End: Shocks Expectations, Reciprocity, and Reinforcement* (Philadelphia: University of Pennsylvania Press, 2013), 3. These figures are derived from the analysis presented in Michael P. Colaresi, Karen Rasler, and William R. Thompson, *Strategic Rivalries in World Politics: Position, Space, and Conflict Escalation* (Cambridge: Cambridge University Press, 2007).

2. David Allen Baldwin, *Economic Statecraft* (Princeton: Princeton University Press, 1985), 41–42.

3. One volume editor and a chapter contributor have written one of the most recent extensions of thinking about economic statecraft. See Jean-Marc F. Blanchard and Norrin M. Ripsman, *Economic Statecraft and Foreign Policy: Sanctions, Incentives, and Target State Calculations* (New York: Routledge, 2013).

4. In chapter 3, Galia Press-Barnathan discusses the connections among the post–World War II resolution of the Franco-German rivalry, American economic statecraft, and European integration.

5. I recognize that I am extrapolating from the Mansfield and Pevehouse chapter to the policy preferences and strategies of negotiators, but the larger point is that their arguments suggest another fruitful avenue for scholarship and policy analysis in the interest of peacemaking.

6. James G. Stavridis, "Strategic Communication and National Security," *Joint Force Quarterly*, no. 46 (3rd quarter 2007): 4–7; Richard Halloran, "Strategic Communication," *Parameters* 37, no. 3 (Autumn 2007): 4–14.

7. Joseph S. Nye Jr., "Public Diplomacy and Soft Power," *Annals of the American Academy of Political and Social Science* 616, no. 1 (March 2008): 94–109.

8. Christopher W. Hughes, "Japan's Military Modernisation: A Quiet Japan-China Arms Race and Global Power Projection," *Asia-Pacific Review* 16, no. 1 (2009): 84–99.

9. Charles F. Hermann, "Changing Course: When Governments Choose to Redirect Foreign Policy," *International Studies Quarterly* 34, no. 1 (March 1990): 3–21.

10. Even a basic introductory text points the way to a deeper engagement with the policy process underlying state behavior. See, for example, Ryan K Beasley, Juliet Kaarbo, Jeffrey S Lantis, and Michael T Snarr, *Foreign Policy in Comparative Perspective: Domestic and International Influences on State Behavior* (Washington, DC: Congressional Quarterly Press, 2012).

11. Valerie M. Hudson, "Foreign Policy Analysis: Actor-Specific Theory and the Ground of International Relations," *Foreign Policy Analysis* 1, no. 1 (March 2005): 1–30.

12. Michael Mastanduno, "The Strategy of Economic Engagement: Theory and Practice," in Edward D. Mansfield and Brian M. Pollins, eds., *Economic Interdependence and International Conflict: New Perspectives on an Enduring Debate* (Ann Arbor: University of Michigan Press, 2003).

13. Christensen and Lægreid trace the ideas behind "whole of government" approaches to the government of British prime minister Tony Blair where the "main aim was to get a better grip on the 'wicked' issues straddling the boundaries of public sector organizations, administrative levels, and policy areas." There are few issues as "wicked" as building peace with the help of economic statecraft. Tom Christensen and Per Lægreid, "The Whole-of-Government Approach to Public Sector Reform," *Public Administration Review* 67, no. 6 (November–December 2007): 1059–66.

14. Mary Kaldor, *New and Old Wars: Organized Violence in a Global Era*, 3rd ed. (Stanford, CA: Stanford University Press, 2012); Peter Andreas, "The Clandestine Political Economy of War and Peace in Bosnia," *International Studies Quarterly* 48, no. 1 (March 2004): 29–52.

15. Peter Andreas, "Criminalizing Consequences of Sanctions: Embargo Busting and Its Legacy," *International Studies Quarterly* 49, no. 2 (June 2005): 335.

16. Peter J. Katzenstein, *A World of Regions: Asia and Europe in the American Imperium* (Ithaca: Cornell University Press, 2005).

17. Ibid., 22–24, 245.

18. Andrew Kydd and Barbara F. Walter, "Sabotaging the Peace: The Politics of Extremist Violence," *International Organization* 56, no. 2. (Spring 2002): 280.

19. Stephen John Stedman, "Spoiler Problems in Peace Processes," *International Security* 22, no. 2 (Fall 1997): 5–53.

20 David Cortright and George A. Lopez, eds., *Smart Sanctions: Targeting Economic Statecraft* (New York: Rowman and Littlefield, 2002); Daniel W. Drezner, "How Smart Are Smart Sanctions?," *International Studies Review* 5, no. 1 (March 2003): 107–10; Daniel W. Drezner, "Sanctions Sometimes Smart: Targeted Sanc-

tions in Theory and Practice," *International Studies Review* 13, no. 1 (March 2011): 96–108.

21. Joy Gordon, "Smart Sanctions Revisited," *Ethics and International Affairs* 25 no. 3 (Fall 2011): 315.

22. Juan C. Zarate, "Harnessing the Financial Furies: Smart Financial Power and National Security," *Washington Quarterly* 32, no. 4 (2009): 43–59.

23. Thomas J. Biersteker, Sue E. Eckert, Aron Halegua, Peter Romaniuk, and Natalie Reid, *Targeted Financial Sanctions: A Manual for Design and Implementation* (Providence, RI: Swiss Confederation, in cooperation with the United Nations Secretariat and the Watson Institute of International Studies, 2001).

24. In recent years Indo-Pakistani trade volume has been less than $3 billion per year, but analysis suggests that this figure could more than triple if impediments to bilateral trade were removed. Michael Kugelman and Robert M. Hathaway, *Pakistan-India Trade: What Needs to Be Done? What Does It Matter?* (Washington, DC: Woodrow Wilson Center, 2013).

25. For an eclectic and wide-ranging meditation on notions of risk, threat, and security, see Ulrich Beck, "The Terrorist Threat: World Risk Society Revisited," *Theory, Culture, and Society* 19, no. 39 (2002): 29–55.

26. Peter Romaniuk, *Multilateral Counter-terrorism: The Global Politics of Cooperation and Contestation* (New York: Routledge, 2010).

Contributors

Jean-Marc F. Blanchard is Distinguished Professor, School of Advanced International and Area Studies, East China Normal University (Shanghai, China). His research interests include Chinese foreign economic policy, Chinese foreign energy policy, multinational corporations, the political economy of national security, and globalization. He is a coauthor of *The Politics of Economic Sanctions and Incentives* (Routledge, 2013), a coeditor of and contributor to *Governance, Domestic Change, and Social Policy in China: 100 Years after the Xinhai Revolution* (Palgrave Macmillan, 2013); and coeditor of *Power and the Purse: Economic Statecraft, Interdependence, and National Security* (Frank Cass, 2000). He is the author of more than 40 book chapters and journal articles, published in, among others, *Geopolitics, Foreign Policy Analysis, Security Studies, Asia Politics and Policy, China Quarterly, China Journal of International Politics,* and *Journal of Contemporary China.*

Peter Dombrowski is Professor of Strategy at the Naval War College, where he serves as the chair of the Strategic Research Department. His research explores the intersection between political economy and national security, with a particular focus on the US defense industry. His authored or coauthored books include *Buying Transformation: Technological Innovation and the Defense Industry* (Columbia University Press, 2006, with Eugene Gholz); *Military Transformation and the Defense Industry after Next* (Naval War College Press, 2003, with Eugene Gholz and Andrew Ross); and *Policy Responses to the Glo-*

balization of American Banking (University of Pittsburgh Press, 1996). He has also edited several books, including *Guns and Butter: The Political Economy of International Security* (Lynne Rienner, 2005), and authored numerous peer-reviewed articles and book chapters.

Yair Hirschfeld is a professor in the Department of Middle Eastern History at the University of Haifa and Director General of the Economic Cooperation Foundation, based in Tel Aviv. He headed the Israeli unofficial track that led to the 1993 Oslo Accords, working with the Norwegians and Palestinians. Following the Oslo Accords, he participated in crafting the Permanent Status Agreement, also known as the "Beilin-Abu Mazen Understanding."

Scott L. Kastner is an associate professor in the Department of Government and Politics at the University of Maryland. His research interests include political economy; conflict and interdependence; and China, Taiwan, and international trade. He is the author of *Political Conflict and Economic Interdependence across the Taiwan Strait and Beyond* (Stanford University Press, 2009) and has published numerous articles in journals such as *International Studies Quarterly, International Security, Security Studies, Journal of Conflict Resolution,* and *Journal of Peace Research.*

Steven E. Lobell is a professor in the Political Science Department at the University of Utah in Salt Lake City. In 2010 he was a Fulbright scholar in Israel and in 2013 a fellow at the Nobel Institute in Oslo. He is the author of *The Challenge of Hegemony: Grand Strategy, Trade, and Domestic Politics* (University of Michigan Press, 2003); *Ethnic Conflict and International Politics: Explaining Diffusion and Escalation* (Palgrave Macmillan, 2004, edited with Philip Mauceri); *Neoclassical Realism, the State, and Foreign Policy* (Cambridge University Press, 2009, edited with Norrin M. Ripsman and Jeffrey W. Taliaferro); *Beyond Great Powers and Hegemons: Why Secondary States Support, Follow, or Challenge* (Stanford University Press, 2012, edited with Kristen P. Williams and Neal G. Jesse); *The Challenge of Grand Strategy: The Great Powers and the Broken Balance between the World Wars* (Cambridge University Press, 2012, edited with Jeffrey W. Taliaferro and Norrin M. Ripsman); and *Neoclassical Realist Theory of International Politics* (Oxford University Press, 2016, with Norrin M. Ripsman and Jeffrey W. Taliaferro). He has published journal articles in *Security Studies, International Studies Quarterly, International Interactions, Review* *of International Studies, Political Science Quarterly, Journal of Strategic Studies, International Relations of the Asia Pacific, International Politics, Comparative Strategy,* and *World Affairs* and coedited a special issue of *International Politics.*

Edward D. Mansfield is Hum Rosen Professor of Political Science at the University of Pennsylvania. His research focuses on international security and international political economy. He has authored or coauthored three books: *Votes, Vetoes, and the Political Economy of International Trade Agreements* (Princeton University Press, 2012, with Helen V. Milner); *Electing to Fight: Why Emerging Democracies Go to War* (MIT Press, 2005, with Jack Snyder); and *Power, Trade, and War* (Princeton University Press, 1994). He has also edited or coedited 13 books and published numerous articles in journals such as *International Security, International Studies Quarterly, International Organization, World Politics, Security Studies, Comparative Political Studies,* and *Journal of Conflict Resolution.*

William Norris is an assistant professor at the George Bush School of Government and Public Service at Texas A&M University. His broad research interests include East Asian security, business-government relations, Chinese foreign and security policy, and international relations theory—particularly the strategic relationship between economics and national security. His recent work focuses on the use of commercial sector actors to achieve national foreign policy objectives in the context of Chinese grand strategy.

Margaret M. Pearson is a professor in the Department of Government and Politics at the University of Maryland. Her research interests include state control of the Chinese economy, China's integration into the global economy and global institutions, Chinese regulatory institutions, and Chinese industrial policy. She is coeditor of "International Political Economy in China: The Global Conversation," a special issue of the *Review of International Political Economy.* Her publications include *Joint Ventures in the People's Republic of China* (Princeton University Press, 1991) and *China's New Business Elite: The Political Results of Economic Reform* (University of California Press, 1997). She has published numerous book chapters and articles in, among other journals, *World Politics, China Journal, Public Administration Review,* and *Review of International Political Economy.*

Jon C. Pevehouse is a professor in the Department of Political Science at the University of Wisconsin–Madison. His research examines the relationship between domestic and international politics. Topics on which he has recently published include regional trade agreements, human rights institutions, exchange rate politics, and international organizations. His books include *While Dangers Gather: Congressional Checks on Presidential War Powers* (Princeton University Press, 2007, with William G. Howell); and *Democracy from Above? Regional Organizations and Democratization* (Cambridge University Press. 2005). He has also published articles in *International Studies Quarterly, International Organization, Security Studies, American Political Science Review, Journal of Politics, American Journal of Political Science,* and *Journal of Conflict Resolution,* among other journals. He is currently editor of *International Organization.*

Galia Press-Barnathan is an associate professor in the Department of International Relations at Hebrew University. Her primary areas of research include international relations theory, political economy of security, transatlantic and Japan, and comparative regional politics. She has published two books, *The Political Economy of Transitions to Peace* (University of Pittsburgh Press, 2009); and *Organizing the World: The United States and Regional Cooperation in Asia and Europe* (Routledge, 2003). She has published several book chapters, and her articles have appeared in *Security Studies, International Studies Review, Cooperation and Conflict,* and *Journal of Peace Research.*

Norrin M. Ripsman is a professor in the Political Science Department at Concordia University in Montreal. He has held prestigious fellowships at the Hebrew University of Jerusalem (1997–98), the Mershon Center at Ohio State University (1998–99), the Belfer Center for Science and International Affairs at the Kennedy School at Harvard University (2010–11), and the Norwegian Nobel Institute (2015). His primary research interests include democracy and national security, postwar peacemaking, constructing regional stability, the political economy of national security, neoclassical realism, and the impact of globalization on national security. He is the author or coauthor of five books, most recently *Peacemaking from Above, Peace from Below: Ending Conflict between Regional Rivals* (Cornell University Press, 2016); and *Neoclassical Realist Theory of International Politics* (Oxford University Press, 2016, with Steven E. Lobell and Jeffrey W. Taliaferro). He is a coeditor of four books, and the author of over 20 peer-reviewed articles published in *International Security, International*

Studies Quarterly, Security Studies, Millennium: A Journal of International Studies, International Interactions, International Studies Review, Geopolitics, International Journal, and *Canadian Journal of Political Science.*

William R. Thompson is Distinguished Professor and Donald A. Rogers Professor of Political Science at Indiana University. His research focus includes international relations theory, conflict processes, international political economy, the rise and fall of major powers, long economic waves and their consequences, and the impact of war. He has authored or coauthored 29 books, monographs, and special issues, including *Sea Power in Global Politics, 1494–1993* (Macmillan, 1988), with George Modelski; *On Global War: Historical-Structural Approaches to World Politics* (University of South Carolina Press, 1988); *The Great Powers and Global Struggle, 1490–1990* (University Press of Kentucky, 1994), with Karen Rasler; *Great Power Rivalries* (University of South Carolina Press, 1999); *The Arc of War: Origins, Escalation, and Transformation* (University of Chicago Press, 2011), with Jack S. Levy; and *How Rivalries End* (University of Pennsylvania Press, 2013), with Karen Rasler and Sumit Ganguly. He has also published over 170 book chapters and articles published in *International Security, International Studies Quarterly, International Interactions, International Studies Review, Security Studies,* and *Journal of Peace Research,* among others.

Marie-Joëlle Zahar is a professor in the Département de science politique at l'Université de Montréal. Her research focuses on substate political violence, peace building, and spoilers of peace processes. Her publications include *Beyond the Arab Spring: Authoritarianism and Democratization in the Arab World* (Lynne Rienner, 2012, with Rex Brynen, Pete W. Moore, and Bassel F. Salloukh); *Intra-state Conflicts, Governments, and Security: Dilemmas of Deterrence and Assurance* (Routledge, 2008, edited with Stephen Saideman); "Territoire et sacré," special issue of *Théologiques* 16, no. 2 (2008, edited with Michel Beaudin); "Intellectuals and the Media: East-West Dialogue on Democracy for the Balkans," special Issue of *Transitions* (Brussels) 45, no. 1 (2005, edited with Mariella Pandolfi, Annie Lafontaine, and Laurence McFalls); and articles in *Global Governance, International Journal, International Peacekeeping,* and other journals.

Index

Note: Page numbers in **bold** refer to tables while page numbers in *italics* refer to figures.